IMAGES
of America

HISTORIC WASHINGTON PARK

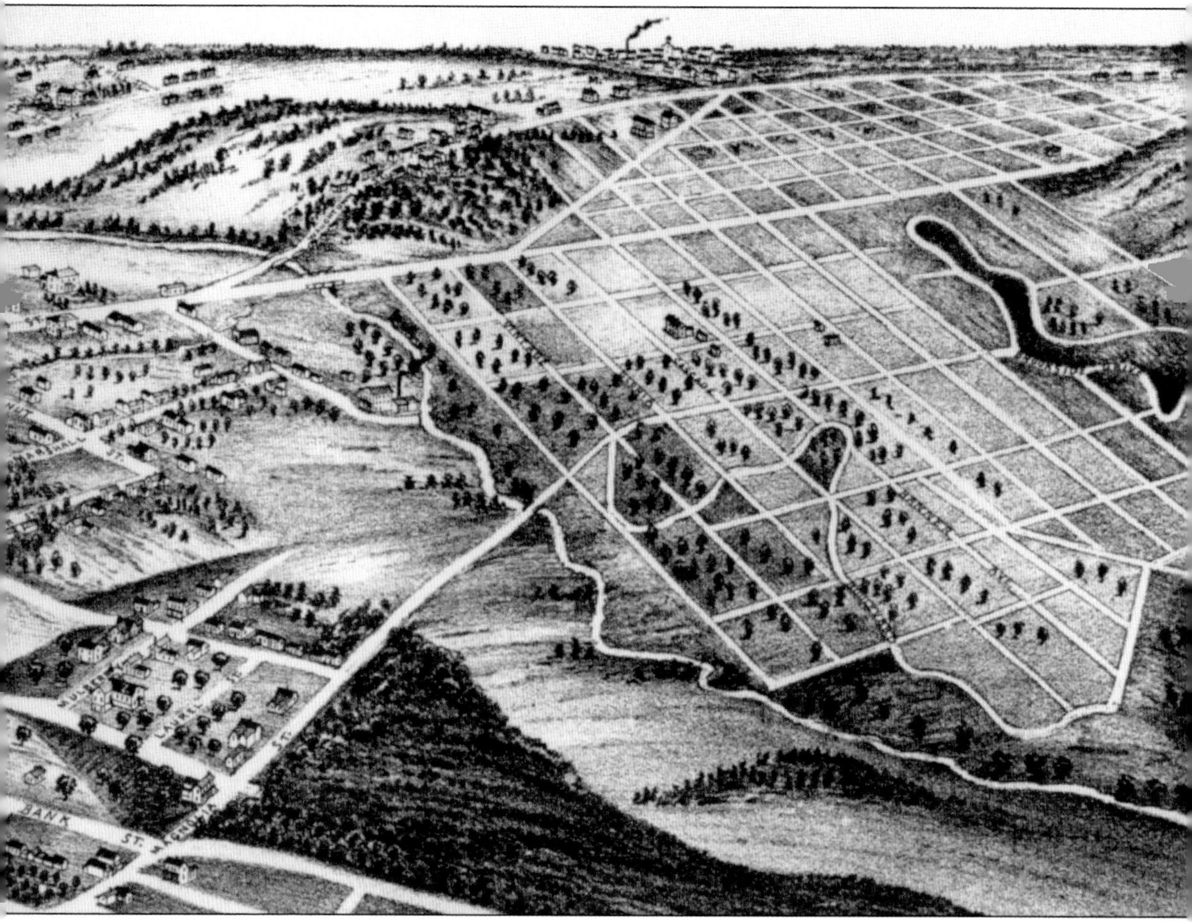

This 1891 bird's-eye view of Winston-Salem shows the area that is now Washington Park. This map shows the neighborhood grid that Joseph Lott Ludlow envisioned, although building of the area had not yet taken place. Two houses with their outbuildings can be seen: the Banner house (now the Burton Craige house) and the old Devonshire farm. Both houses are still standing today. The Blum Mill, located in what is now the Southeast Gateway area, is located along Salem Creek. There are three bridges leading to the Southside and Sunnyside areas: Waughtown bridge, South Main Street bridge, and Magnolia Street bridge. Broad Street, then a small street four-blocks long, ended at Bank Street. Today this is one of the main thoroughfares through the Washington Park neighborhood. The housing project known as Happy Hill Gardens was forest, and the next hill over was—and still is—called Happy Hills. The smokestack in the top is Henry E. Fries's Southside Mill in the Sunnyside Community. (Collection of the Wachovia Historical Society; photograph courtesy of Old Salem Museums and Gardens.)

ON THE COVER: Rodney Boggs (left) and Danny Walters play along the stone bridges in Washington Park. This photograph, *c.* 1974, was taken during a neighborhood residents' picnic. Shortly before, the *Winston-Salem Journal* had run an article declaring the neighborhood was in a decline, which prompted the citizens of Washington Park to form a neighborhood association. (Forsyth County Public Library Photograph Collection.)

IMAGES
of America

HISTORIC WASHINGTON PARK

Suzanne Wildrey Bragg

ARCADIA
PUBLISHING

ISBN 978-0-7385-5295-8

Published by Arcadia Publishing
Charleston SC, Chicago IL, Portsmouth NH, San Francisco CA

Printed in the United States of America

Library of Congress Catalog Card Number: 2007928791

For all general information contact Arcadia Publishing at:
Telephone 843-853-2070
Fax 843-853-0044
E-mail sales@arcadiapublishing.com
For customer service and orders:
Toll-Free 1-888-313-2665

Visit us on the Internet at www.arcadiapublishing.com

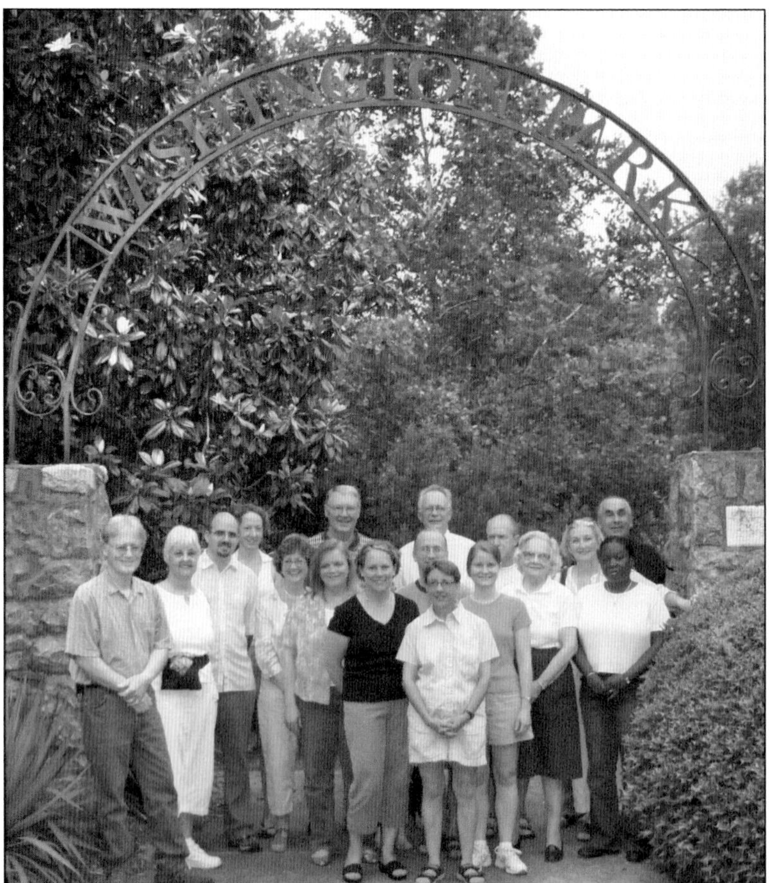

This book is dedicated to the many people, those pictured and those who are not, who spent the last 33 years revitalizing and preserving one of the most loved areas in the Piedmont. Your hard work, dedication, and drive have made this neighborhood one of the safest, most beautiful places in Winston-Salem. I have lived in many cities in my adult life, but there is none I have loved more than where I live now. Thank you for all you have done.

Contents

Acknowledgments

There are many people who have helped with this book and made it possible. First, thanks to my wonderful husband, Patrick, who supports and believes in me. Second, thanks to the neighbors and friends who donated their time and effort in making this book a reality. Special thanks to the members of the Washington Park Neighborhood Association for your donation. In alphabetical order (by first name), they are Arthur Easter, Bert Bahnson, Beverly Paszkowski, Bill Benton, Chad Davis, Cindy and Chris Sheaffer, David Gall, Debbie and Anthony Transou, Debra Collins, Deidre Johnston, Donny Swan, Eddie Ingle, Eugene Hayes, Frances Barrow, Frank Frye, Gary Vernon, Gregg Errett and Carmen Caruth, Hannah Ashford and Mike Oder, Hans Zachman, Heidi Moore, Jack Graham, Jane Handly, Jean Hayes Mahaffey, Jessica Richard and Tim Blackman, Jennifer Bean Bower, Joe Tappy, Julie Harris, Julie Palm, Karen Byrd, Katie Moosbrugger, Kay McKnight, Kim Mitchell, Kriss Dinkins and Stephan Dragisic, Laura Turner, Leslie Kamtman, Lisa McConnell, Lois Hipp, Marianne DiNapoli-Mylet, Matthew Johnson, Molly Rawls, Nancy and Nick Bragg, Nancy Hart and Bob Fitzgerald, Nancy and Denis Kissane, Nancy Shelton Bean, Norma McNeil, Patrice Slattery, Rachel and Keith Wilson, Richard Starbuck, Rodney Reich, Sarah and Kevin Higgins, Sarah Johnston Hunter, Sherry Dagenhardt Griggs, Stacy Brendle, Stephen Turner, Sue Stanley, Tom Dillon, and Walter Leonard. If I left anyone's name off this list, please forgive me, as it was not intentional. Thanks to Maggie Bullwinkel at Arcadia Publishing for believing in this project and for supporting me through the entire process. It is greatly appreciated. Also, there were many pictures that I was not able to use because of space restrictions. Please check the neighborhood Web site for continuous updates: www.washingtonparkneighbors.org.

Introduction

When people ask where I live, I usually get the response, "you live over there?" "Over there" is the south side of Winston-Salem, up the hill from historic Old Salem. It's a neighborhood with tree-lined streets, sidewalks filled with people walking their dogs, and a park filled with hills that echo laughter, music, and the screams from softball games. When people think of Southside, their minds fill with thoughts of gang violence, break-ins, houses filled with drug abusers, and dead bodies under the bushes in the park. Nothing could be further from the truth. I moved here in February 2005, shortly after arriving in Winston-Salem, and knew nothing about the reputation of the area. From the moment I laid eyes on my house and the neighborhood, I fell in love. Huge trees canopied the streets, kids rode their bikes and drew hopscotch boxes in chalk on the sidewalks, and people dropped off cookies on our porch to welcome us to the neighborhood. Neighbors actually spoke to us when we walked by. It reminded me of home in Wilmington, North Carolina—back when it was a still a small town—where people spent more time outside than inside, and more time sharing than just driving by and waving.

As I started researching the history for this book, I heard the words community, hospitable, beautiful, and friendly when asked to describe the area. I discovered a pattern of longtime residents who have lived here since they were children, and another pattern of people who moved here, outgrew their homes, and found another two blocks over. Tracing their steps, they may have lived in five houses, but they never left the neighborhood. Many more "came back," as they have stated, back to their family home and the area in which they felt the most comfortable. It inspired me to keep digging for more information.

The neighborhood is significant, as it is one of the early residential suburbs developed as a result of the streetcar. It reflects the city's development from a small business town to one of the leading manufacturing cities of the South and contains the residences of many of Winston's and Salem's most prominent leaders of that period. It represents middle- and upper-income homes and as such is a symbol of the affluence of the boom times Winston-Salem enjoyed in the early decades of the 20th century. In the 1920s, Winston-Salem became the largest city between Atlanta and Washington, D.C., and the increasing sophistication and prosperity of its residents continued with Washington Park's residents until the 1960s.

What is unique to Washington Park is the layout of the homes. The grandest homes stand along the ridge of the bluff on Cascade Avenue, Main Street, and Banner Avenue. As one travels down the hill toward town, each subsequent street's homes decrease in size. The factory and landowners lived on the large lots with mansions and grand gardens; the streets below them housed the executives and accountants, then the next housed managers, and the day workers, etc.

The neighborhood received its origins from a land trust company. In an article from the *Twin-City Sentinel* dated May 4, 1935, the former president of the Sunnyside Company reminisced about what life was like back in 1890. He stated that his company's land was composed of three farms, upon which there was a single residence, and that it was purchased by a group of Winston and Salem people, among them Dr. Henry Bahnson, Henry E. Fries, and seven other gentleman from New Bern, High Point, and other towns. To develop this property, they had to extend Main Street by a straight line across Salem Creek, and southward through the property, build an iron bridge, macadamize the street (now Waughtown Road), and extend the car line practically to the southern limit of the property. In less than a year, the development was a success, and every stockholder could have sold out for a profit.

Sunnyside is believed to have gotten that name from a plantation owned by E. A. Volger. Other documents give that name to another plantation, owned by the distinguished author and poet Henry E. Harman. After the Sunnyside Company (name later changed to the Winston-Salem Land and Investment Company) bought the farmland to the Southeast, it is believed that they purchased the land and plantations to the southwest (known as Southside at the time) and named it Washington Park.

Many of the families that moved to this new neighborhood were related: the Siewerses, the Frieses, the Bahnsons, the Fogles, the Ellers, the Brawleys, and the Craiges, to name a few. Each played a significant role in the founding of Winston-Salem as an industrial epicenter and educational hub. Over the last century, it has become an urban neighborhood that has successfully weathered the destruction that many others have suffered.

Whether you love old homes, old neighborhoods, or new ones, there is a little something in here for everyone. I hope you enjoy what you read.

One

Industry

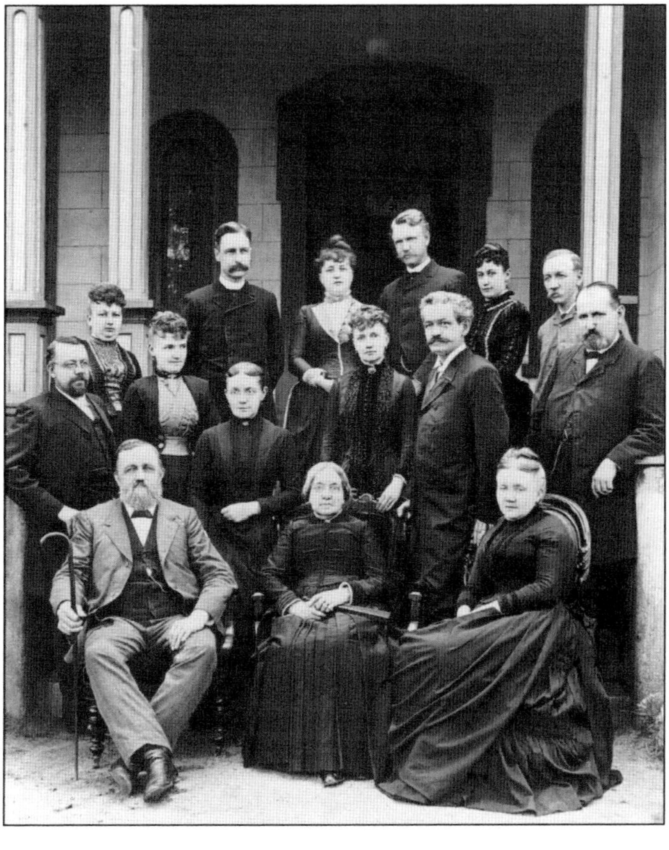

According to a newspaper report in the *Winston-Salem Journal*, the name Fries meant power in a city that today is more often linked with families named Reynolds and Hanes. The Fries family members were leaders in bringing industry as we know it to Winston-Salem. The textile mill Francis L. Fries built in 1840 survived well into the 20th century and was the forerunner of all the factories that made Winston-Salem a manufacturing giant. His descendents went on to found Wachovia Bank and Trust, build power plants, start railroads, run companies, act as land developers, own the *Winston-Salem Journal*, and champion public schools. (Private collection; photograph courtesy of Old Salem Museums and Gardens.)

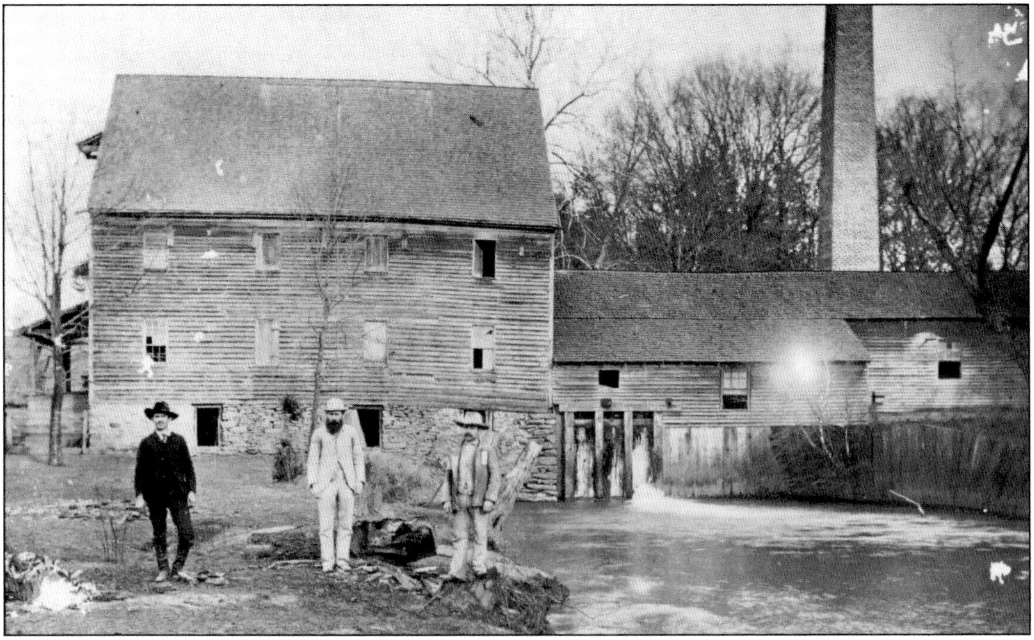

Located along Salem Creek in what is now called the Southeast Gateway area, Blum's Mill is believed to have a been corn and wheat facility. This photograph, taken sometime between 1890 and 1900, shows the mill and water flow of Salem Creek. When construction for the Summit Building in the new Gateway began in 2007, pilings had to be drilled into the earth to compensate for the water that ran underneath it. (Collection of Old Salem Museums and Gardens.)

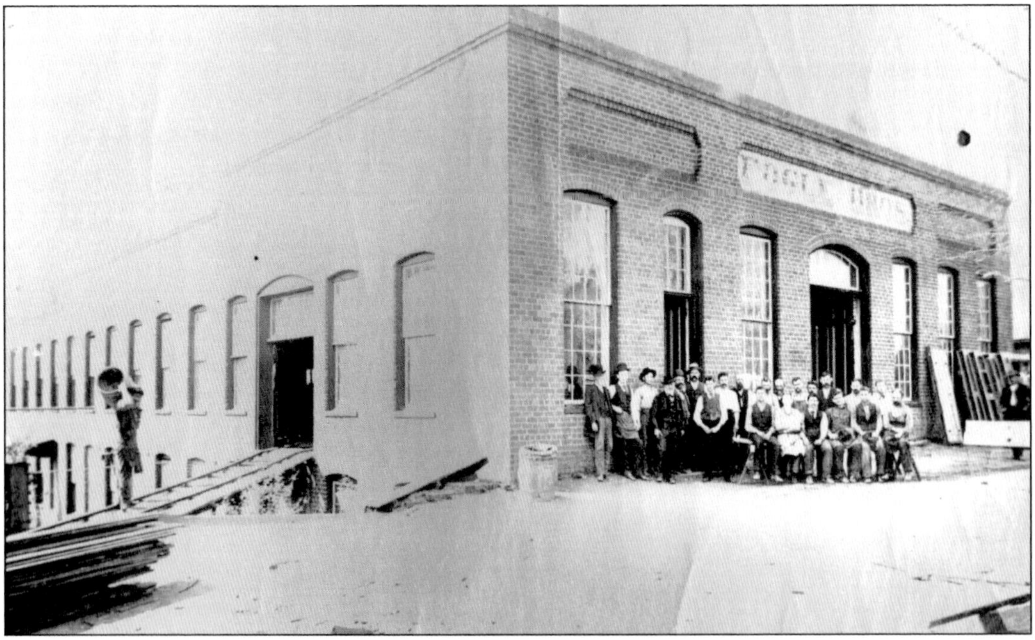

Brothers Christian H. and Charles A. Fogle, sons of Augustus Fogle, who served as steward of Salem Academy, sheriff of Forsyth County, and mayor of Salem, founded the Fogle Brothers Lumber Company in 1871, employing men in the Salem area. The plant was located at the corner of Belews Creek Street and Water Street. (Collection of Old Salem Museums and Gardens.)

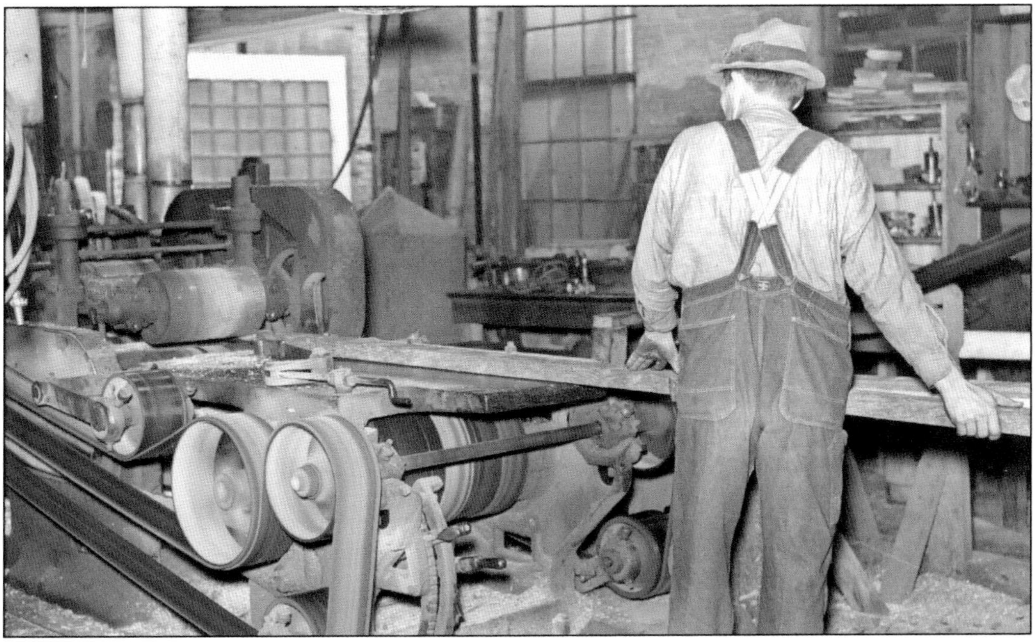

The Fogle Brothers Lumber Company engaged in general millwork, such as sash doors and fireplace mantles, and in home building and business construction. For several years, the Fogle Brothers company manufactured tobacco boxes for many of the 37 tobacco companies in the area. They were responsible for building many of the structures in Winston and Salem during the real estate boom of the 1890s through the 1920s, including many of the homes in the Washington Park area. In 1892, Charles A. Fogle left the partnership because of health issues, and his brother continued as sole proprietor until he died in 1898. The Fogle Lumber Company and its subsidiaries remain in existence through the Fogle heirs. (Forsyth County Public Library Photograph Collection.)

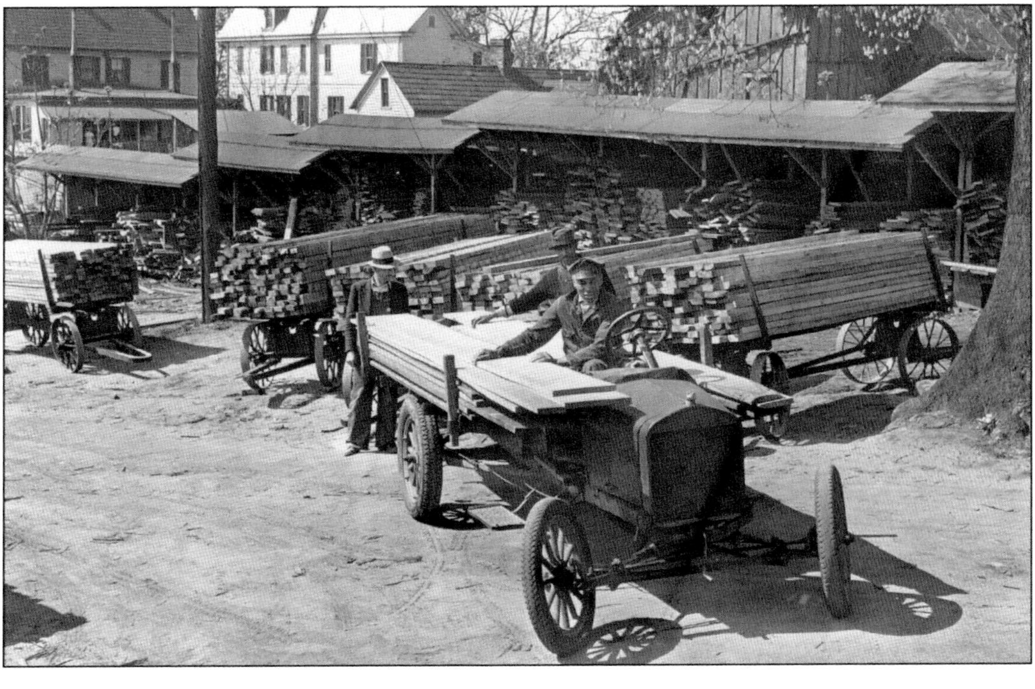

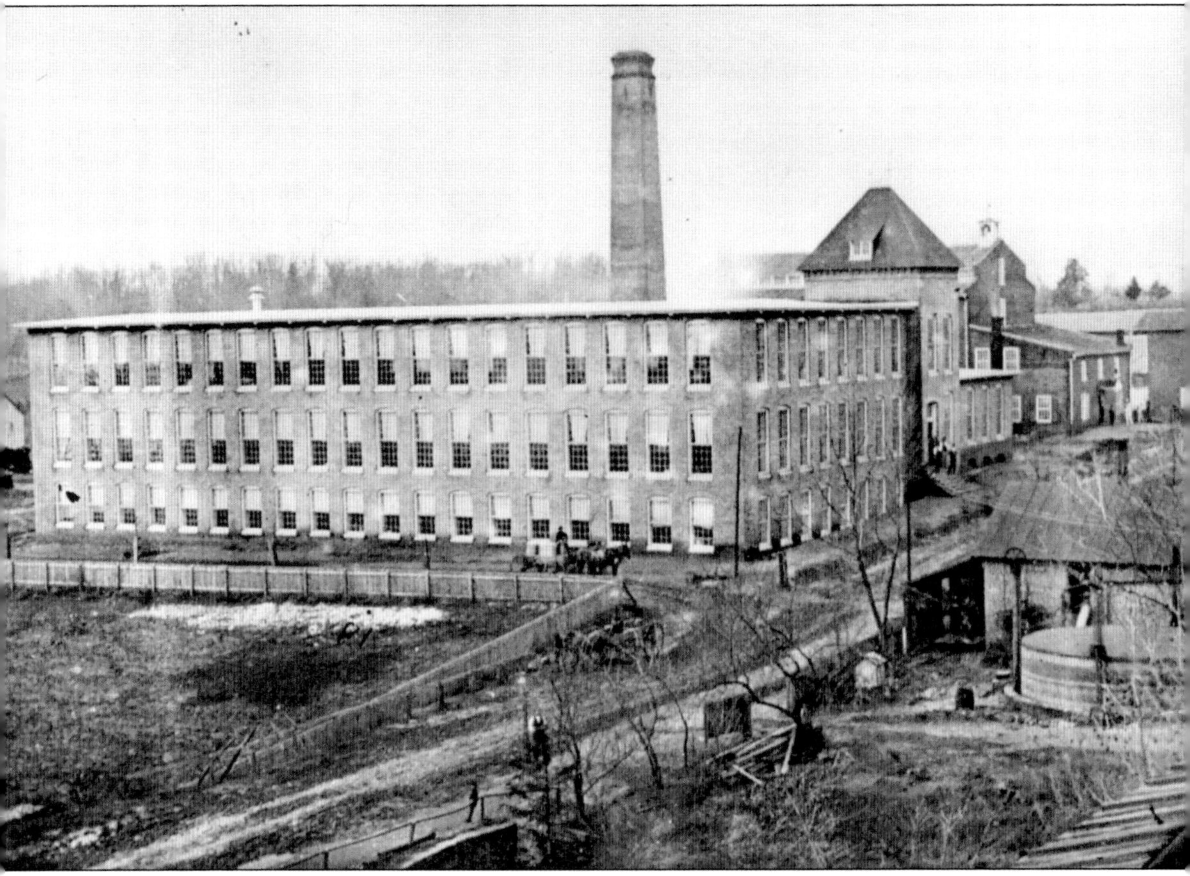

Francis L. Fries built Fries Woolen Mills at the site of the Old Salem Manufacturing factory, at what is now the Brookstown Inn. In 1846, his younger brother Henry became his partner, and the company was renamed F&H Fries Company. It consisted of a woolen mill, cotton mill, and a smokehouse. At the outbreak of the Civil War, the Frieses' slaves and hired hands worked day and night to weave the gray cloth needed for Confederate uniforms and heavy denim jeans. After Francis's oldest son Colonel Fries took over the business, the company moved all its cotton milling under the name Arista Cotton Mill. Arista Mills Company was formed in 1903 by the merger of Arista and Southside Cotton Mill, which was owned by Francis's youngest son, Henry E. Fries. Arista Mills abandoned their Brookstown plant in 1927 and moved all of its milling to Henry's Southside factory on Goldfloss Street. Arista Mills entered data processing in 1956 and ended its textile production in 1970. (Collection of Old Salem Museums and Gardens.)

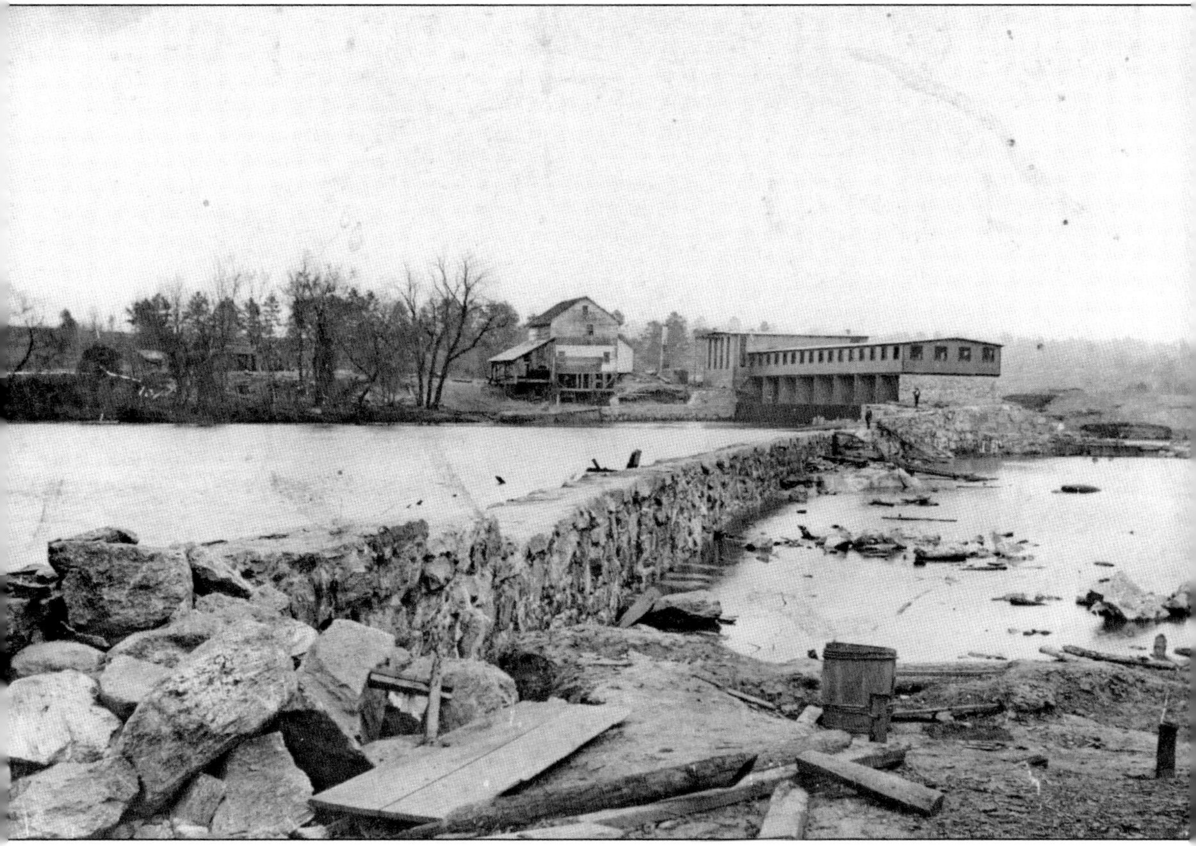

As an owner and manager of several textiles mills and a grain mill, Francis L. Fries' son Henry developed an interest in the use of electricity to power industrial machinery in the 1880s. Upon meeting an engineer at an 1896 New York event honoring former president Glover Cleveland, Henry inquired about the feasibility of the long-distance transmission of electrical power. When he received the answer he wanted, Fries immediately wired his uncle, who owned the Douthit's Ferry location Fries wanted to use, asking permission to precede with a hydropower design. When it was completed on April 18, 1898, the station on the Yadkin River provided power for textile and fertilizer mills, an electric railway system, electric street lighting, and wood and metal shops in Salem and Winston. The power generated enabled the area to become a significant industrial and manufacturing center in North Carolina. Thomas Edison and Frank J. Sprague were among the early shareholders in Fries's business venture. The plant, renamed Idols Mill, is still used today by Duke Power. (Collection of Old Salem Museums and Gardens.)

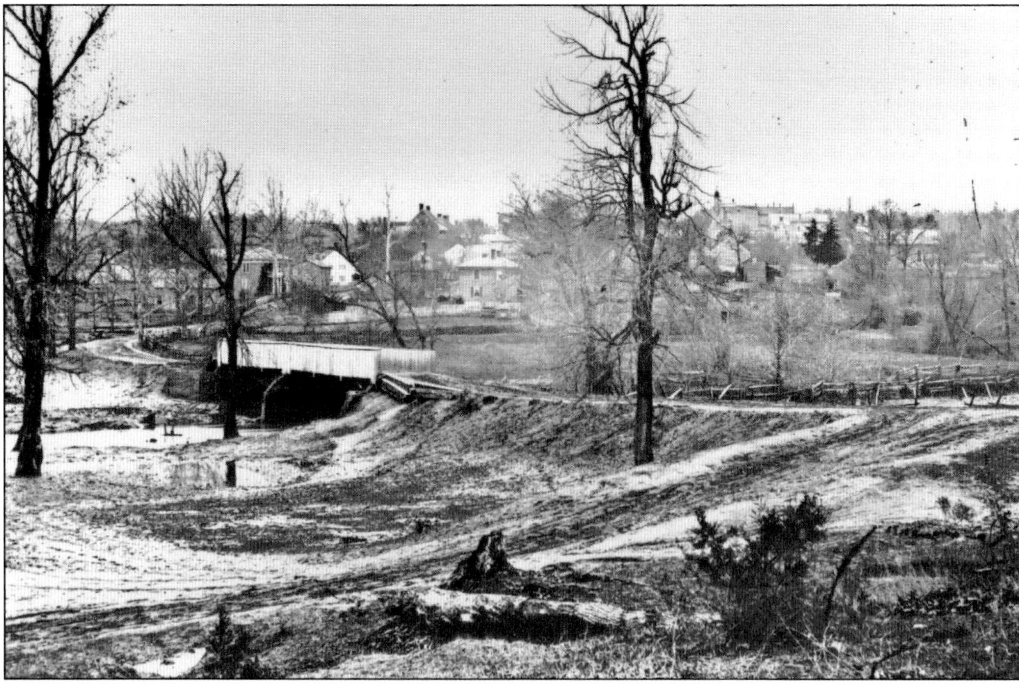

After the Sunnyside Company was formed to develop the land south of Salem, they extended Main Street to run straight across Salem Creek. This photograph, taken c. 1890, shows the way the street looked before development began. (Collection of the Wachovia Historical Society; photograph courtesy of Old Salem Museums and Gardens.)

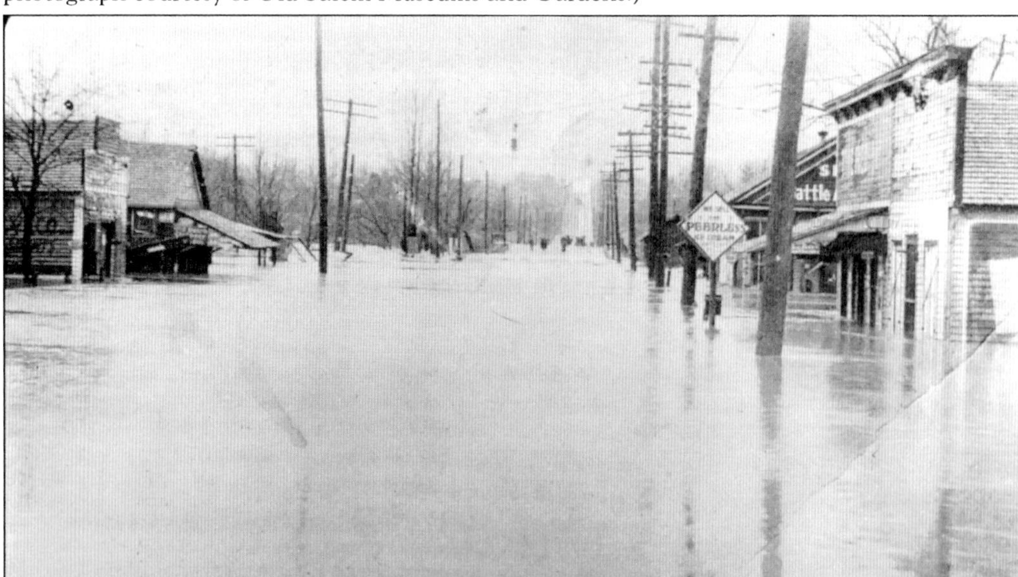

The March 15, 1912, Salem Creek flooded, drowning many of the businesses in Salem township. Throughout history, Salem Creek has flooded its banks and turned the surrounding areas into moving bodies of water. This photograph, taken from North Main Street looking south, shows the extent of one flood Salem Creek produced. (Collection of the Wachovia Historical Society; photograph courtesy of Old Salem Museums and Gardens.)

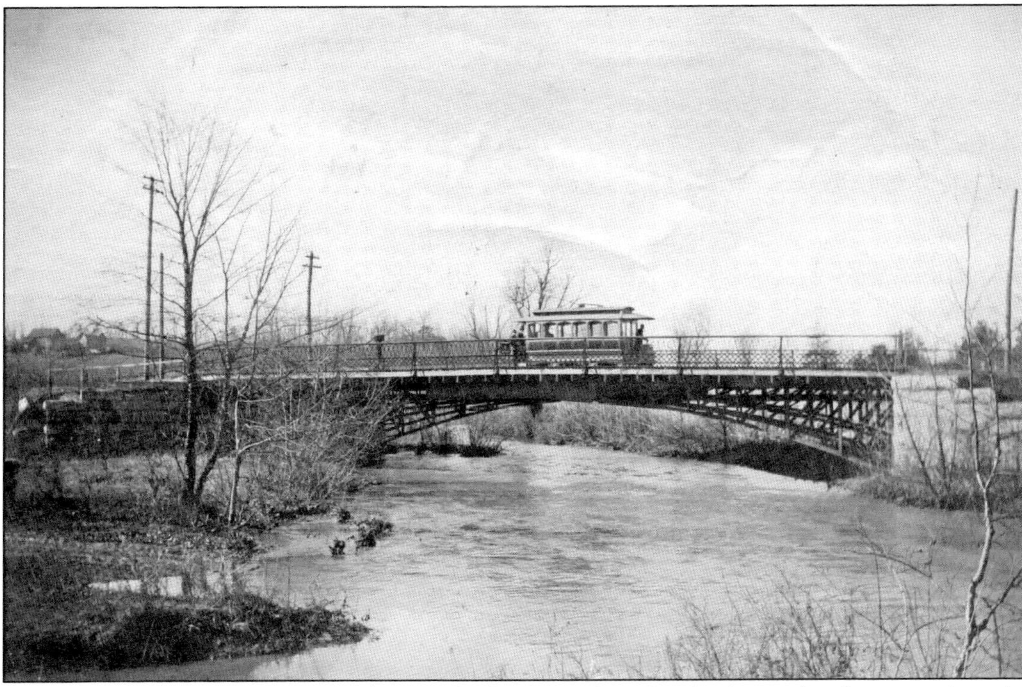

In 1891, a new stone-and-iron bridge was built over Salem Creek. A couple of years earlier, the Winston-Salem Railway and Electric Company was incorporated, organized by Thomas Edison and Frank Sprague. In 1900, Henry E. Fries bought the company. Streetcars began running through Salem and up the hills to the south on July 14, 1890. (Forsyth County Public Library photograph collection.)

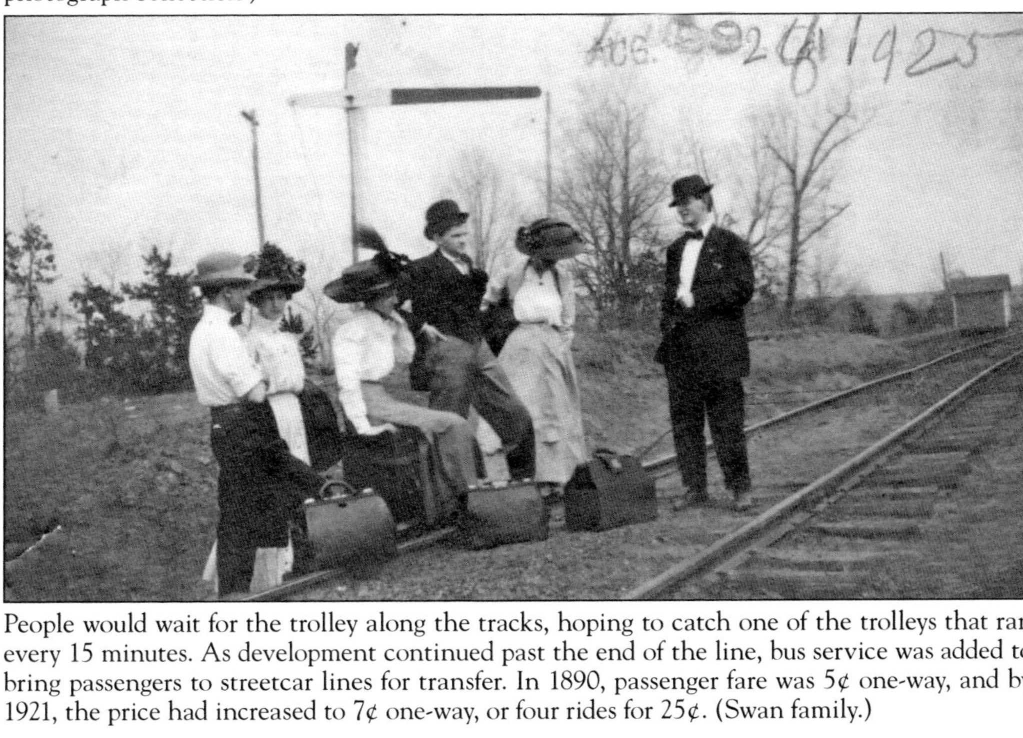

People would wait for the trolley along the tracks, hoping to catch one of the trolleys that ran every 15 minutes. As development continued past the end of the line, bus service was added to bring passengers to streetcar lines for transfer. In 1890, passenger fare was 5¢ one-way, and by 1921, the price had increased to 7¢ one-way, or four rides for 25¢. (Swan family.)

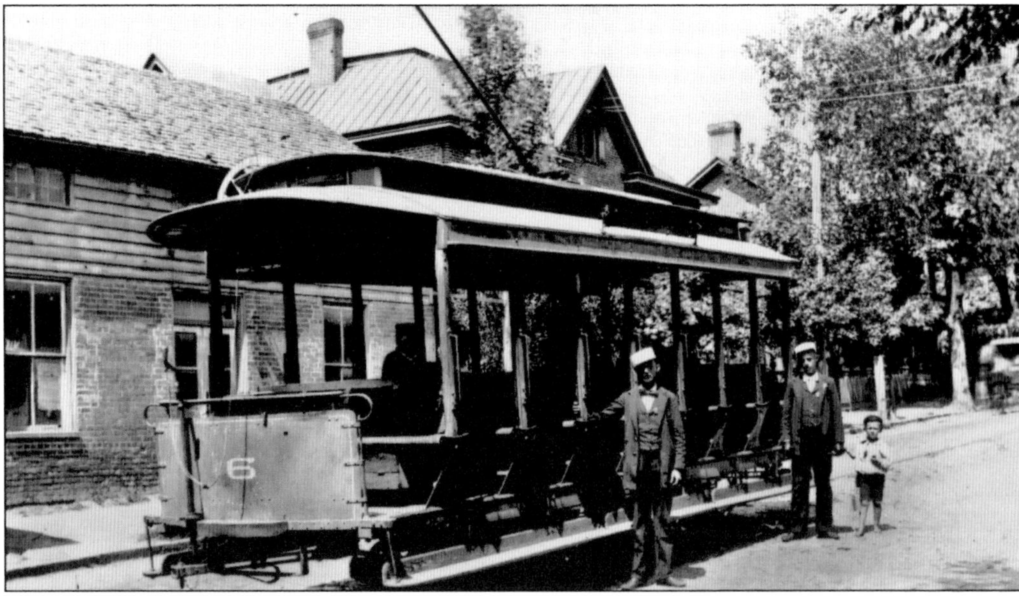

Summer cars, such as the one pictured above, were open on both sides with seats that spanned the cars. The winter streetcars, such as the one pictured below, had a different seating arrangement, with closed sides and a central aisle. Long seats on each end housed an electric heater and a sand box with a mechanism to release sand on the icy tracks when needed. A former trolley motorman remembered that "without the sand, it'd run away from you." Around Halloween, youngsters in the neighborhood would grease the tracks at the bottom of the hill near a curve. The *Winston-Salem Journal* stated that the slippery rails "made for a harrowing ride. You [were] lucky if you'd stay on the track, it'd go so fast." The average trolley speed was about 30 miles per hour. (Above, collection of the Wachovia Historical Society, photograph courtesy of Old Salem Museums and Gardens; below, the Moravian Archives, Winston-Salem, North Carolina.)

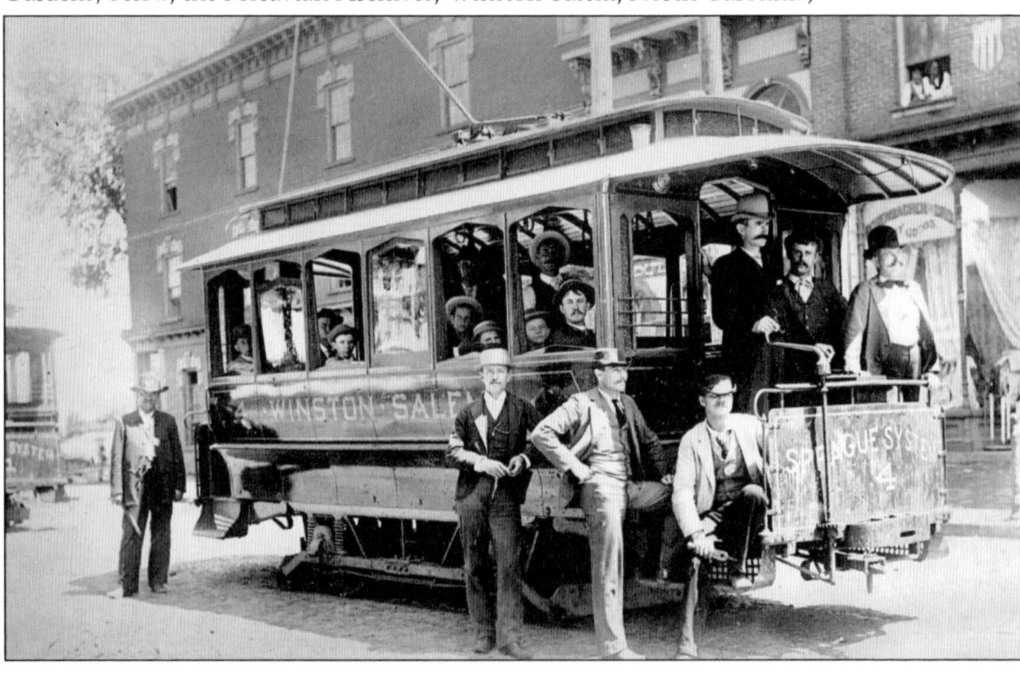

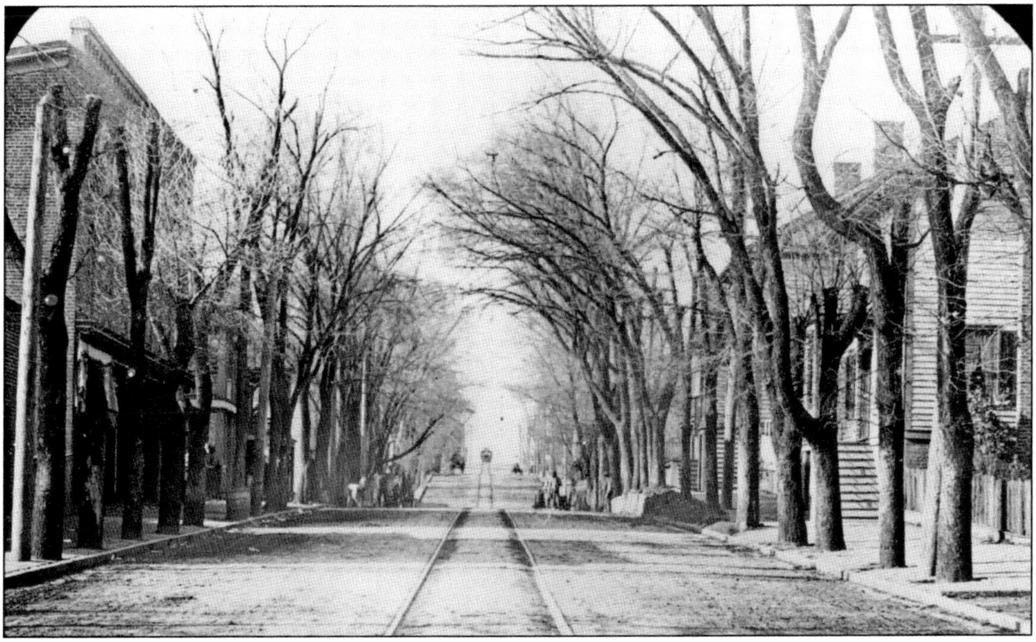

Construction companies and developers were the primary owners of the railway, and development in the West End and Washington Park closely paralleled trolley routes. The streetcars ran in as far south as Nissen Park in the Waughtown area. This image shows the southern route on North Main Street in what is now Old Salem. (Collection of the Wachovia Historical Society; photograph courtesy of Old Salem Museums and Gardens.)

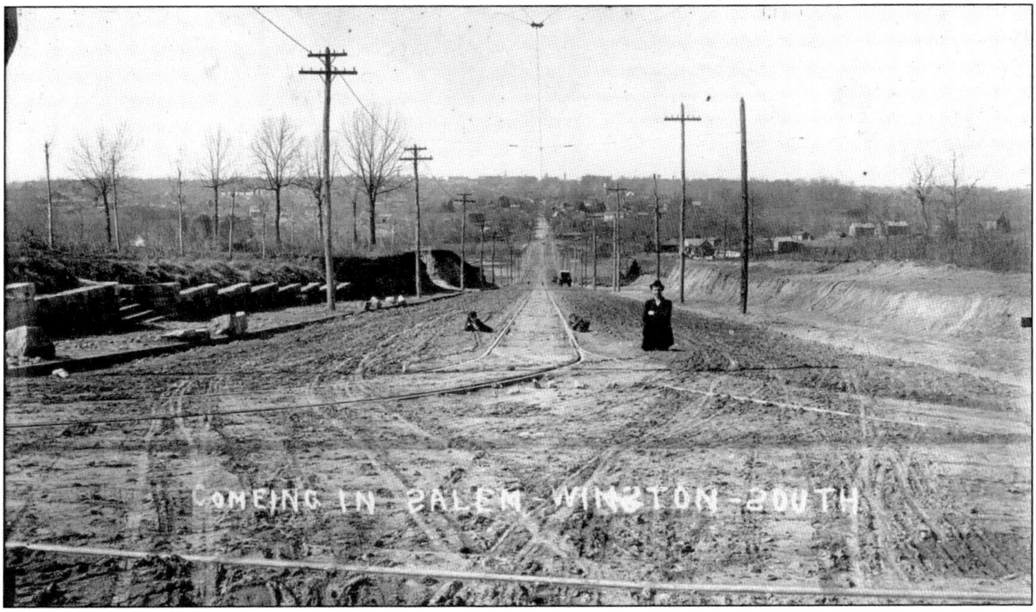

The streetcar line ran south from Salem, along Main Street, where it forked west on Cascade Avenue and stopped just past the Henry E. Fries house at 104 Cascade Avenue. Since the streetcar was the major means of transportation, property along or near the line was more expensive and fashionable. This view is looking north from the corner of Cascade Avenue and Main Street. The men are unidentified. (Forsyth County Public Library Photograph Collection.)

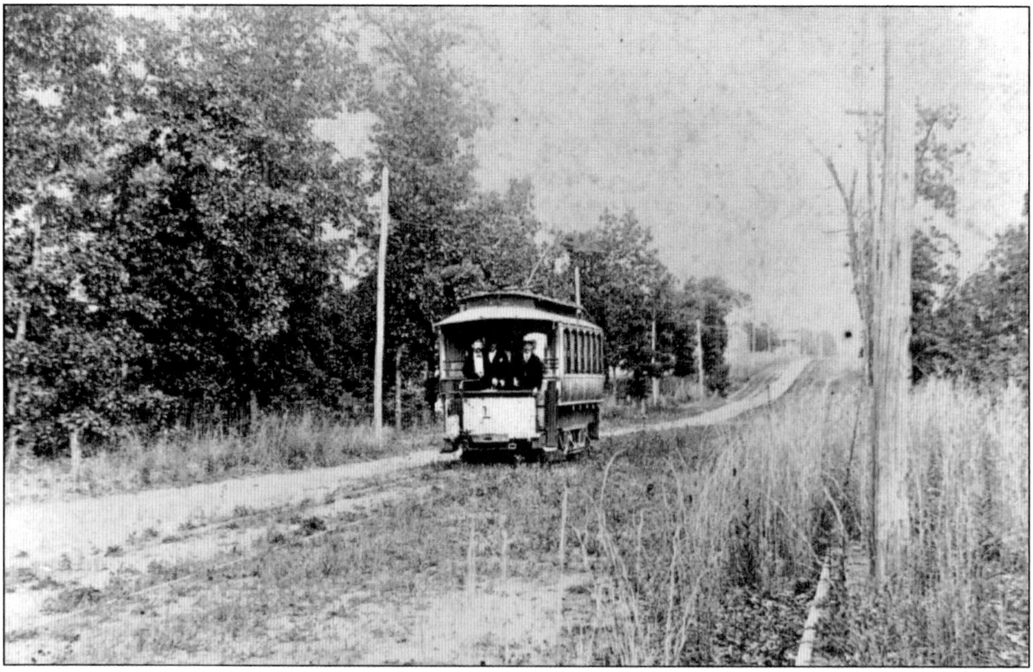

The Main Street line extended south to East Sprague Street to Peachtree Street, where Nissen Park once stood. This park was created by the Winston-Salem Southbound Railway in 1900 to entice people to take the 30-minute trolley ride to the outskirts in Waughtown. Nissen Park's heyday lasted until the rise of the automobile, and by the 1920s, the park had lost its luster and the Sprague Street line ended before it got to Nissen Park. This photograph shows the trolley rolling along Sunnyside Avenue. (Moravian Archives, Winston-Salem, North Carolina.)

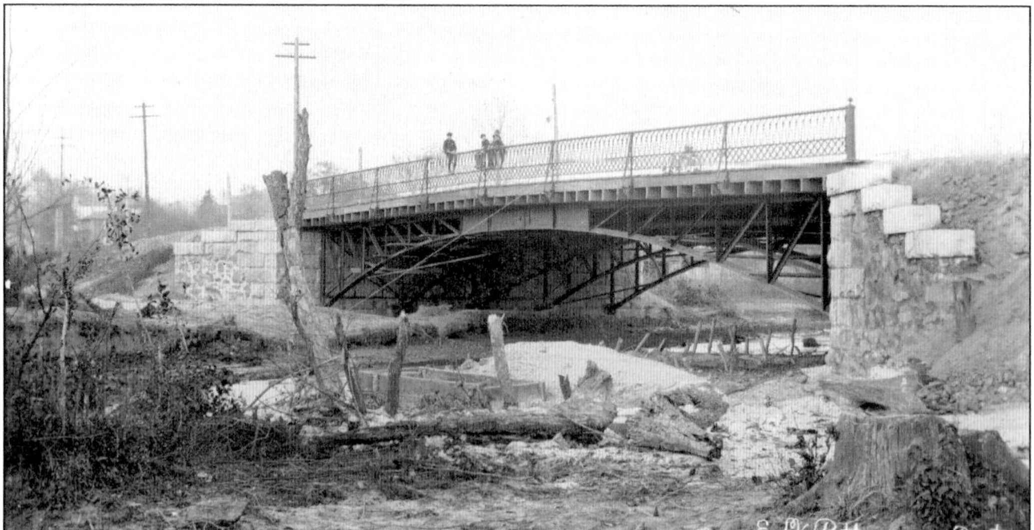

Although a few wealthy individuals had cars in 1908, the automobile did not appear in any sizable number until 1915. Henry E. Fries was the first to own a car in the neighborhood, and his great-niece remembers being taken for rides by his gardener and that it was "electric and completely quiet." This photograph shows the steel-truss bridge of Main Street over Salem Creek, near the present-day Southeast Gateway YWCA. (Forsyth County Public Library Photograph Collection.)

Two

FOUNDING FAMILIES AND THEIR HOMES

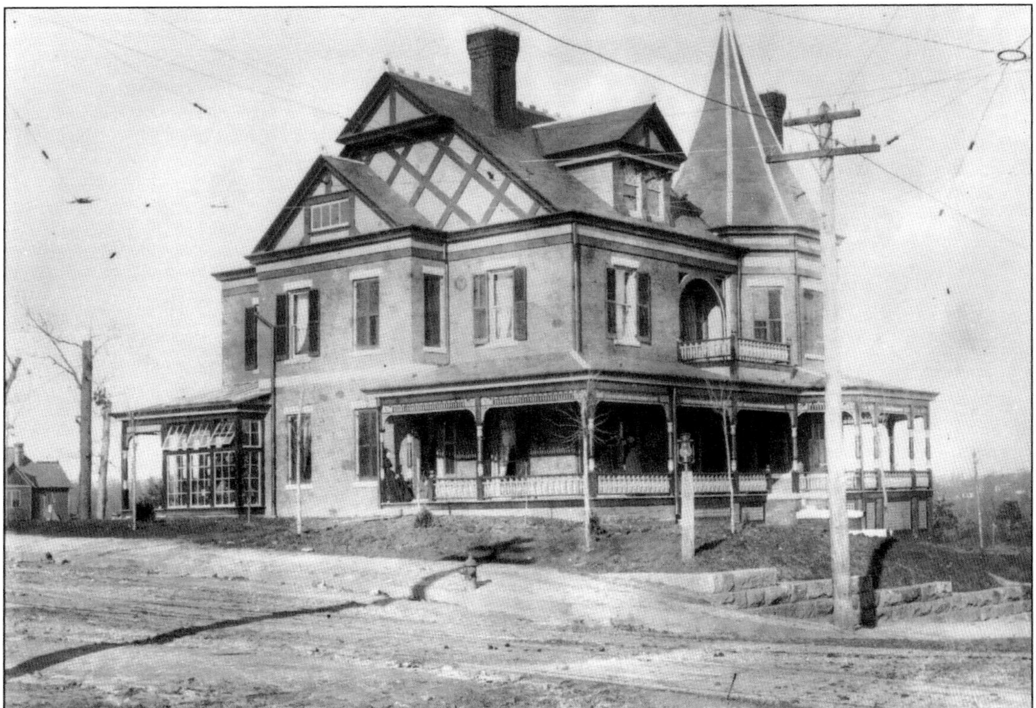

The David S. Reid House is a Victorian brick mansion at the corner of Cascade Avenue and South Main Street. Reid lived on East Second Street when he bought this property in August 1891 and completed the house in 1894. Later the home was the residence (bought in 1920) of Dr. Paul Schallert, his wife, Grace, and their four children. Dr. Schallert eventually turned the house into apartments and moved to Florida. The house became known as the Charlotte House because of the mispronunciation of Dr. Schallert's name. (Collection of the Wachovia Historical Society; photograph courtesy of Old Salem Museums and Gardens.)

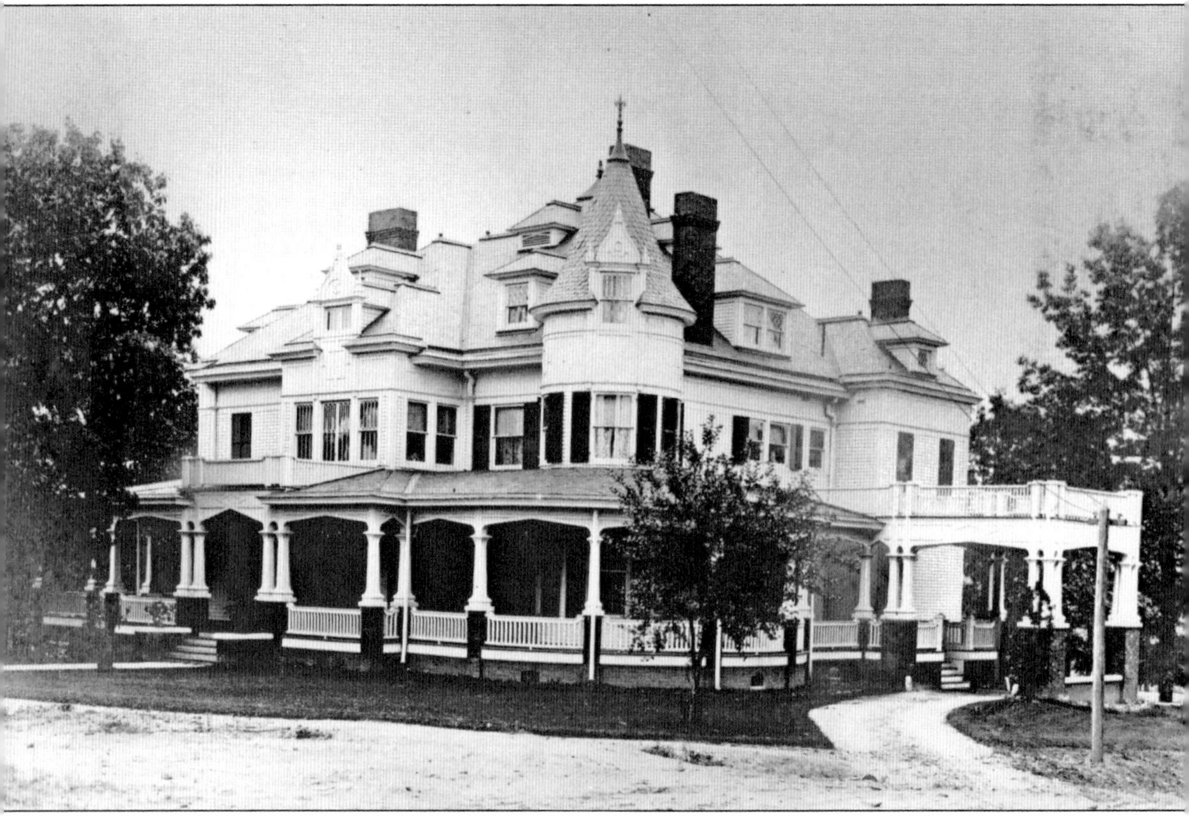

This home, which stood at 205 Cascade Avenue and covered the city block of Cascade Avenue, Broad Street, Gloria Avenue, and Park Boulevard, was built by Jesse Lagenour and his wife around 1900. It was reportedly designed by the same Washington architect who build R. J. Reynolds's home at 666 West Fifth Street. Lagenour's wife, the former Mary Alice "Minnie" Volger, "was the Dresden China type," according to her nephew, and was always beautifully dressed. She was the youngest daughter of E. A. Volger and Emma Antoinette Reich, who owned the Sunnyside Plantation, for which this area of town is named. A *Winston-Salem Journal* article reported that neighbors recalled seeing the childless couple cross the porch and leave from the porte cochere in a carriage with livery. The couple moved to Woodland, California, in 1917, where they remained unil they died. The Thomas Shirley Fleshman family bought the house when they relocated from Kernersville. (Moravian Archives, Winston-Salem, North Carolina.)

Mina Pepper Fleshman lived at 205 Cascade Avenue for 30 years before she died. Her husband was from Appomattox, Virginia, and had been a traveling salesman for a large firm in Lynchburg, Virginia. In 1898, he transferred to Salem, and on December 14 of that year he married Mina. They had four children—two sons and two daughters—three of whom died in infancy or childhood. (Forsyth County Public Library Photograph Collection.)

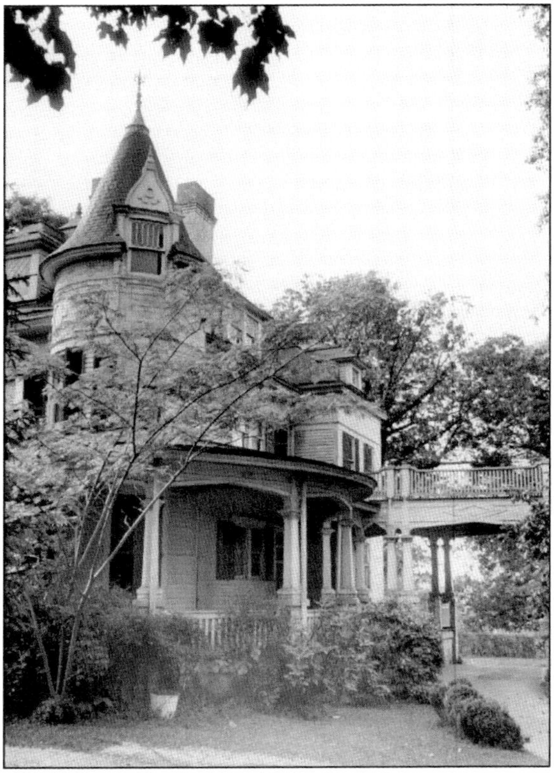

When Thomas S. Fleshman lived on Cascade Avenue, he became the district manager for Mutual Life Insurance Company of New York and invested in real estate and R. J. Reynolds stock. He retired from active business to devote his time to managing his private assets. At the time of his death, he had amassed a great fortune. (Forsyth County Public Library Photograph Collection.)

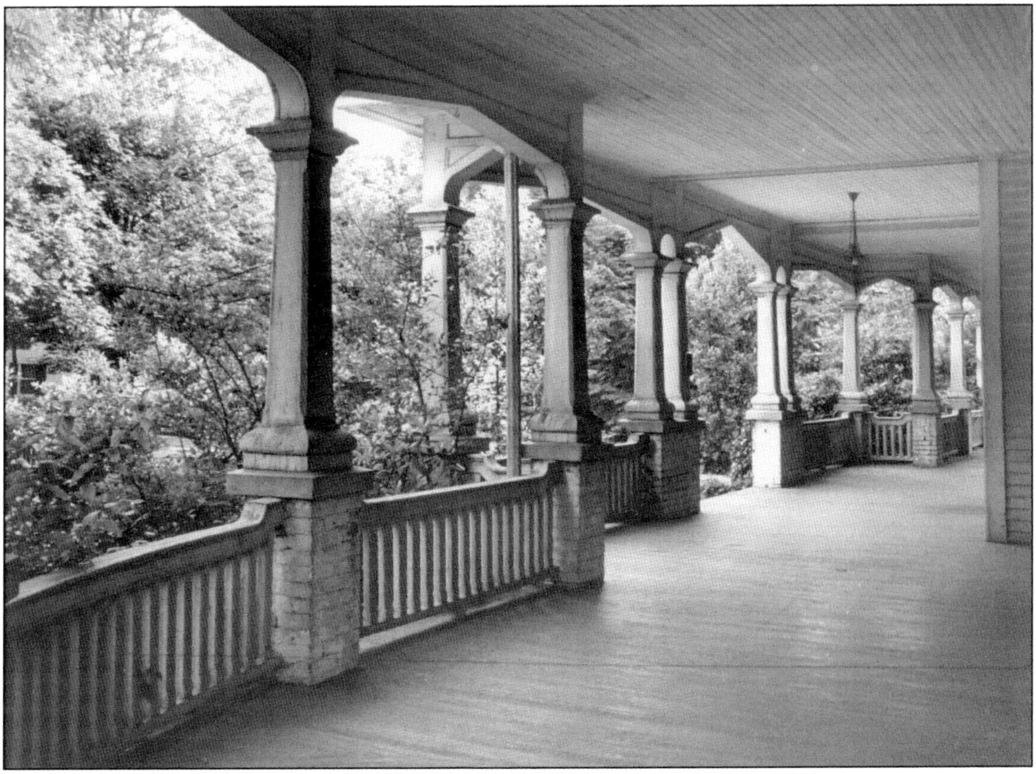

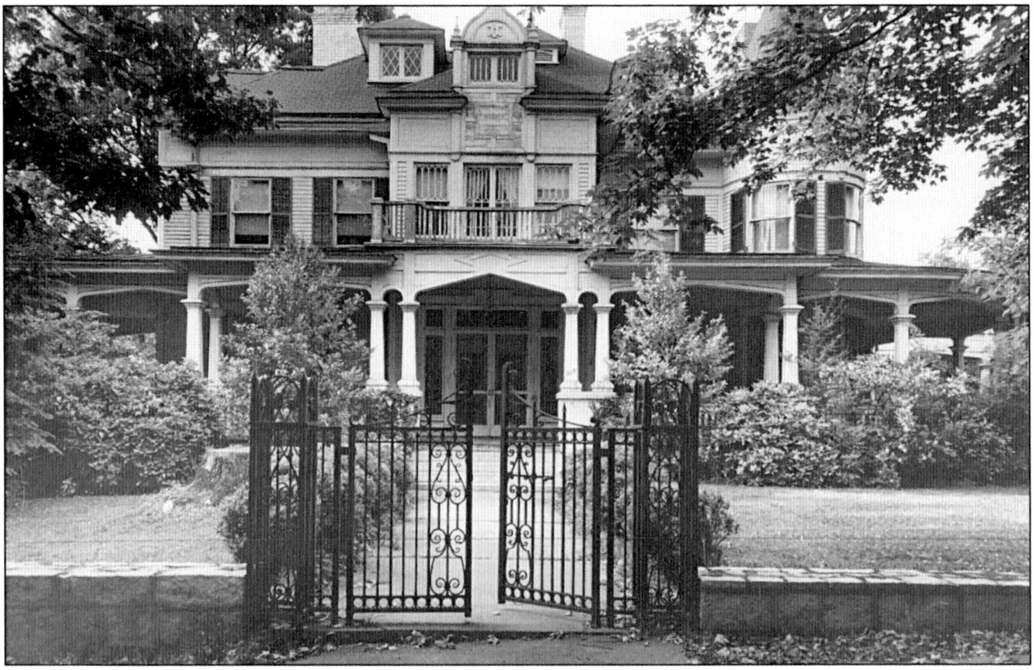

Mina Fleshman was an ardent gardener, and her house at 205 Cascade Avenue was named Eglantine after the wild roses that grew everywhere. After she passed away in 1965, her daughter Geraldine had the place torn down. The existing stone wall and gateposts and some scattered trees and daffodils are all that remain of the stately mansion and its gardens. (Forsyth County Public Library Photograph Collection.)

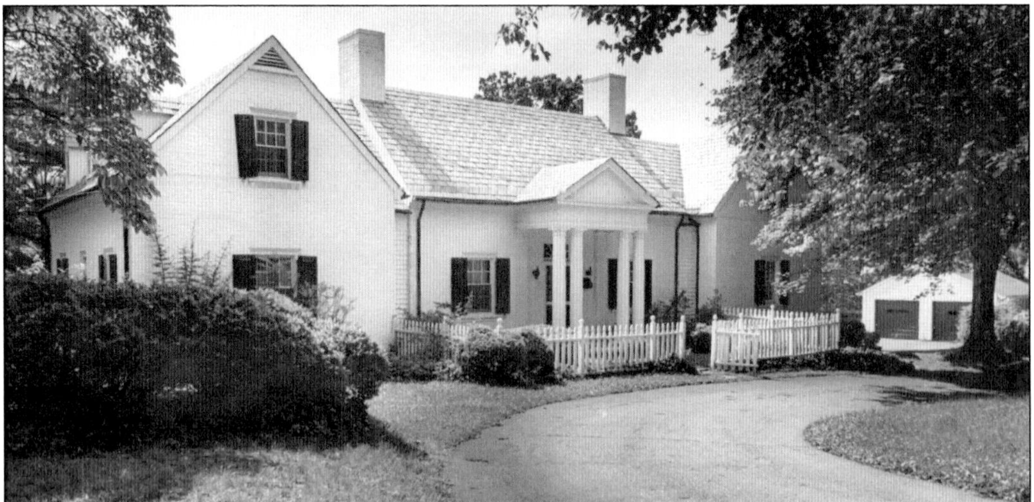

The Fleshman-Graham house was built in 1925 for the Fleshman's daughter Geraldine and her husband, Gregory Graham. It was built on the back corner of Eglantine's property, on the corner of Park Boulevard and Cascade Avenue. It was the first house designed by Luther Lashmit, the architect who designed Graylyn, and it won him a national design award. Many neighbors remember when Geraldine's husband hanged himself in the early 1940s, and Geraldine promptly moved to the other side of town. She eventually married Stewart C. Pratt and had one daughter. (Kriss Dinkins and Stephan Dragisic.)

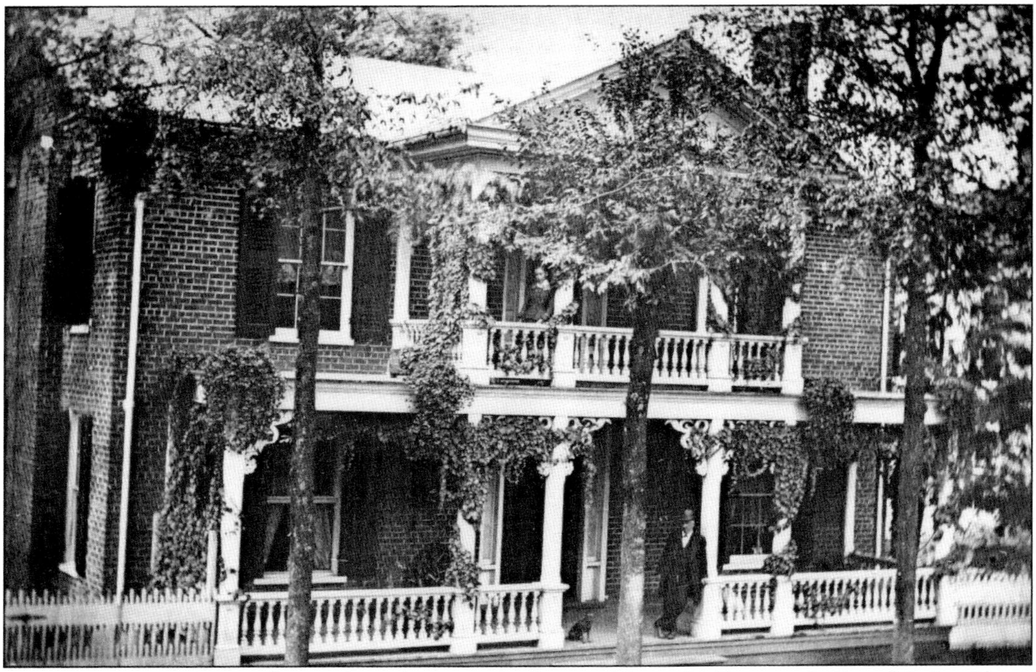

Among the wealthy residents of Washington Park were Henry E. Fries, wife Rosa Mickey Fries, and daughter Anna Marguerite Fries. They moved from their first house, located on South Main Street in Salem (shown above), to their new home at 104 Cascade Avenue (shown below). Henry was instrumental in the development of the neighborhood with his involvement in the Winston-Salem Land and Investment Company; his power plant, which generated the power for the streetcars; and his mill on Goldfloss Street. He was also head of the gas company, president of the Winston-Salem Southbound Railway, and a mayor of Salem. In 1884, he helped create the North Carolina Industrial Exposition in Raleigh and was a member of the three-man committee that helped plan the North Carolina College of Agriculture and Mechanic Arts (now North Carolina State University). For 53 years, he was a trustee of what is now Winston-Salem State University. (Above, Moravian Archives, Winston-Salem, North Carolina; below, Forsyth County Public Library Photograph Collection.)

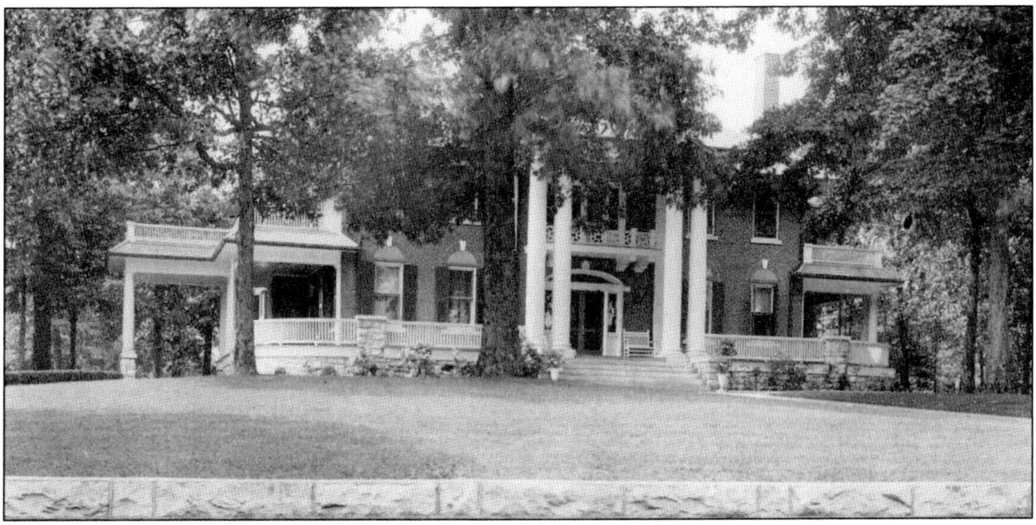

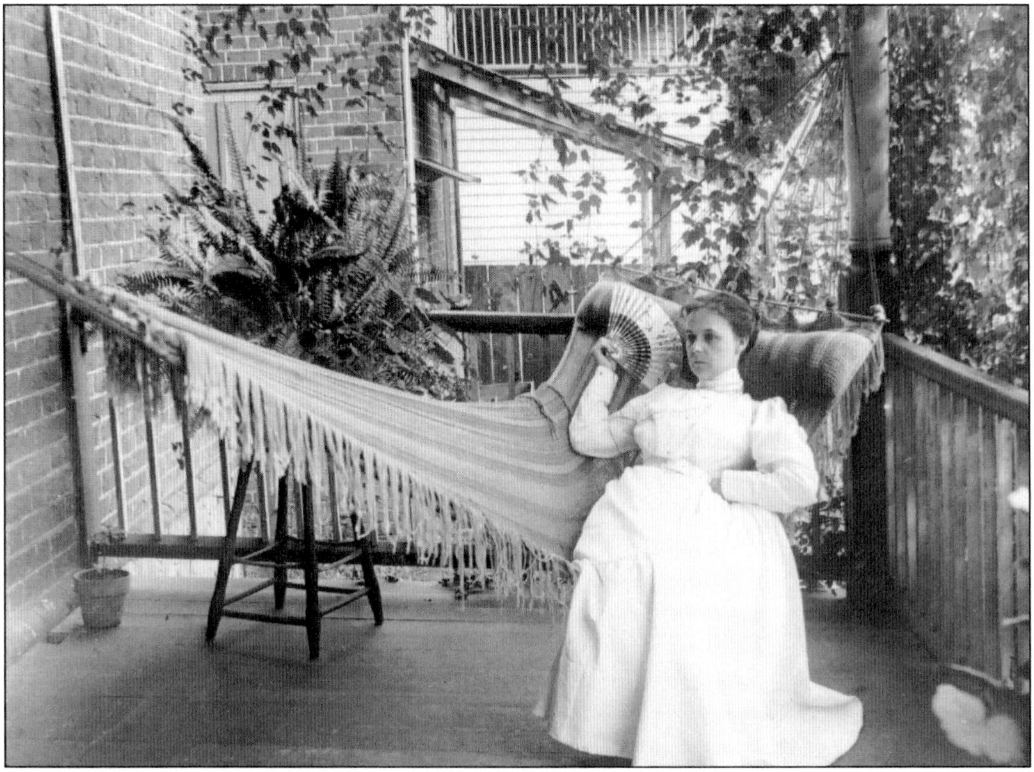

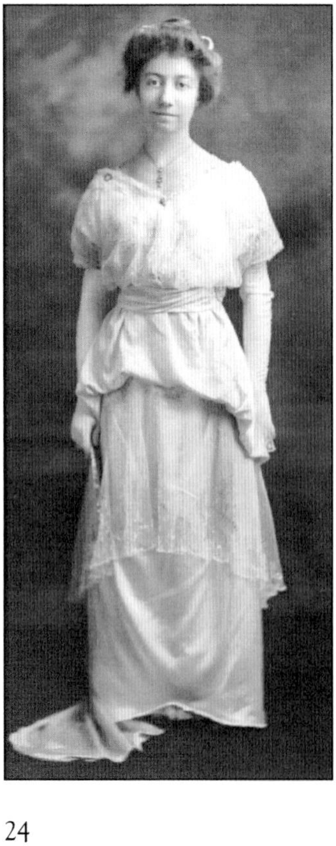

Henry E. Fries and Rosa Mickey were married on April 20, 1881. Two years before her husband helped organize the North Carolina Industrial Exposition in Raleigh, Rosa organized a wheat fair at Pace's Tobacco Warehouse on North Liberty Street in Winston. The fair was so popular that it continued to be held, with the scope widening to include many agricultural products. (Collection of Old Salem Museums and Gardens.)

The only child of Henry and Rosa Fries, Anna was only 24-years-old when she died of scarlet fever in 1916. She awoke with it Sunday morning April 2, and died Friday evening, April 7. According to her obituary in the Moravian archive, she was described as "dear to her parents as the apple of the eye, and all the arrangements of the home were constantly being made for her happiness, and yet she grew up strangely unselfish." (Moravian Archives, Winston-Salem, North Carolina.)

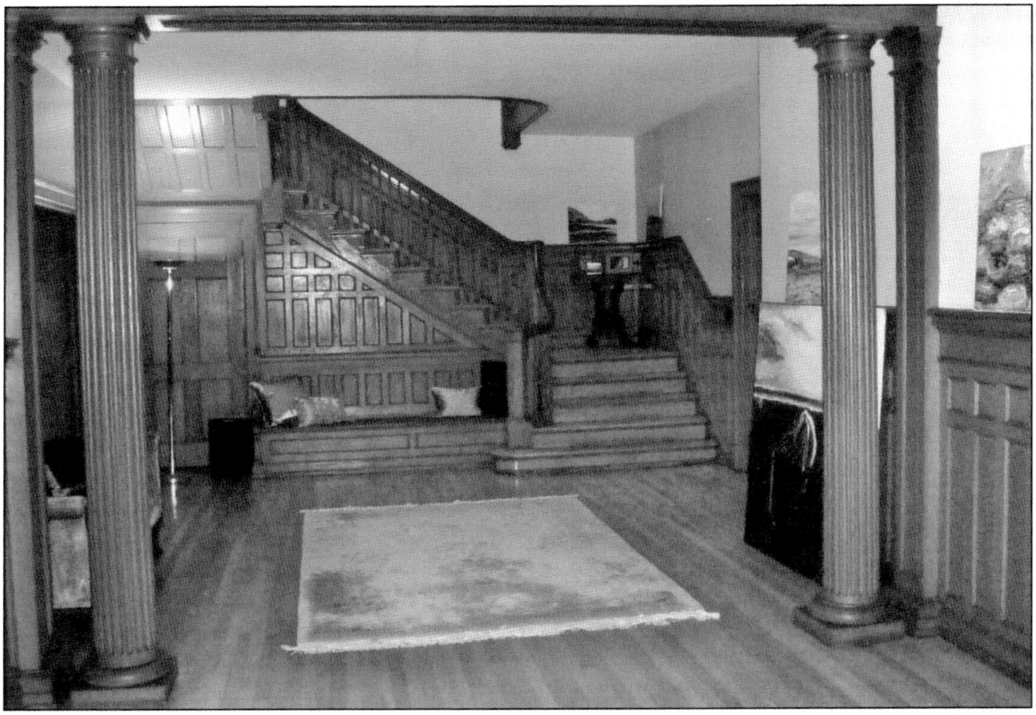

When the Frieses' envisioned their home at 104 Cascade Avenue, they imagined throwing open the doors on the front porches and having large affairs for everyone to attend. But after the sudden death of their daughter, Anna, they were devastated, and although they entertained, it was never quite the same. It is said that Henry did more than any other in the city, and probably in the state, for harmony between the races. (Deidre Johnston.)

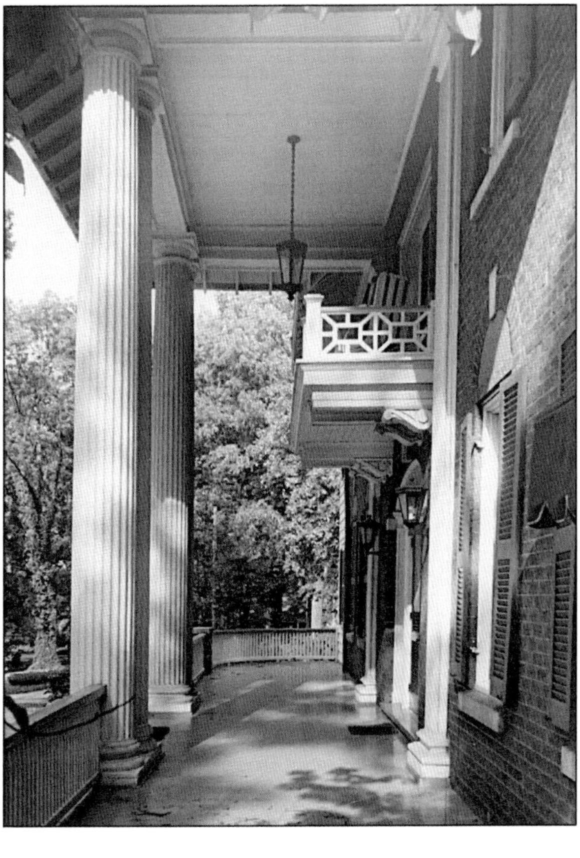

After Henry and Rosa died, the William F. Fishel family bought the house in 1945 and converted in into seven apartments (including the carriage house) to help alleviate the housing shortage. Work began about December 1, and by March 15, 1946, six apartments in the main house and a seventh in the carriage house were ready for curtains. The house was restored back to the original, single-family residence when Paul McCann and Deirdre Johnston bought the house in 1995. (Forsyth County Public Library Photograph Collection.)

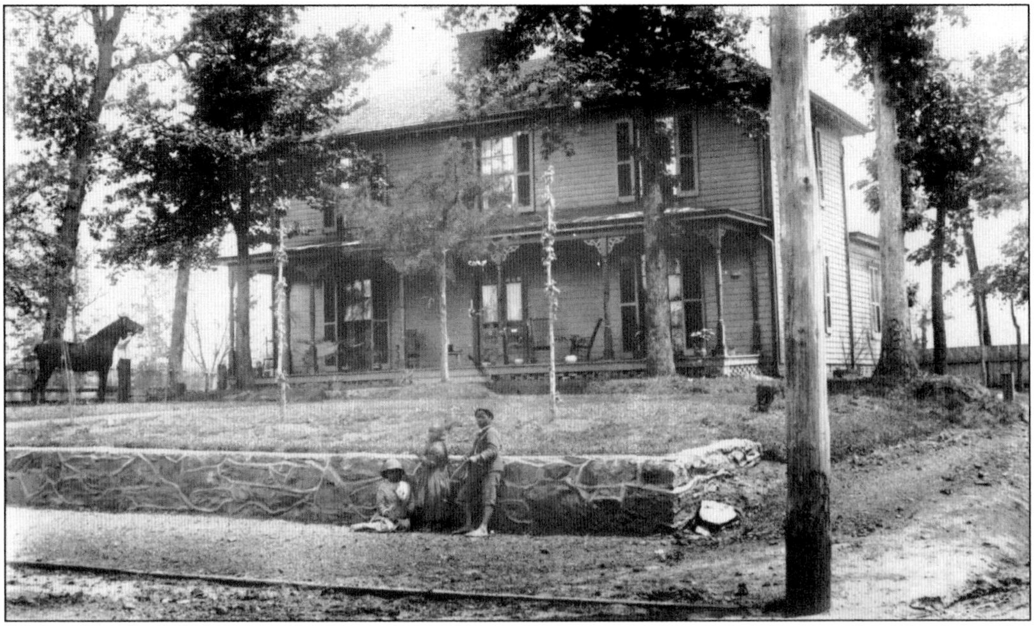

This house at 134 Cascade Avenue started as a farmhouse built by the Banner family in the mid-1800s. Between 1890 and 1905, a dining room and small den were added. In 1928, under the direction of architect Luther Lashmit, a total remodeling took place. The people in the photograph are unidentified. (Collection of the Wachovia Historical Society; photograph courtesy of Old Salem Museums and Gardens.)

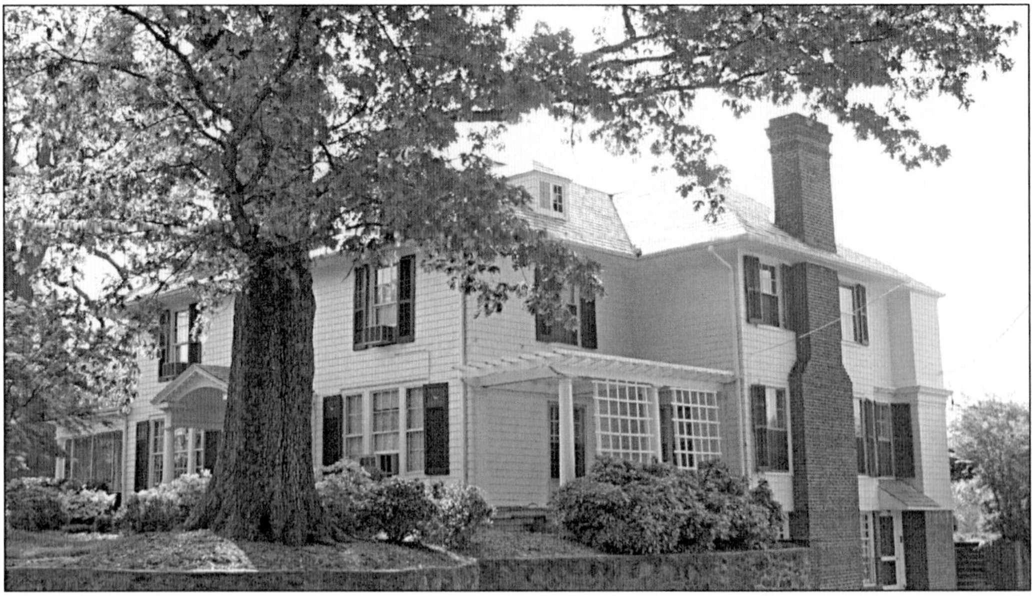

The renovated house at 134 Cascade Avenue had been home to two families that were closely related—the Craiges' nephew, Robert V. Brawley, lived across the street in the Cicero Lowe house. Jane Boyden Craige and her husband, Burton, lived here with their two children. They chose to remain on Cascade Avenue in order to maintain their close ties to the Boyden and Brawley families in Salisbury. The Brawleys later acquired this home and moved into it in the early 1970s. (Chris and Cindy Sheaffer.)

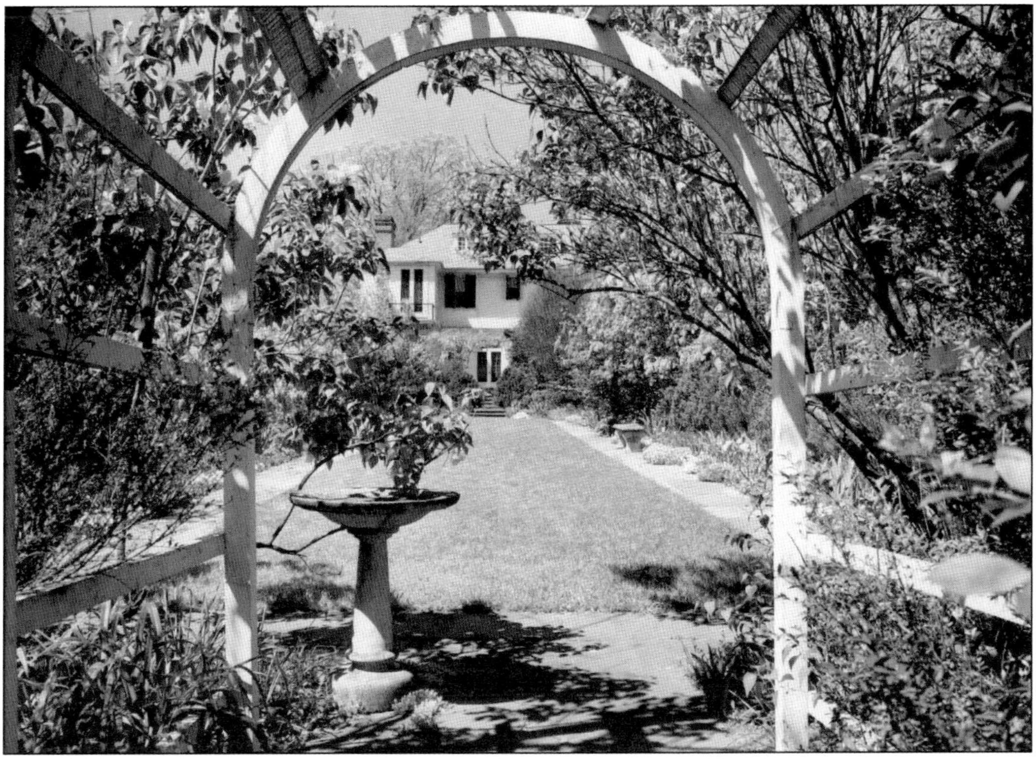

The gardens at 134 Cascade Avenue were designed by Thomas Sears, who also landscaped R. J. Reynolds's estate, Reynolda, and Bowman Gray's estate, Graylyn. The original plans were designed in September 1928 and revised in March 1929, when work began. The gardens retain the same configuration today, including the rose garden and the pool. When Emmy Brawley owned this house, she opened up the pool to the neighborhood and it was dubbed "Club Cascade." (Above, Forsyth County Public Library Photograph Collection; below, Chris and Cindy Sheaffer.)

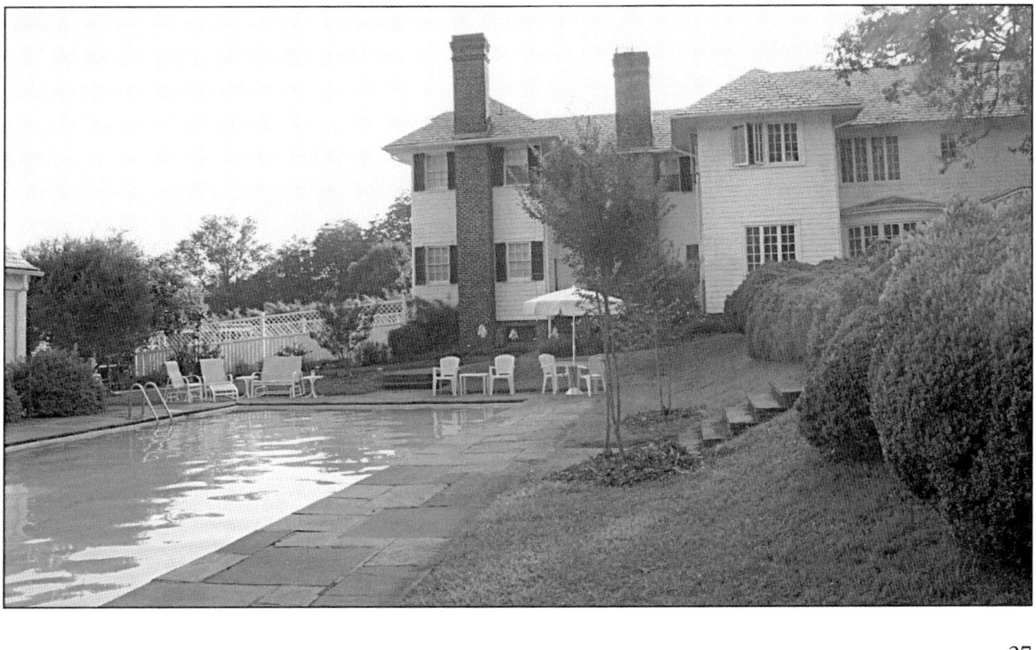

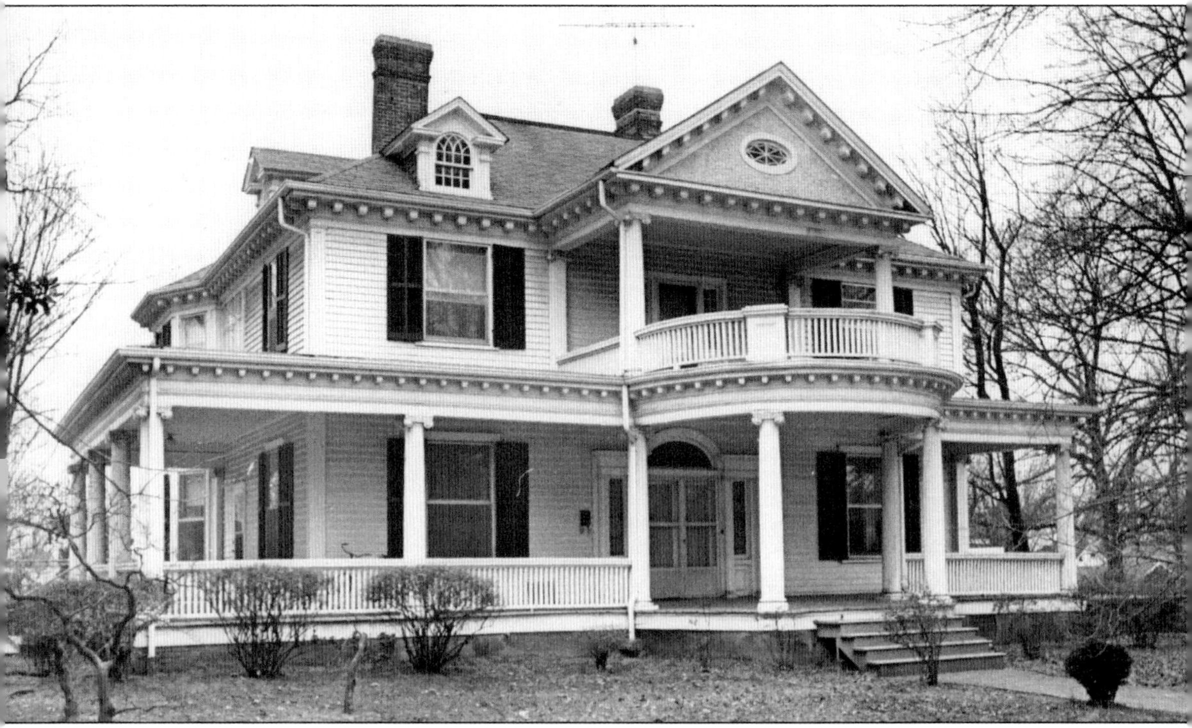

Janet Rawlings, one of Lowes' children, was three when their house at 204 Cascade Avenue was built in 1911. Her father was secretary and later vice president of Brown-Rogers-Dixson Hardware Company. She remembers her mother arranging flowers in the sink in the butler's pantry and that the nurse and cook lived in the quarters in the back. When the stock market crashed in 1929, Lowe's finances went with it, leaving a Norfolk, Virginia, bank with the deed of trust. The house changed hands, first going to a mortgage company and in May 1932 to W. S. Lindsay and his wife, Sethelle. The house was later purchased by the Robert V. Brawley family, which eventually sold it in 1981 after moving into Robert's aunt's house at 134 Cascade Avenue 10 years earlier. (Forsyth County Public Library Photograph Collection.)

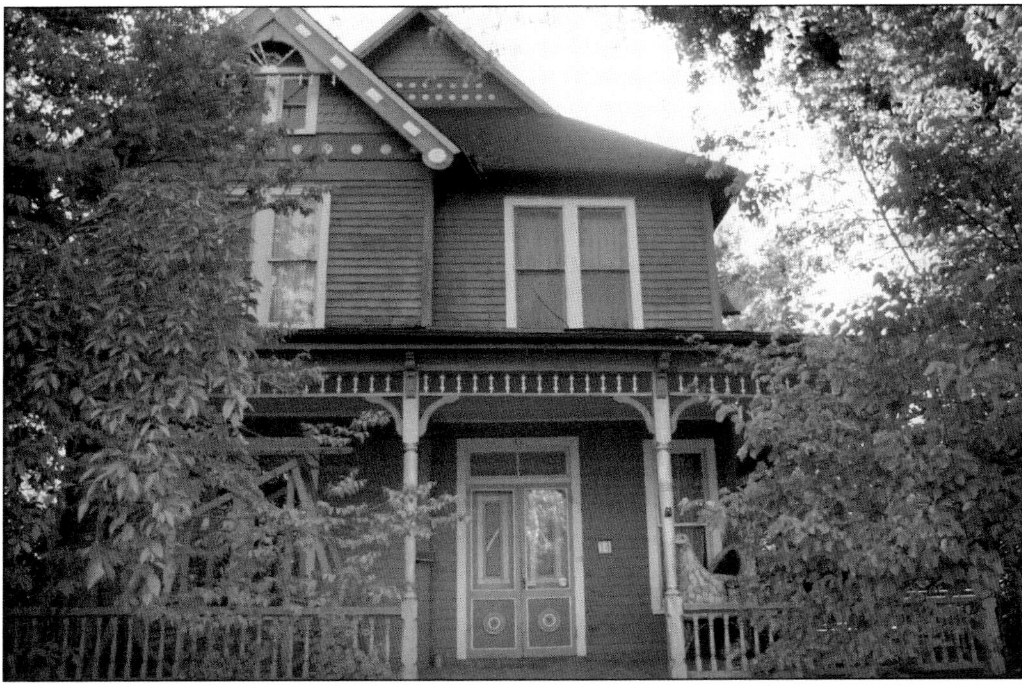

Adolphus Eller and his wife moved the Victorian house at 129 Cascade Avenue, shown above, to 14 Park Boulevard in 1918. They sold it to Thomas C. Davis, who lived here with his wife, Francis, and two daughters. On the newly vacant property of 129 Cascade Avenue, the Ellers built a new Dutch colonial home designed by the firm Northup and O'Brien. The property used to extend to Gloria Avenue, but it is believed to have been sold to build the pool. Three smaller houses were constructed in the 1960s on the former garden property. (Forsyth County Public Library Photograph Collection.)

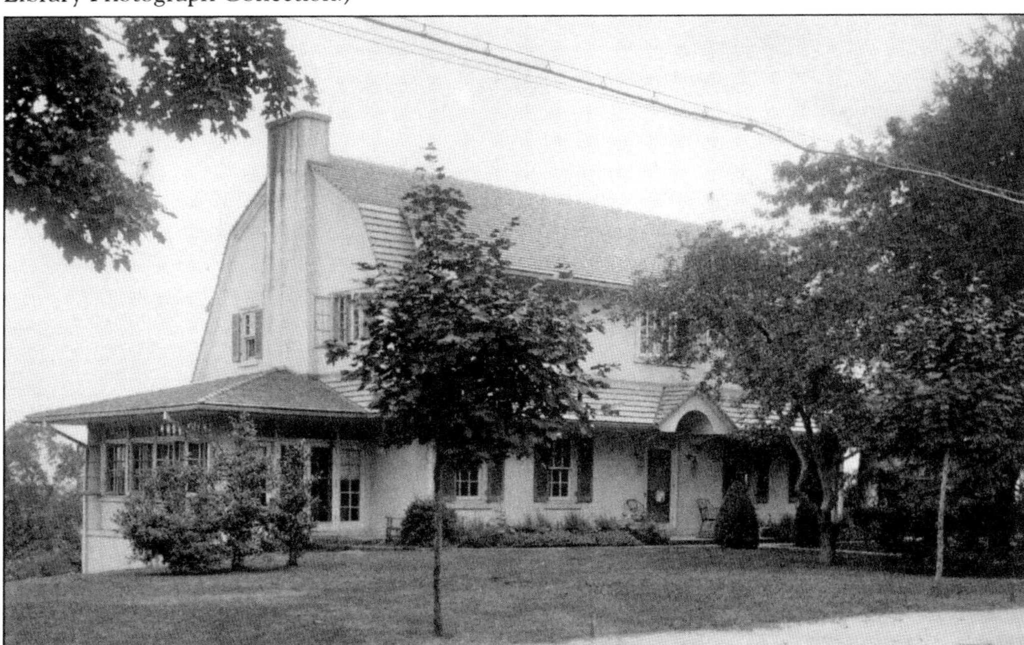

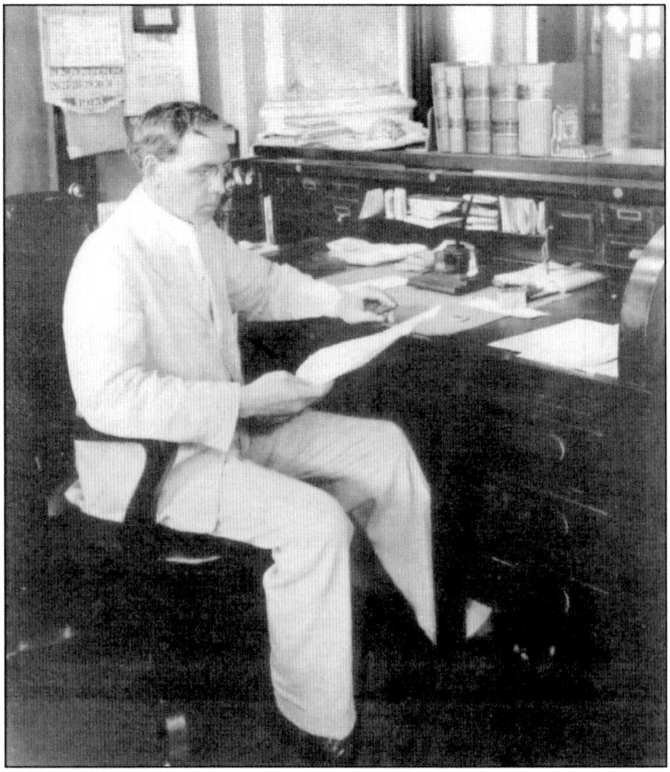

Adolphus Eller, shown here at his desk, was a lawyer whose business interests lay in banking, railroads, and politics. He practiced law until 1914, when he became a trust officer and vice president of Wachovia Bank and Trust. He served in the North Carolina Senate from 1905 to 1907 and was secretary and treasurer of the North Carolina Railroad from 1908 to 1912. He was also cofounder of Baptist hospital and the Slater Industrial Academy (now Winston-Salem State University). (Doris McMillan Eller.)

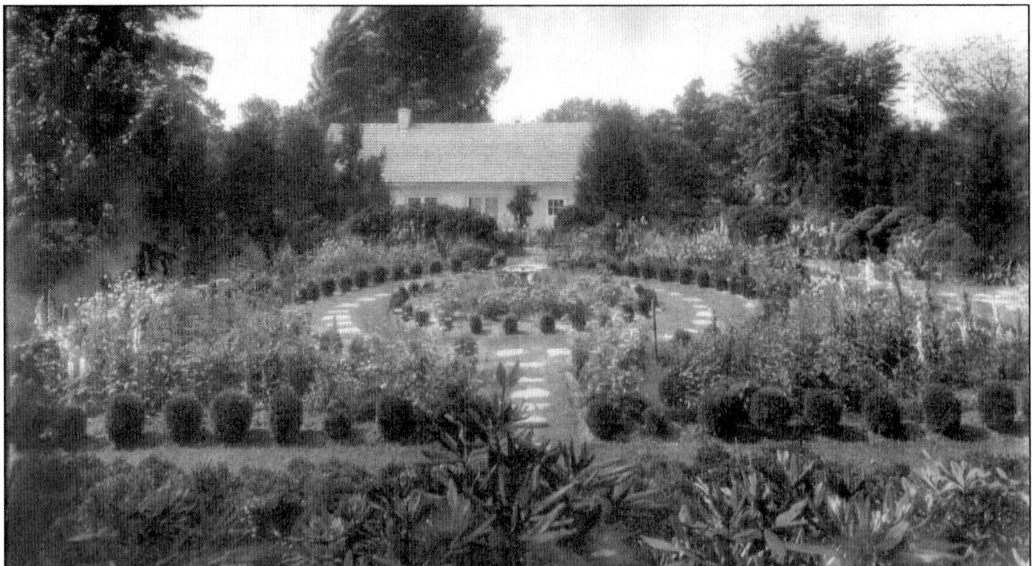

According to a *Winston-Salem Journal* article dated May 23, 1931, the Eller garden, located at 129 Cascade Avenue, was featured in a garden tour. It stated, "the formal garden which is slopping alongside the sun parlor of the handsome Eller home, [named] Sunnyside" described the trees, boxwoods, lovely blossoms, and roses. It also described the apple orchard in which "happy little boys rode their pony amid a setting historic and appealing." The gardens were located along Broad Street and Gloria Avenue. (Doris McMillan Eller.)

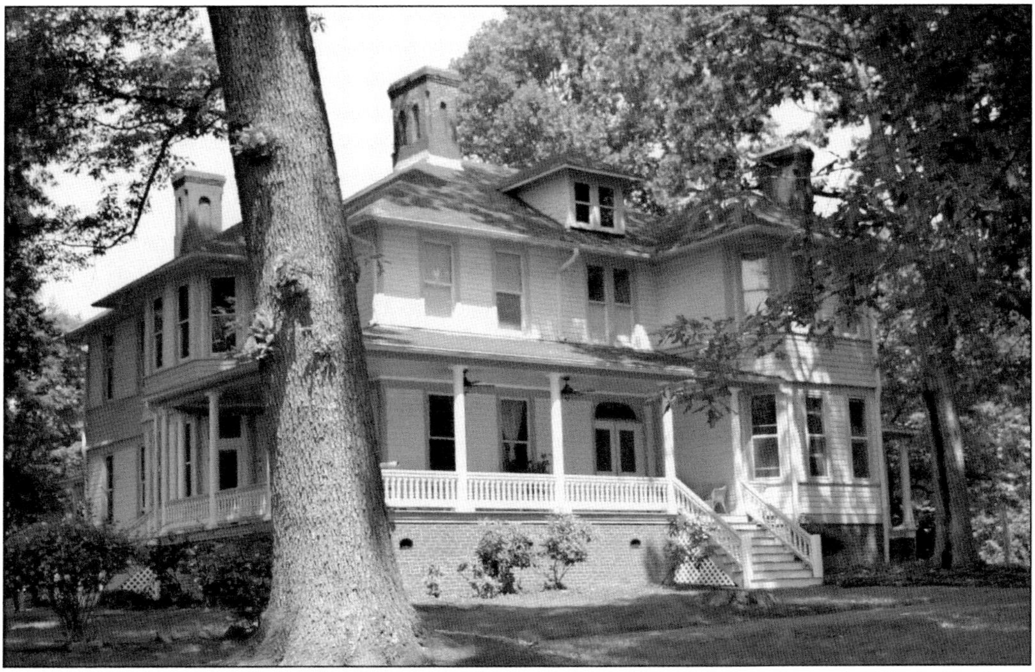

Built between 1896 and 1898 by Christian H. Fogle, a founder and partner in the Fogle Brothers Lumber Company, this house, located at 514 West Banner Avenue, was originally part of a working farm, with vegetable gardens, an orchard, and acres of fenced pasture for cattle. Now the barn, the only one left in the neighborhood, and several small outbuildings are all the remain of the farm. Christian died before the house was completed, but his widow, Emma, moved here from their house on Belews Street. Older residents remember people arriving for a visit in a carriage drawn up under the porte cochere and seeing Japanese lanterns strung through the tress for summertime parties. With its many architectural details, the house is believed to have been constructed to showcase the supplies, services, and fine cabinetry that Fogle Brothers could provide their customers. (Nancy Hart and Bob Fitzgerald.)

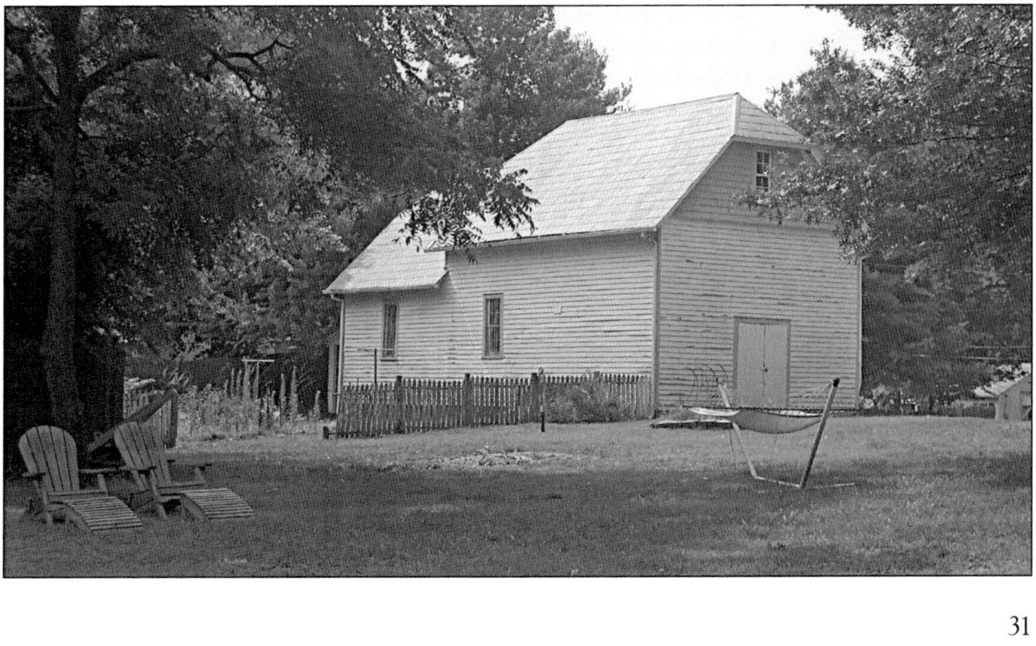

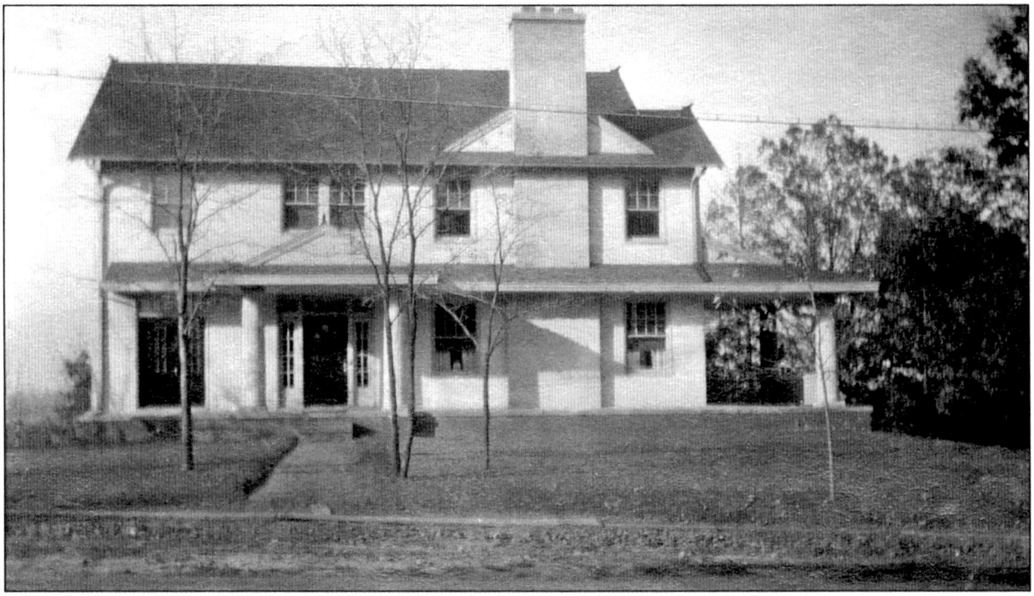

Charles Rudolph Fogle, the son of Charles Alexander and the nephew of Christian H. Fogle of the Fogle Brothers Company, built his home at 29 Cascade Avenue (shown above and below). Charles began work in his family's business, Orinoco Supply Company (later known as Builders Supply Company or House), in 1912 and became its vice president. His partner was E. T. Mickey, who married Charles' sister Ada. Charles's obituary said that he was the last representative of a generation who was born in Salem, educated at the Salem Boys School, furthered his education elsewhere, and came back to make a lasting contribution to this area. At the time of his death, he was the oldest member, and past master, of the Salem Masonic Lodge, at age 92. (Arthur Easter and Michael Ryden.)

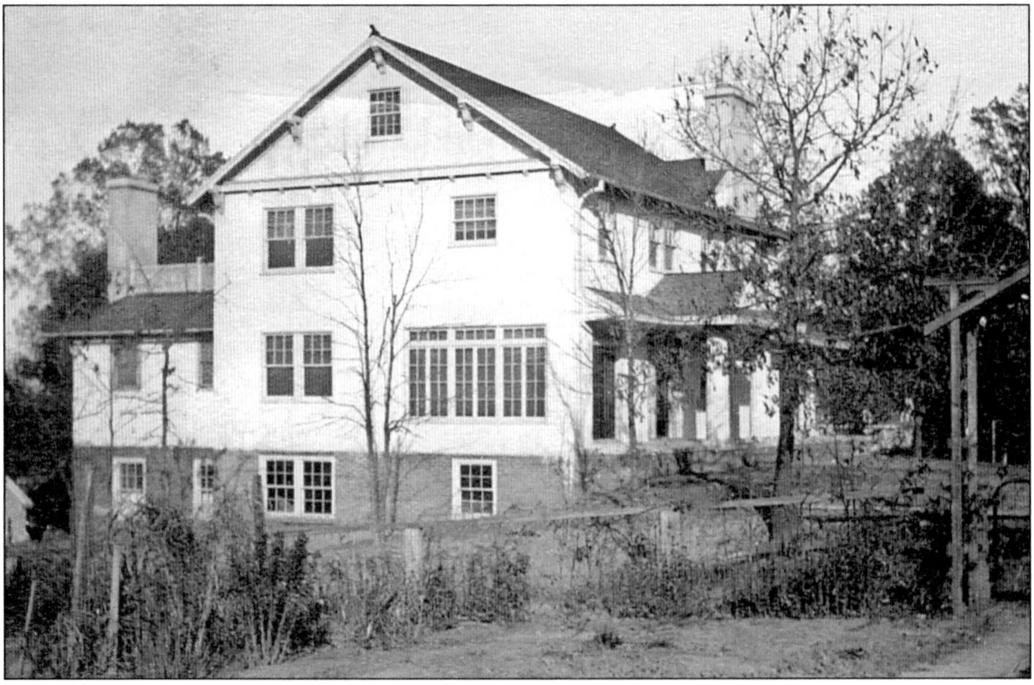

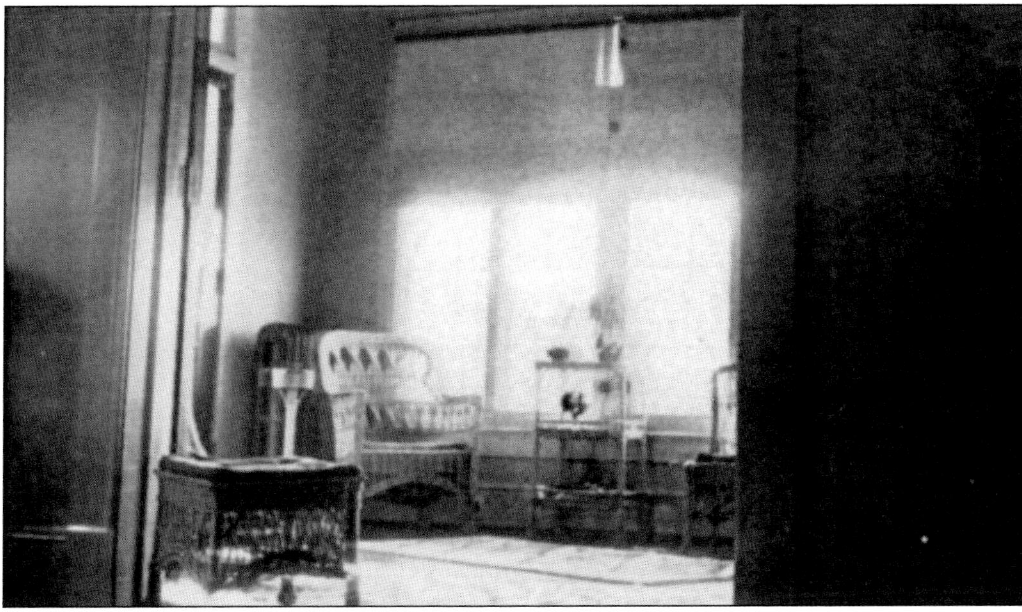

When the contents of Charles R. Fogle's house were auctioned off in 1972, the standing floor clock was bought by the Single's Brothers House in Old Salem. According to his daughter Anna Wray Fogle Cotterill, Charles kept birds, fish, and animals all about the place. His friend was a taxidermist, so heads and whole animals were displayed in some rooms of the house. All the lumber for the house came from Pilot Mountain, and the house sits on one of the highest elevations in the city. The property retains its original landscape, such as a boxwood garden, walls, pathways, and a fishpond. The rooms shown in these photographs are the living room and sitting room, located on either side of the front entrance. (Arthur Easter and Michael Ryden.)

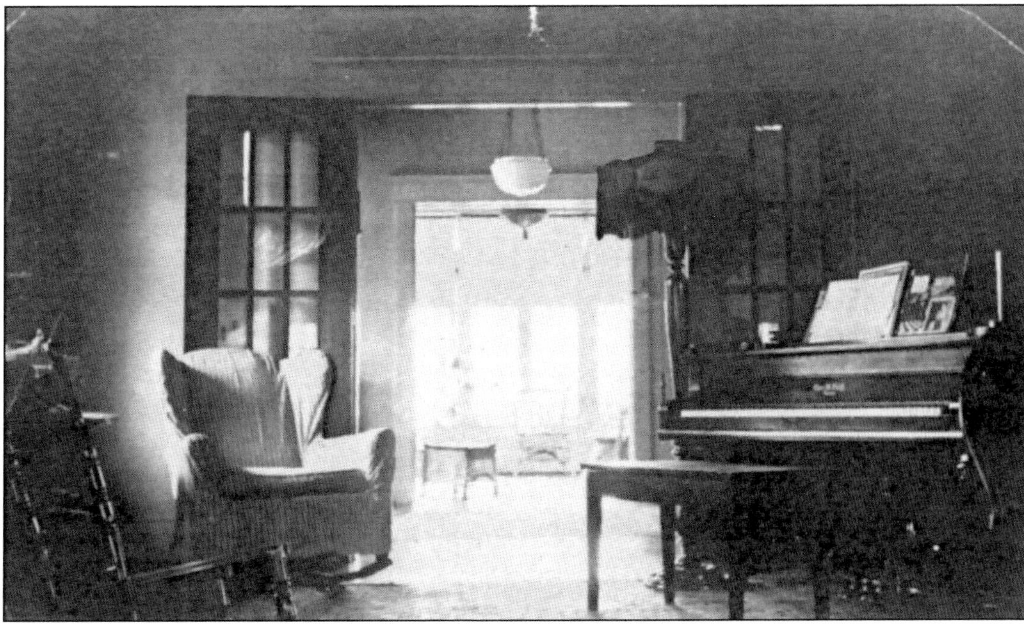

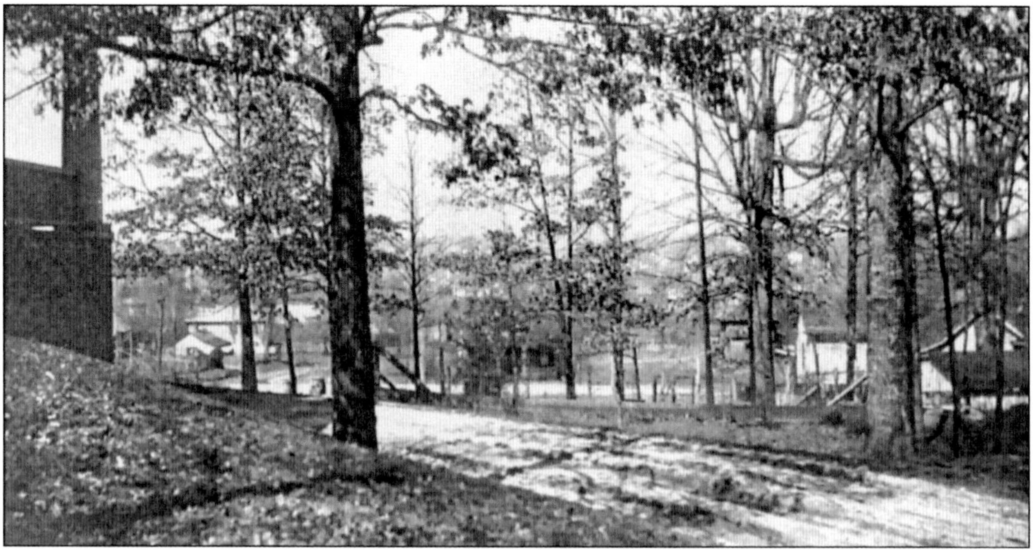

All the lots in the original Washington Park plan contained large parcels of land with an alley running between them. This alley was located behind the Charles R. Fogle home at Cascade Avenue and Doune Street. Today there are a few alleys still in existence in the neighborhood. (Arthur Easter and Michael Ryden.)

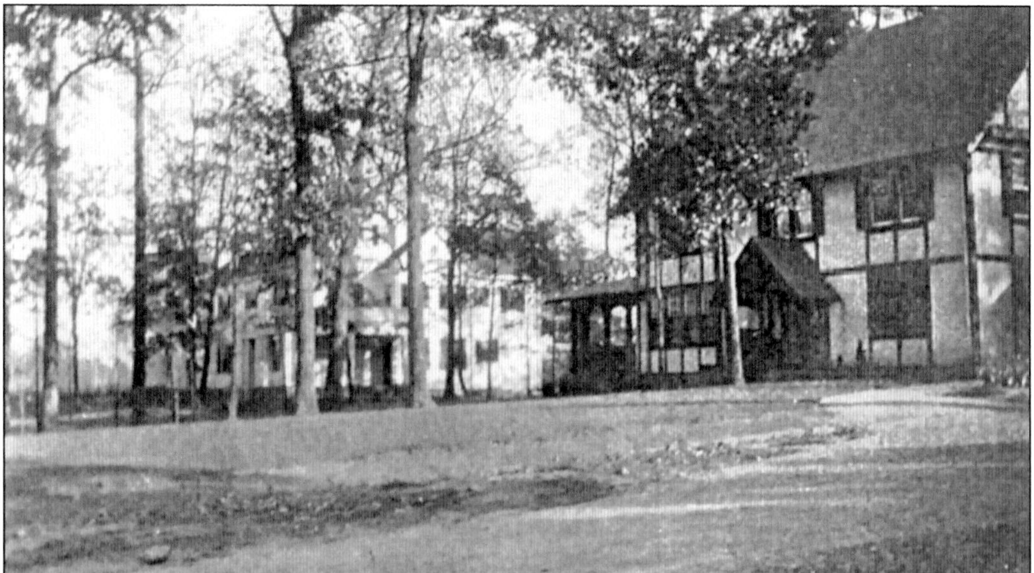

After the Civil War, good friends Henry T. Bahnson and Nathanial Siewers wanted to attend medical school in Pennsylvania. At the time, Henry did not have the financial means to pay for college, but Nathanial's family did, so they paid for his tuition. Two generations later, after the Depression, and when their finances were reversed, the Bahnsons paid for their son Hank and the Siewers' son Christian to attend medical school together. Their sons, Charles Siewers (house on left) and Frederic Bahnson (house on right) became next-door neighbors on Cascade Avenue. (Arthur Easter and Michael Ryden.)

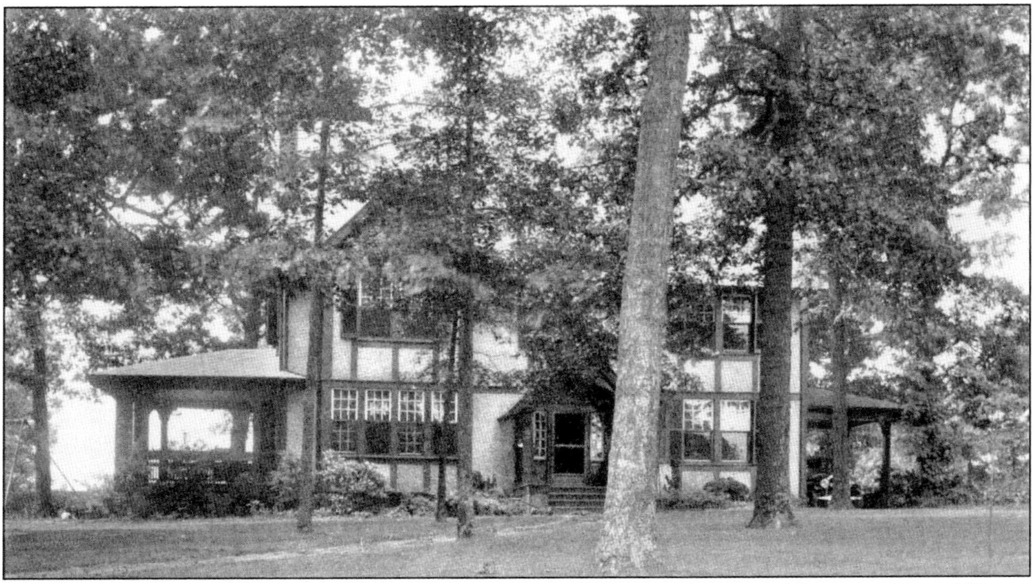

Frederic Fries Bahnson, the son of Dr. Henry T. Bahnson and Emma Christina Fries (Henry E. Fries' sister), built his home at 28 Cascade Avenue. He planned to be a doctor but had to drop out because of serious eye trouble. He turned to the field of engineering and worked for his uncle John W. Fries as an experimental scientist with humidifiers. In 1929, he organized the Southern Steel Stamping Company, along with his son Frederic Jr. (Forsyth County Public Library Photograph Collection.)

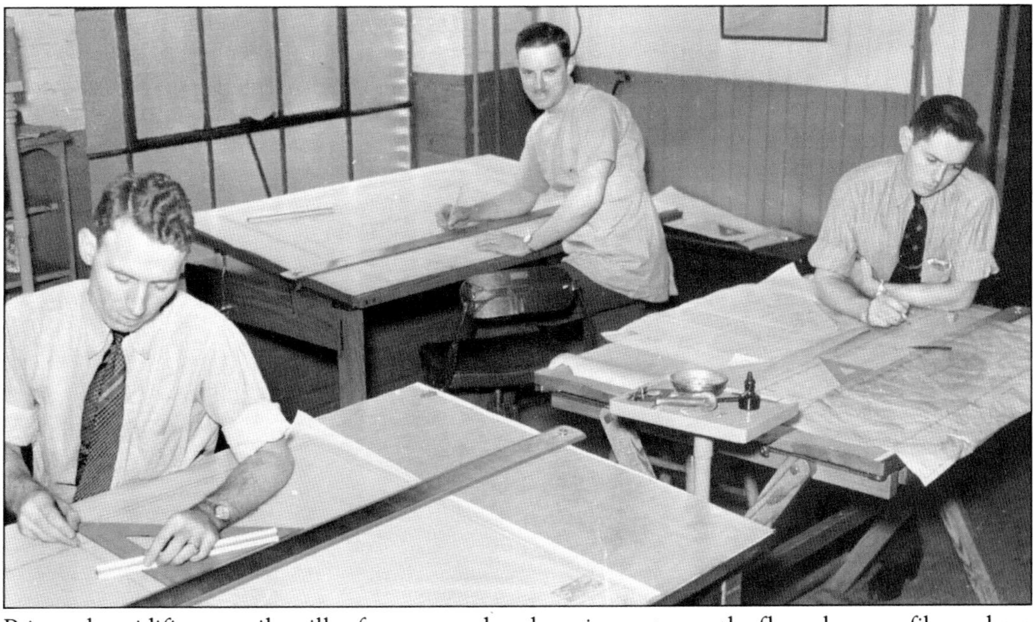

Prior to humidifiers, textile mills often resorted to throwing water on the floors because fibers where easier to work with when the air was moist. John W. Fries's humidifier patent proved successful, and he sold it to his nephews, Frederic and Agnew Bahnson. In August 1915, the Normalair Company was formed. By 1929, the name was changed to the Bahnson Company, employing over 1,000 people, including the draftsmen shown here, at its peak. Fred sold his interest to his brother Agnew in 1940. (Forsyth County Public Library Photograph Collection.)

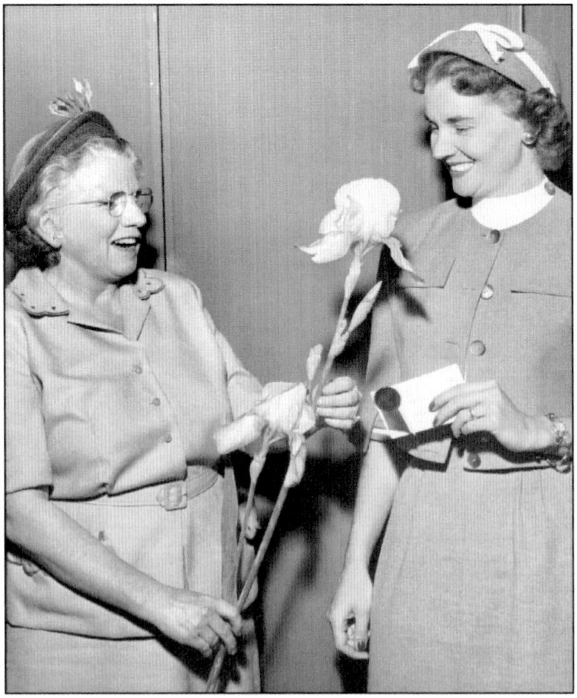

Mrs. Fred Bahnson Sr., the former Bleeker Reid of Charlotte, was a well-known horticulturist who was a charter member of the Twin City Garden Club. She is credited for planting hundreds of flowers throughout Washington Park. After her death in 1968, the house was donated to the North Carolina School of the Arts to be used as the chancellor's residence. She is pictured here with her daughter-in-law Cora Louise Bennett "Bennie" Bahnson. (Forsyth County Public Library Photograph Collection.)

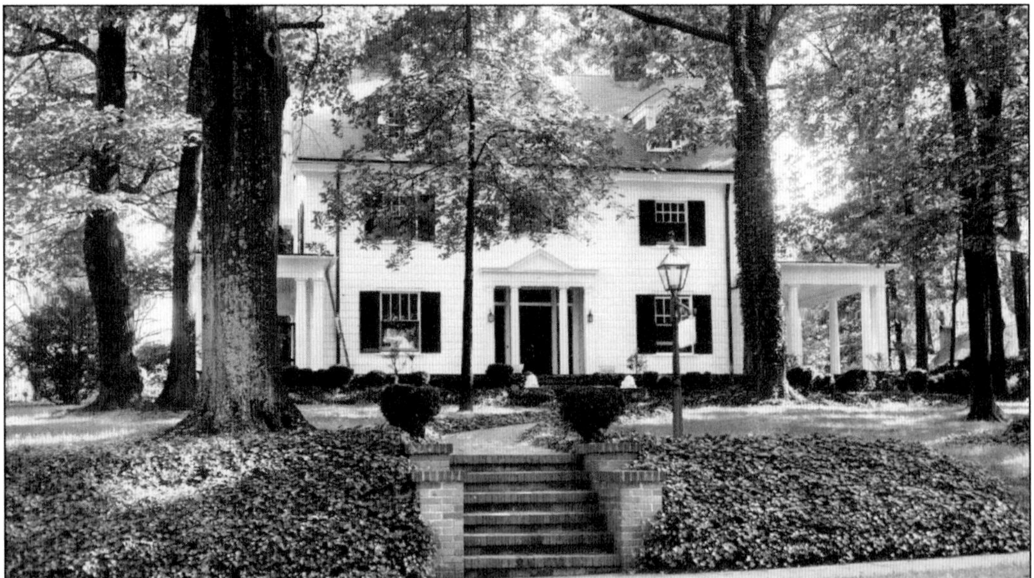

Charles Shober Siewers, son of Dr. Nathaniel Siewers, was president of the Forsyth Chair Company and the Forsyth Dining Room Furniture Company until the Depression, when the company folded. His partners in business were J. A. McDowell, Henry. E. Fries, Edward. T. Mickey, J. A. Lineback, and R. A. Spaugh. From the back porch of his house at 20 Cascade Avenue, he could view the top of his company's building, located on the corner of South Main Street, Acadia Avenue, and Sunnyside Avenue. After his wife's death, the house became the Moravian Music Foundation until 2001, when his grandson bought the property. (Forsyth County Public Library Photograph Collection.)

Charles Siewers was the second oldest of seven children of Dr. Nathanial Shober Siewers and Eleanor Elizabeth de Schweinitz of Salem. Through marriage on his mother's side, his uncles are John W. Fries, Henry E. Fries (his neighbor on Cascade Avenue) and "Colonel" Francis Henry Fries. Charles married Clara Vance on October 5, 1875. (Dr. Charles and Laura Turner.)

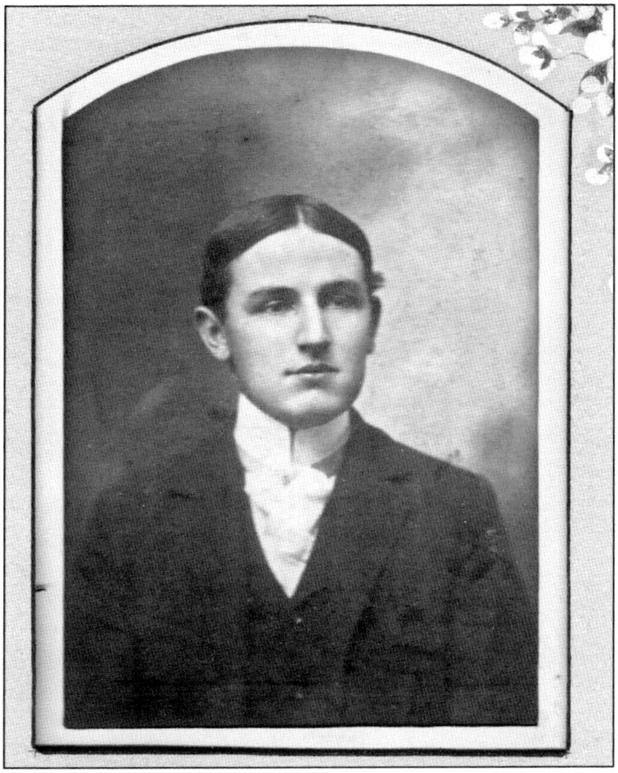

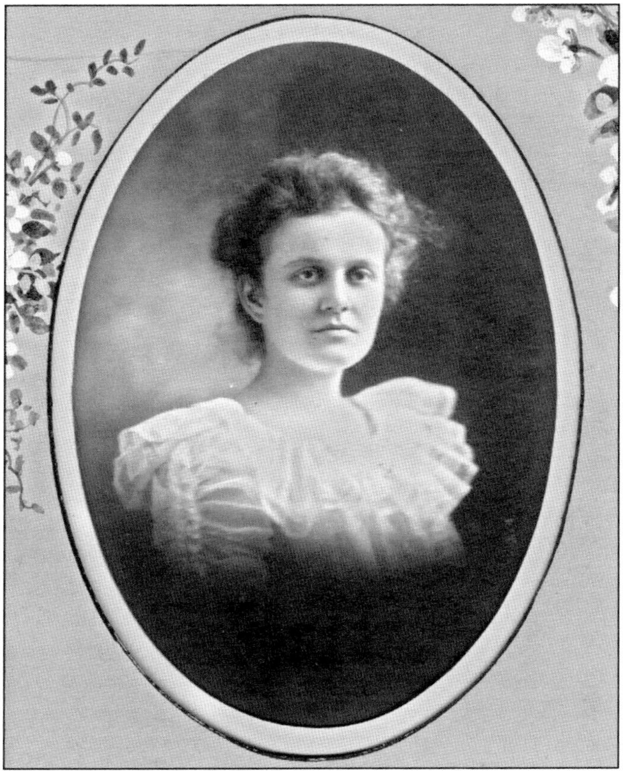

During and after the World War II, Clara Vance Siewers let rooms to single young women in Winston-Salem to help make ends meet. Her youngest child, Christian, was only 12 when his father passed away. Prior to marrying Charles, Clara studied in New York and was known for her beautiful voice. (Dr. Charles and Laura Turner.)

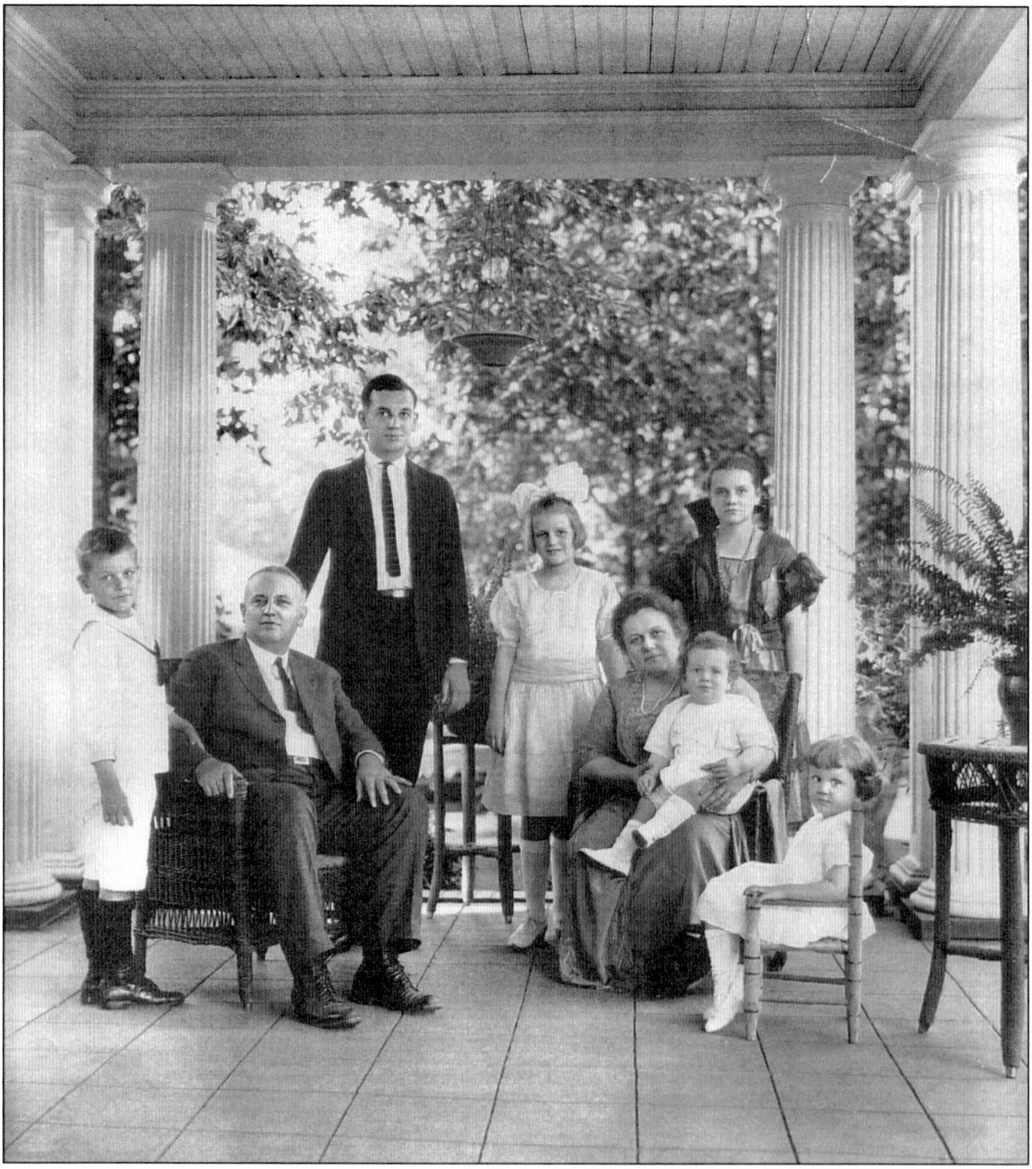

Charles and Clara Siewers had eight children, six of whom survived and prospered. Pictured from left to right are John, Charles Sr., Charles Nathanial, Margaret, Carolyn, Christian, and Mary Louise. Clara Vance Siewers lived here until she died on January 20, 1960. Her oldest son, Charles Nathanial, sat on the board of the Moravian Music Foundation and after her death made arrangements for the Moravian Music Foundation to relocate their offices here in 1962. The foundation owned the house until 2001 when Margaret's son, Dr. Charles Siewers Turner, bought the house and, with the aid of McNair Construction, restored the family home back to its original state. He currently resides there with his wife, Laura. The Moravian Music Foundation turned a portion of the basement into a climate-controlled vault to house rare manuscripts. The Turners use it for a wine cellar. (Dr. Charles and Laura Turner.)

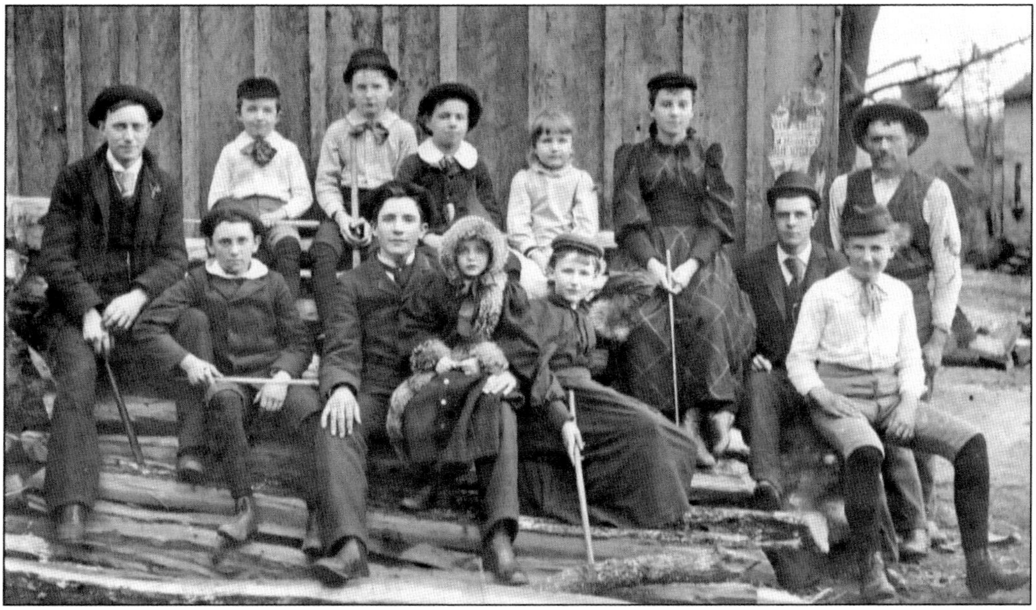

The Charles Shober Siewers siblings are pictured here in Salem. In the first row are Grace Siewers (fourth from left) with the hood, and next to her is Agnes Siewers (second from right). The older boy in the white shirt is Charles Shober Siewers. The two boys in the second row are Ralph Siewers (first from left) and Ledoux Siewers (second on left). (Dr. Charles and Laura Turner.)

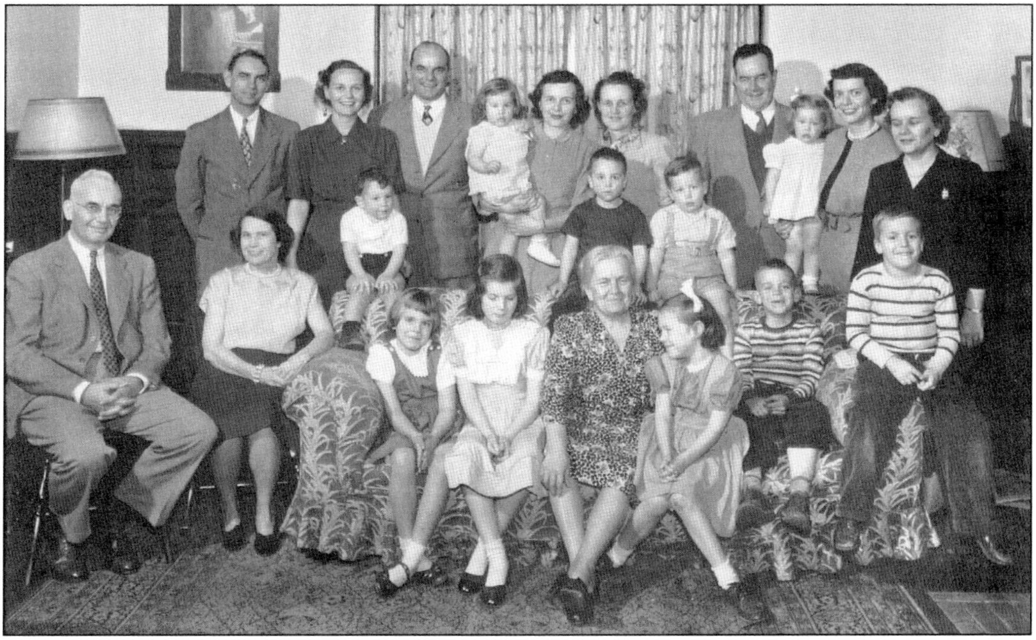

The Siewers family, c. 1950, pose with "Grandmother Clara," Clara Vance Siewers, in her home at 20 Cascade Avenue. Her children are Mary Louise (second from left, standing); Charles Nathanial (left, seated), Margaret Siewers Turner (fifth from right, standing); Christian Fogle Siewers (fourth from right, standing); and Carolyn (first on right, standing). The owner of the house today, Dr. Charles Siewers Turner, is sitting on the arm of the couch on the right. (Dr. Charles and Laura Turner.)

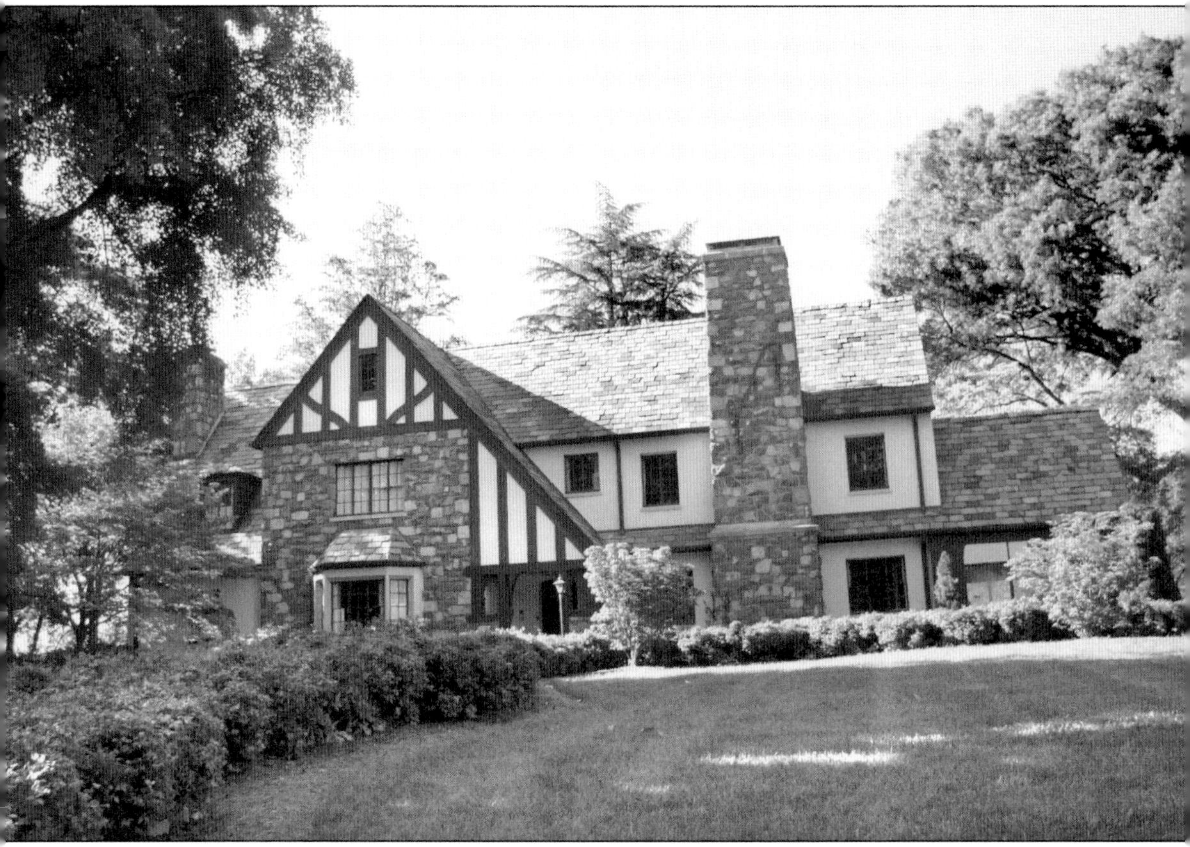

This Tudor Revival–style house and garden located at 631 West Banner Avenue used to be owned by Christian H. Fogle's son Frederick. Christian's wife, Emma, built this house for her son two blocks down from her home at 514 Banner Avenue. Fred was one of the organizers, along with Charles Shober Siewers, of the Forsyth Furniture Company, located on the corner of South Main Street and Acadia Avenue. In 1922, he organized Fogle Furniture Company. He served two terms as the mayor of Salem—he was mayor when the towns merged in 1913—and served as alderman. When his mother passed away, he moved into her home and left his wife, Beryl Pratt Fogle, to "carry on in this house." After his death, this house was lived in by a couple of families before being sold to the Winston-Salem State University for their chancellor's residence. The home is now owned by a private family again. (Washington Park Neighborhood Association.)

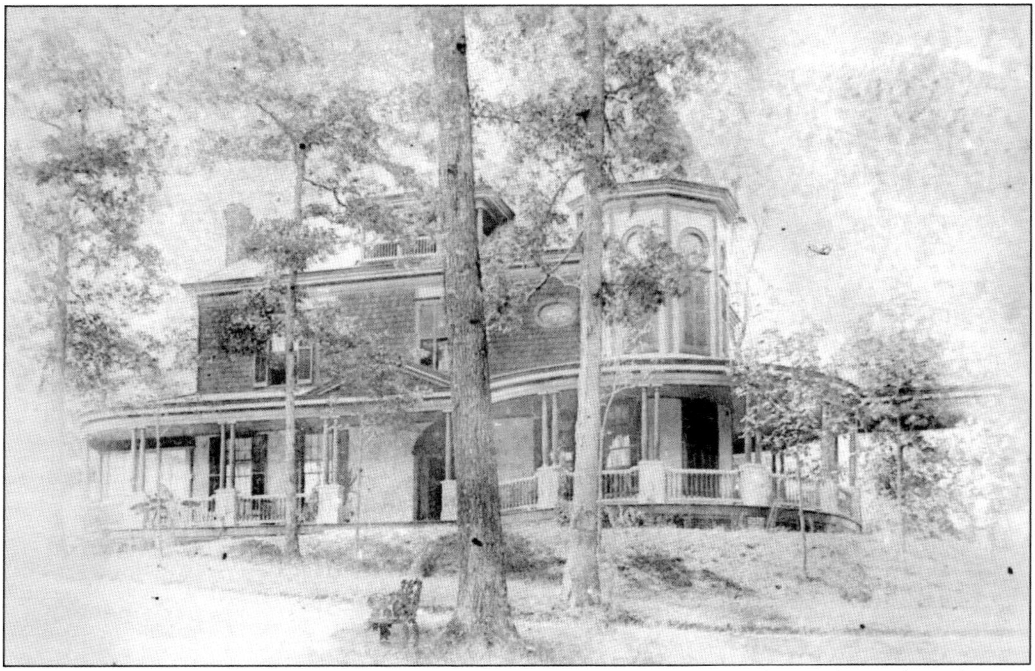

Before 1926, a number of small bus companies operated in Winston-Salem. John Gilmer formed the Camel City Coach Company in 1926 by purchasing a number of smaller lines and began operation with six buses. In 1930, the Camel City Coach Company merged with the Blue and Gray Lines of Charleston, West Virginia, to become the Atlantic Greyhound Lines. Gilmer's original house (shown above), located at 605 Cascade Avenue, burned around 1929, and they couldn't find anywhere else they're rather live, so they rebuilt on the same lot (shown below). The large acreage, including a large flower garden on the southwest corner of Leonard Street and Cascade Avenue, was subdivided and developed in the 1940s. The house remains on a hill overlooking Washington Park with a view of Winston-Salem's downtown skyline. (Forsyth County Public Library Photograph Collection.)

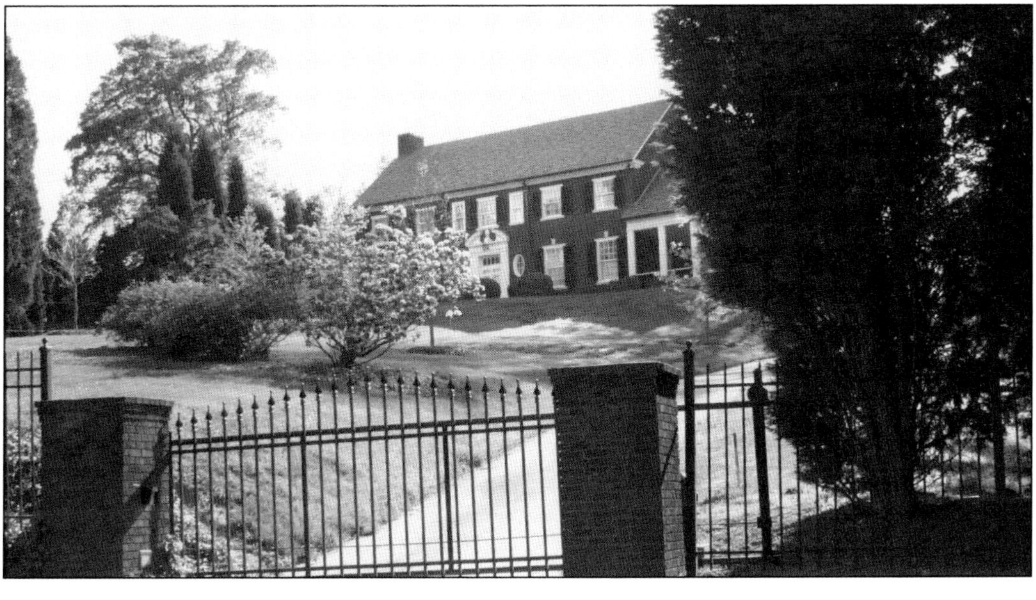

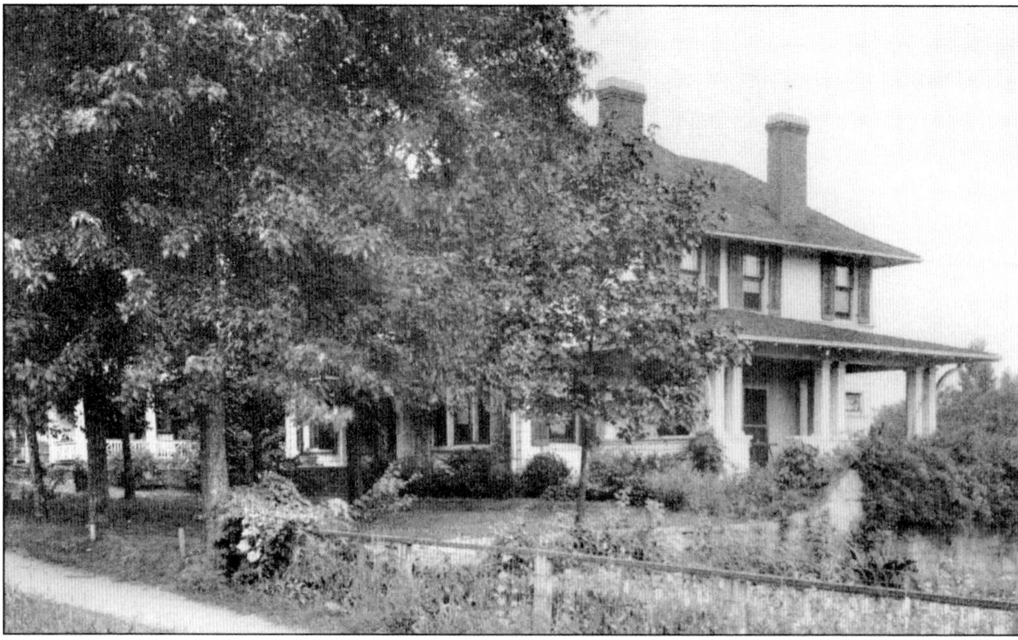

The Reed-McKaughan home, located at 115 Cascade Avenue, was built in 1913 by William P. Reed, a freight agent for the Winston-Salem Southbound Railway. He sold the house to Luther C. McKaughan, a lawyer and partner in Sapp and McKaughan Law Firm in 1917. This photograph, taken from the Fries family's formal gardens next door, shows the main entrance facing east. (Forsyth County Public Library Photograph Collection.)

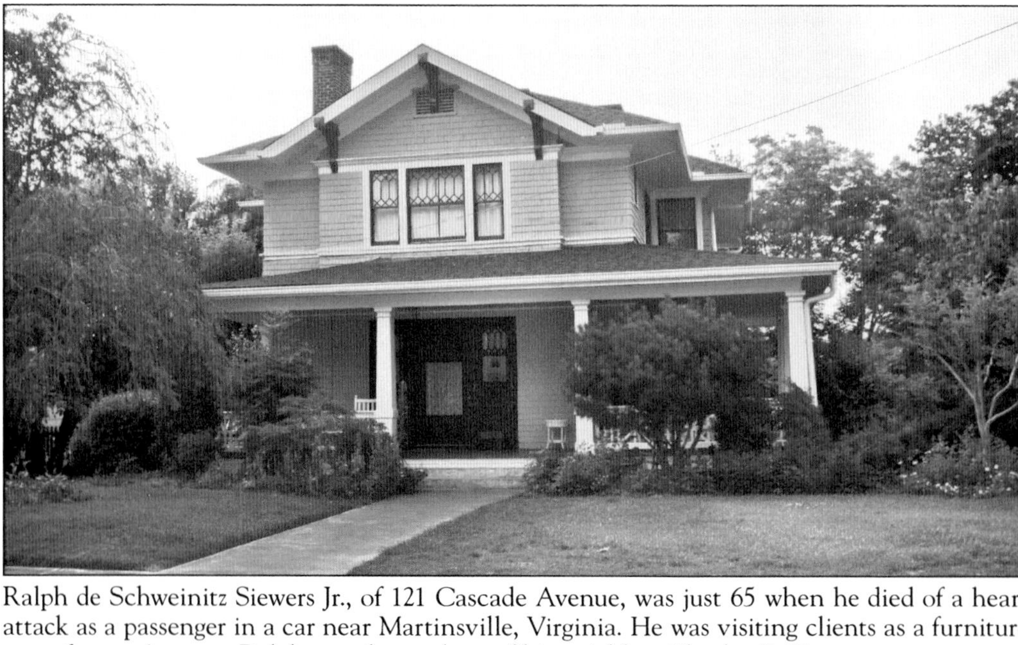

Ralph de Schweinitz Siewers Jr., of 121 Cascade Avenue, was just 65 when he died of a heart attack as a passenger in a car near Martinsville, Virginia. He was visiting clients as a furniture manufacturer's agent. Ralph was the nephew of his neighbor Charles S. Siewers, was a veteran of World War II and fought in the Battle of the Bulge. His son, Ralph III, is a doctor who worked with his neighbor Fred Bahnson's son, Hank, in Pittsburgh. Hank Bahnson was the chairman of the Department of Surgery at the University of Pittsburgh's Presbyterian hospital.

Edna, the wife of Ralph Siewers Jr., was well-known in Winston-Salem social circles. When she and Ralph bought the house at 121 Cascade Avenue in 1946, she stated in a newspaper article that the porch covering two sides of the house was pure enjoyment for them. They had "tea now and then on the porch and, traditionally, served homemade ice cream out there on the fourth of July." (Reich family.)

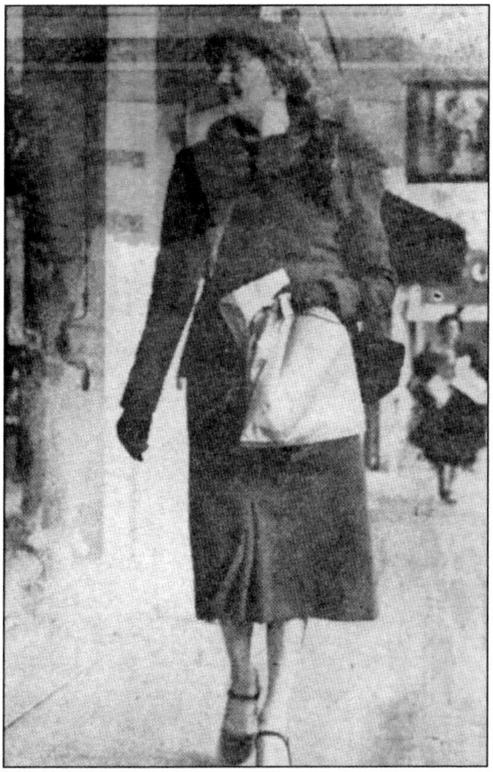

Lucretia Siewers, left, and Jeannie Turner of Greensboro (sister of Dr. Charles Turner) greet their cousin Ann Bondurant and Ann's new husband, Dr. William B. Young, the morning after their wedding. Lucretia Siewers was the daughter of Charles Nathanial Siewers. Jeannie Turner was the daughter of Margaret Siewers Turner, and Ann Bondurant was the daughter of Dorothy Siewers Bondurant (daughter of Ledoux Siewers). (Reich family.)

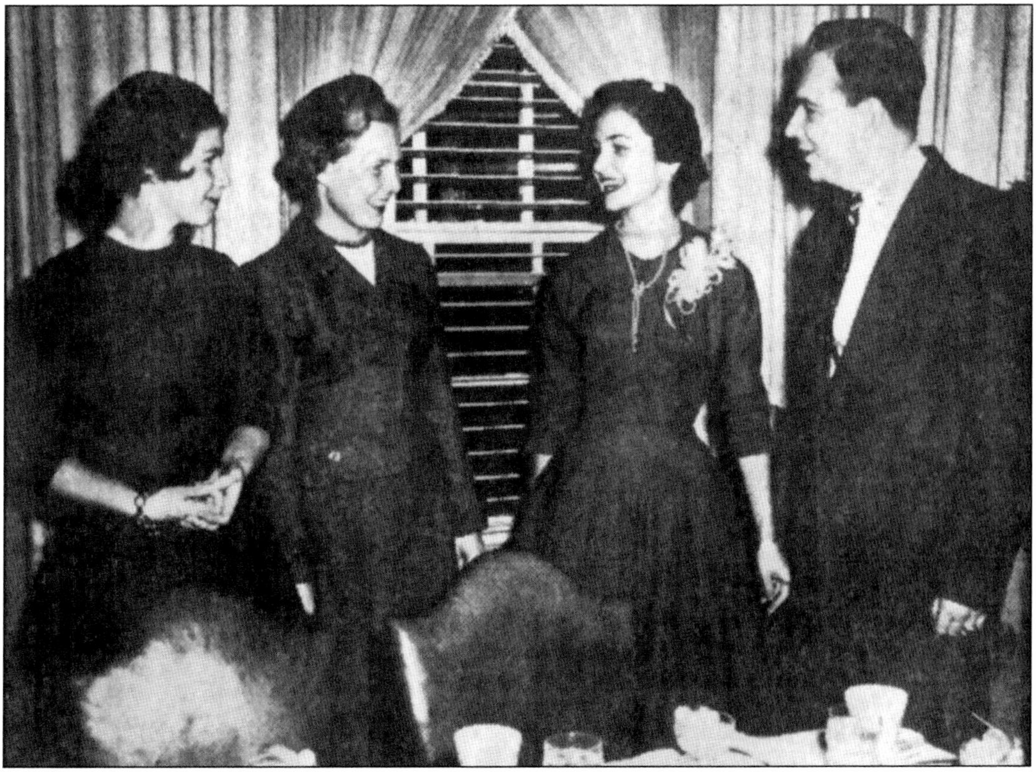

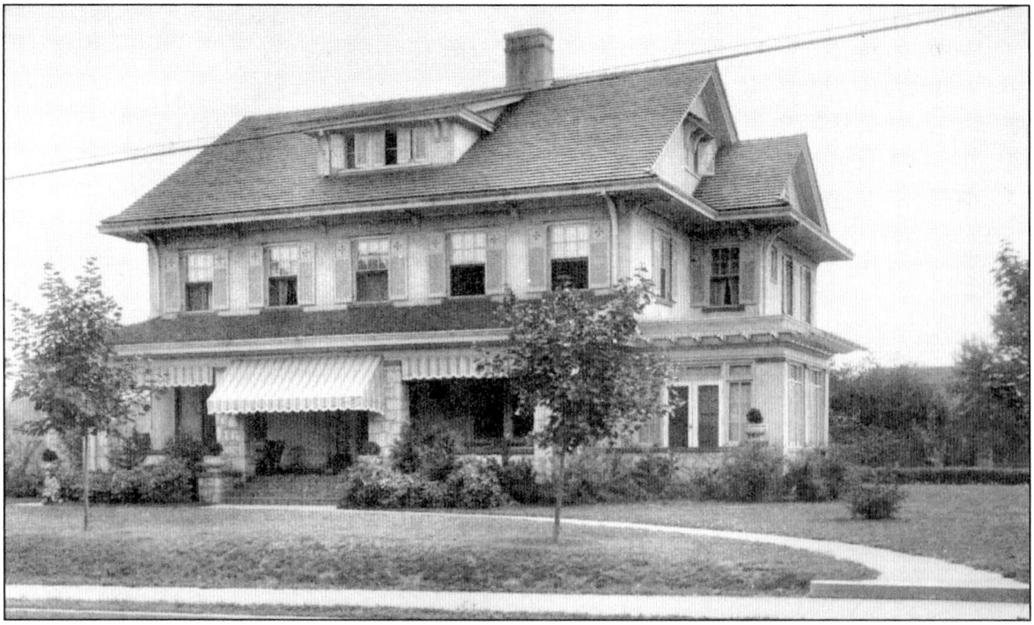

Lindsay E. Fishel, of 1919 South Main Street, was an automobile mechanic for the first cars in this community. In 1909, he worked for the Gilmer Motor Company and later established the Lindsay Fishel Buick Company. At the time of his death, he was a salesman for the Motor Sales Company. This house is now part of the North Carolina School of the Arts. (Forsyth County Public Library Photograph Collection.)

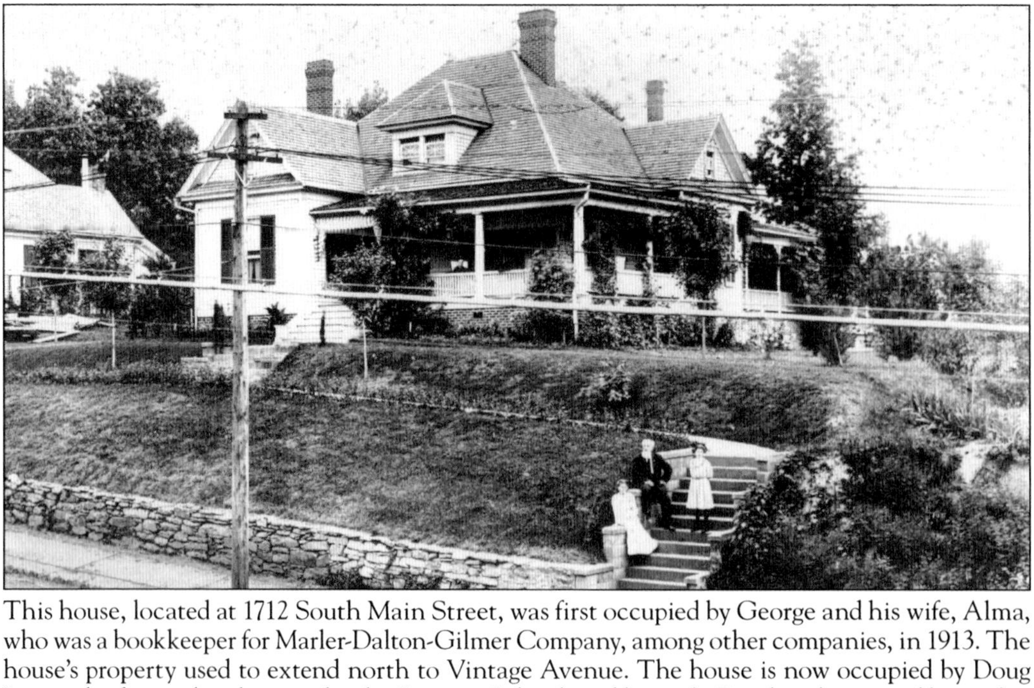

This house, located at 1712 South Main Street, was first occupied by George and his wife, Alma, who was a bookkeeper for Marler-Dalton-Gilmer Company, among other companies, in 1913. The house's property used to extend north to Vintage Avenue. The house is now occupied by Doug Lewis, the former headmaster for the Summit School, and his wife, Bingle, who moved here after he retired. The house offers one of the best views of the Winston-Salem skyline. (Collection of Old Salem Museums and Gardens.)

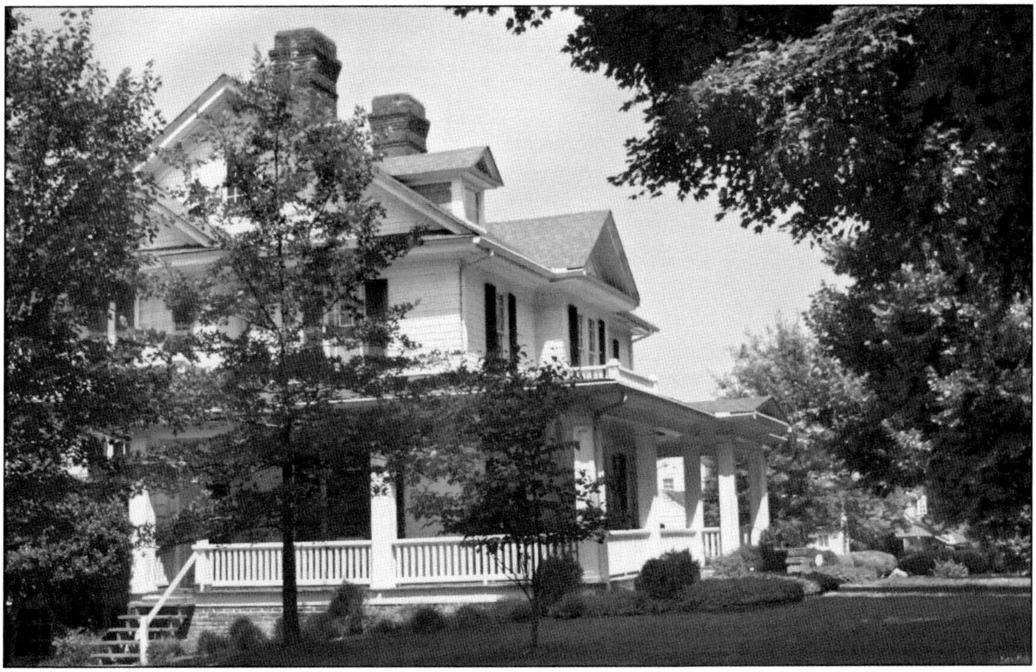

Two families of brothers started building companies, the Fogles and the Millers. The Miller Brothers Company was started by John S. and Gideon L. Miller in 1872 and was successful for two decades. In 1893, they turned to furniture manufacturing. One of the descendants, William F. Miller, went on to become the vice president for Fogle Brothers and with Wachovia Development Company. His house, located at 42 Park Boulevard, is shown here. (Washington Park Neighborhood Association.)

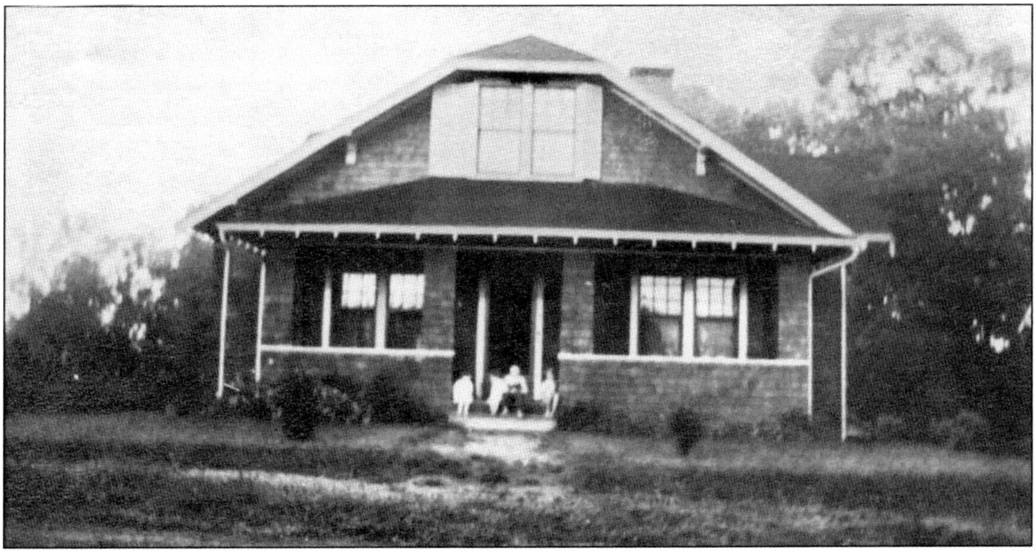

This frame house, located at 60 Park Boulevard, may have been built for L. C. Stinson and his family. The house is located around the corner from the park and has been renovated since the time this picture was taken. The front door is enclosed within a large front porch, the cedar shingles have been painted yellow, and an addition has expanded the back of the house. (Butter and Balint Birkas.)

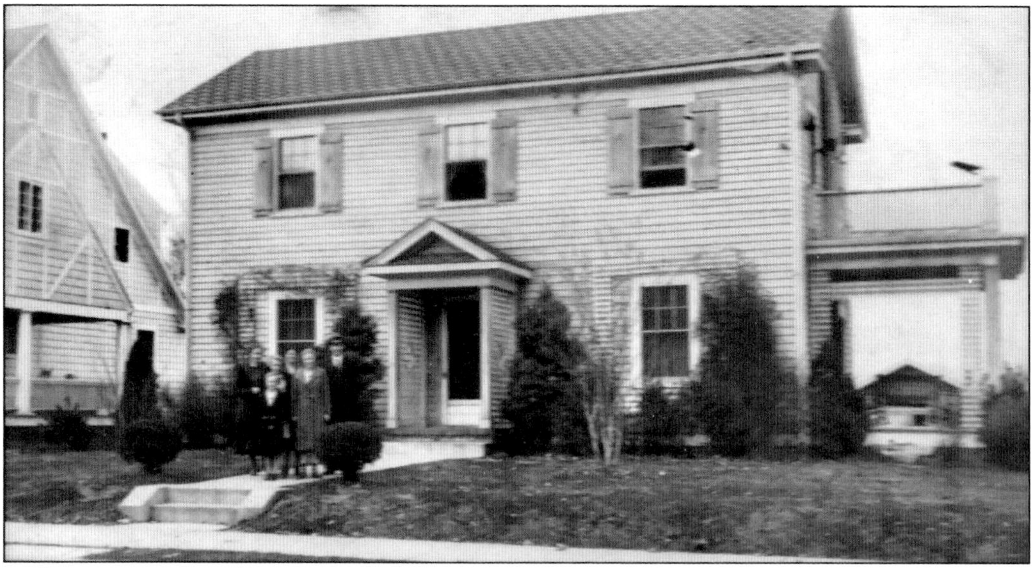

William T. Baynes and his wife, Vera, built this house at 107 Gloria Avenue in 1926. Vera designed it from a building she admired in Virginia. William worked as secretary-treasurer and later office manager for Clinard Electric Company. This photograph shows the family with their four children in the mid-1930s. (Tim Blackwell and Jessica Richard.)

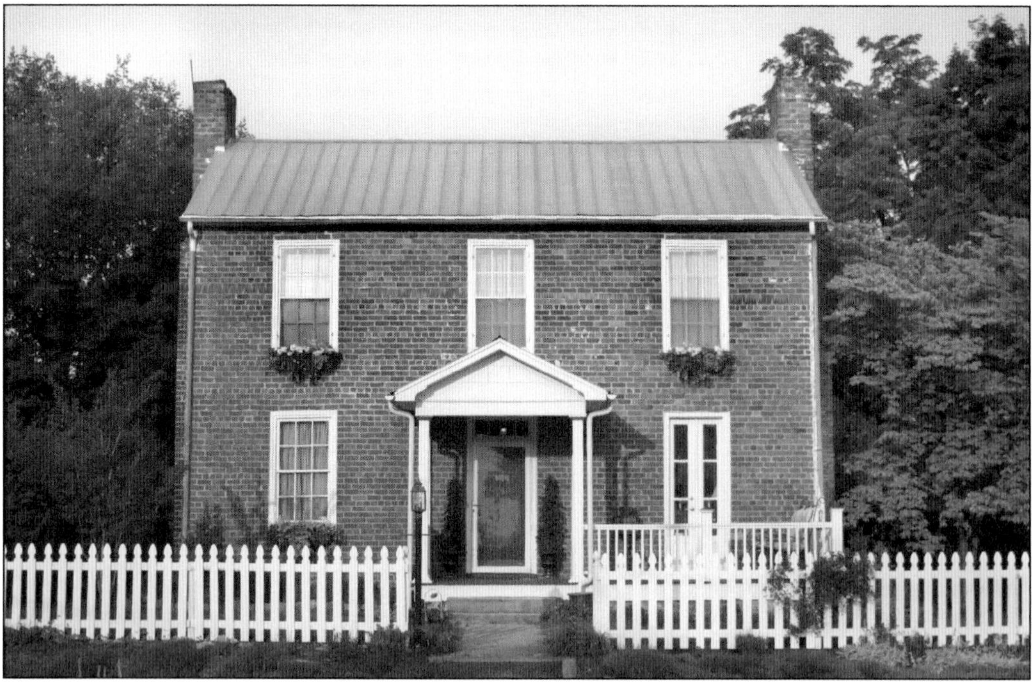

In 1867, Claude Thomas's grandfather bought this 1857 farmhouse, located at 24 West Devonshire Street, in the hills south of Salem. Thomas's mother grew up in the house and continued to live there after she married Charles Franklin Thomas. He added four back rooms to the original two-story brick house for their five daughters. The front porch has been removed, but it still retains the 12-inch-thick walls and low doorways. (Washington Park Neighborhood Association.)

Three

Washington Park

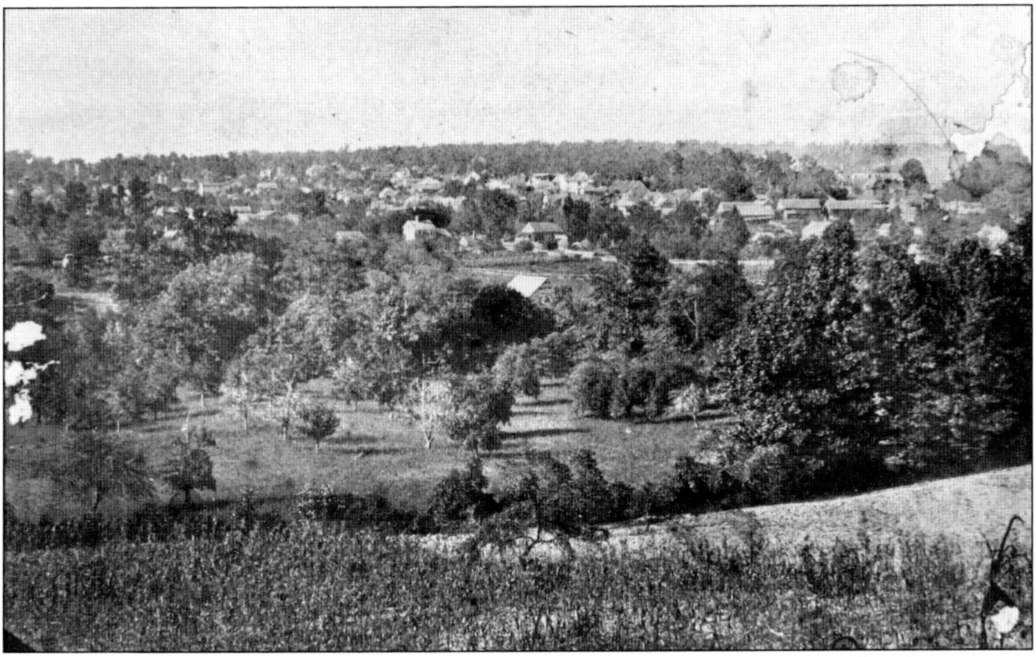

In 1892, a little over 17 acres were designated as a park by the Winston-Salem Land and Investment Company, who developed the neighborhood. In July 1955, the city purchased an additional 47 acres from the Moravian Church, and over the years acquired more to bring the total to over 75 acres. It is generally accepted that Washington Park was named in honor of George Washington, who passed through the area on his way to Salem on May 31, 1791. His route through the South brought him in town on Old Lexington Road, today's Rawson Street. Most believe the park has always been named Washington Park, but the development designer, Jacob Lott Ludlow, referred to it in his drawings as "Sunny Side Park," and the city directories refer to it as "Southside Park." In 1928, the Daughters of the American Revolution (DAR) dedicated the stone gateway at the foot of Gloria Avenue with the name Washington Park. The ceremony extolled the virtues of George Washington, but did not give any indication if this was a new or continuing name for the park. (Moravian Archives, Winston-Salem, North Carolina.)

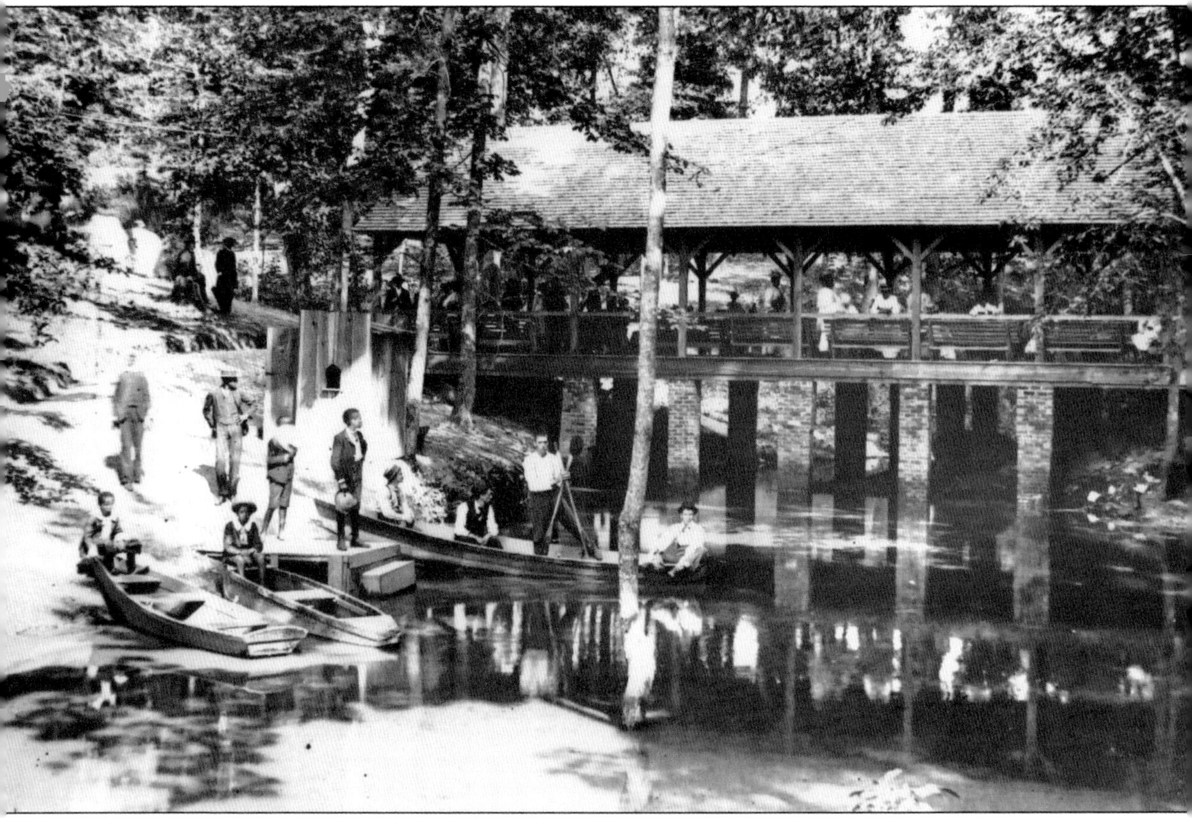

The Winston-Salem Land and Investment Company planned two neighborhoods along the streetcar lines in the southern side of Salem: Washington Park, then referred to as Southside, and Sunnyside, just to the southeast. Washington Park was meant to be classier with prominent citizens, a park superintendent, and ice-skating rink, and a bakery. Older residents of the neighborhood remember ice skating on the pond and sailing boats in it. The pond was believed to have been fed by a stream or spring near Cascade Avenue and flowed northwest to Salem Creek. Pictured are the pond, boathouse, and boats. At some point the pond was drained, but the contours of where it stood can be seen today. (Collection of the Wachovia Historical Society; photograph courtesy of Old Salem Museums and Gardens.)

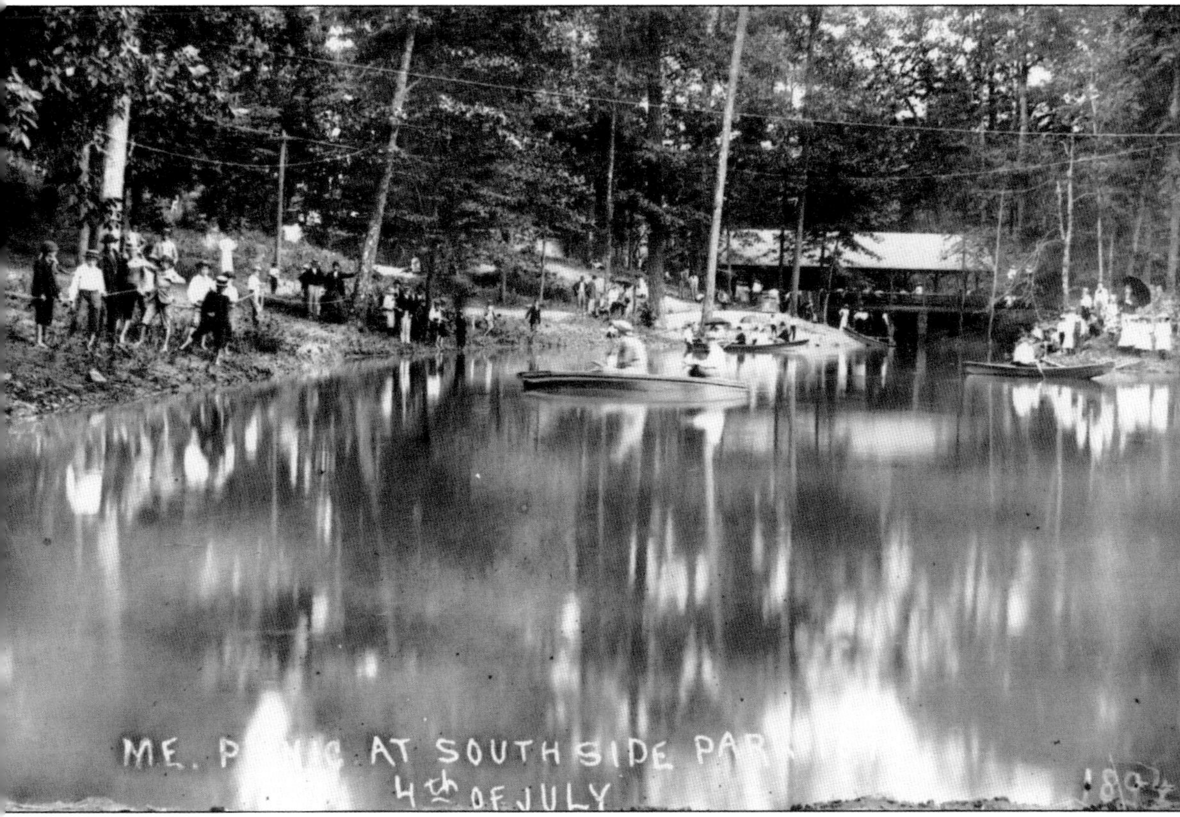

Based on interviews, the pond was located from the corner of Cascade Avenue and Park Boulevard, and flowed to the edge where the children's playground ends today. A dam held the water in place. The pathways are now paved, and the landscape still shows the same indentions where the lake once stood. The covered bridge was removed sometime in the early 1900s, although nobody knows what happened to it. On either side of the lake were concrete-and-wood pavilions built out of tree trunks (not shown in the photograph.). The park contained three pavilions that were built in the 1930s, but one burned down shortly after it was built. According to numerous reports, a woman committed suicide by dousing herself with some type of inflammatory substance and lighting herself on fire while standing inside one of the pavilions. (Collection of the Wachovia Historical Society; photograph courtesy of Old Salem Museums and Gardens.)

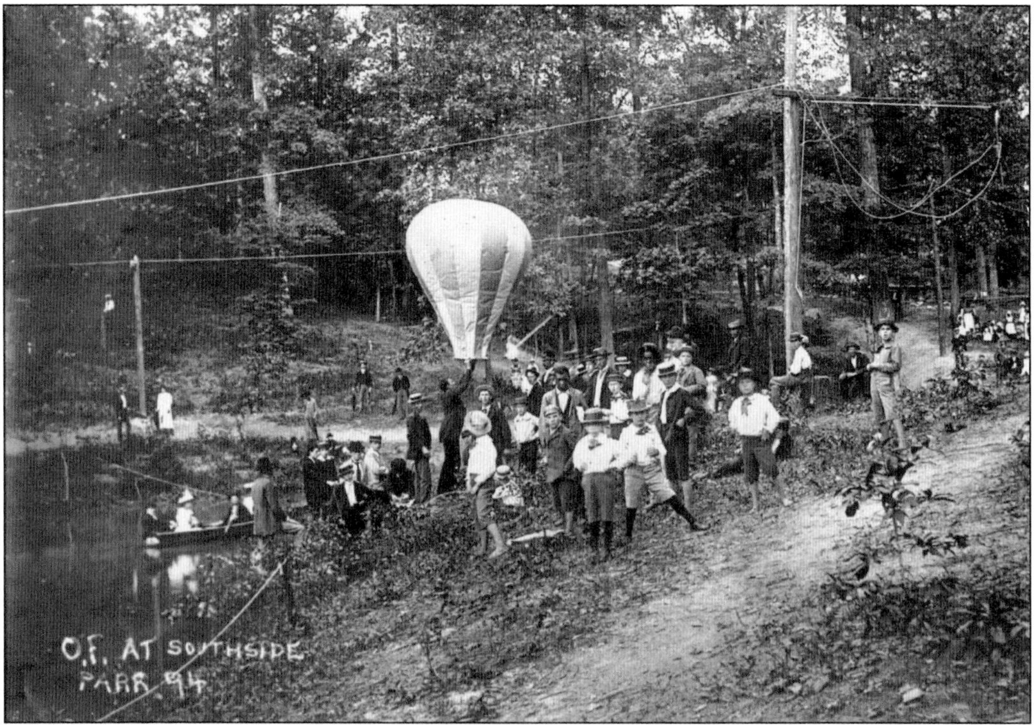

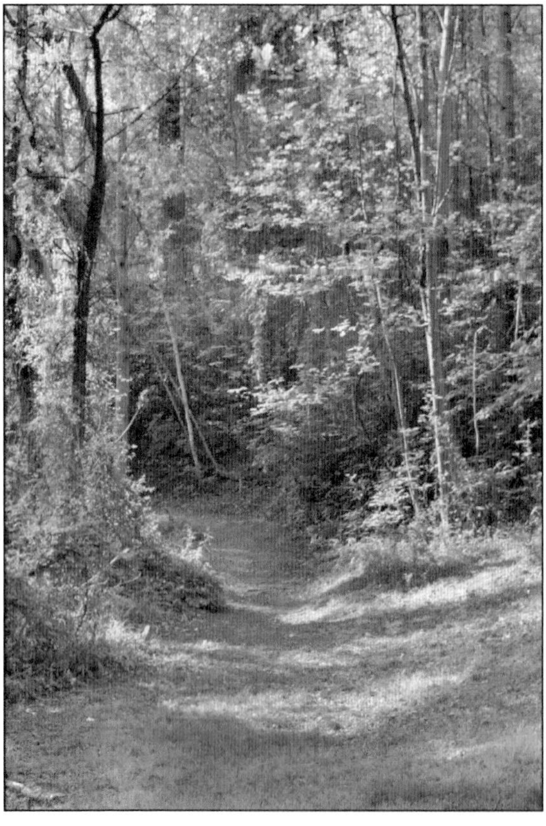

The Order of the Odd Fellows gathered for a day in Washington Park, referred to as Southside, in 1894. The landscape of the park has remained almost the same, minus the lake and the power lines. The pathways are now paved but follow the same route as shown in this picture. A large storm in 1989 destroyed the park's large trees and underbrush, leaving many bare patches seen today. A large planting project was undertaken and many of the trees have been replaced. Today the rolling hills are manicured, and the grass is mowed, losing its wilderness feel, seen here. (Courtesy of Forsyth County Public Library Photograph.)

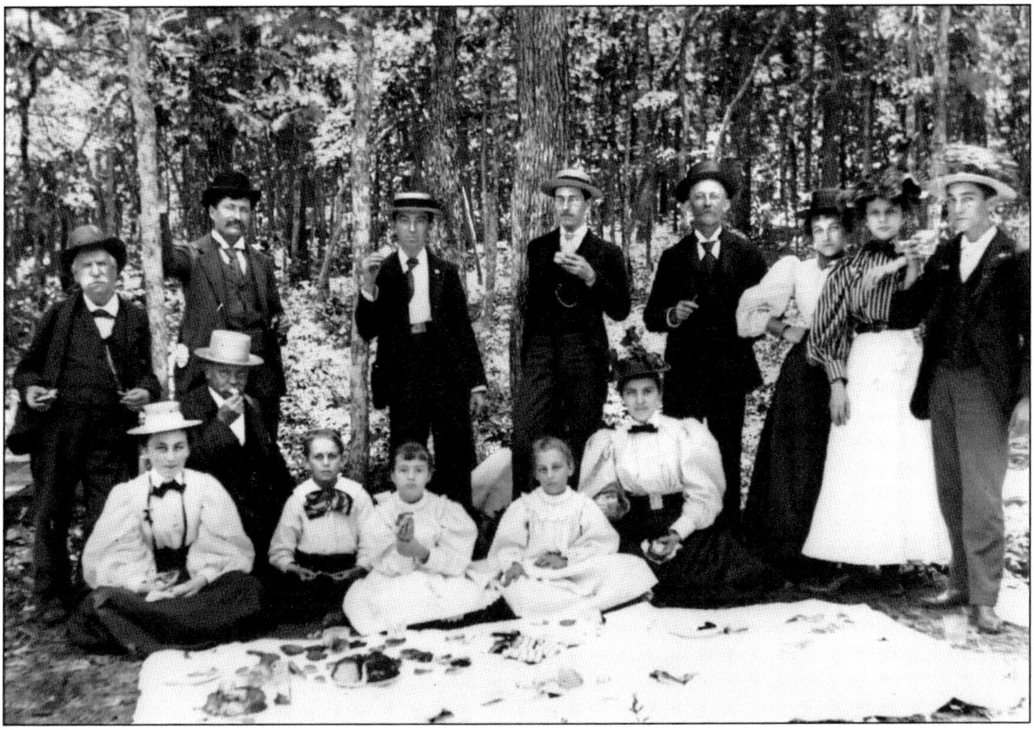

Church groups and fraternity organizations used the park frequently for outings. An article from the *Winston-Salem Journal* in 1928 reported on its "green and shadowed hills, its winding walks, its leaf-flecked lakes and tumbling streams." It told in detail how the land had been donated in 1890 for a wilderness park to be used for Sunday picnic outings. At that time, the park was in the country and churches were in the heart of the town. Youth groups, church ministries, and families from the area would have picnics under the thick foliage and row boats in the lake. Full meals and desserts would be served, as evidenced by the Bundt cake sitting on the blanket. (Above, collection of the Wachovia Historical Society, photograph courtesy of Old Salem Museums and Gardens; below, the Swan family.)

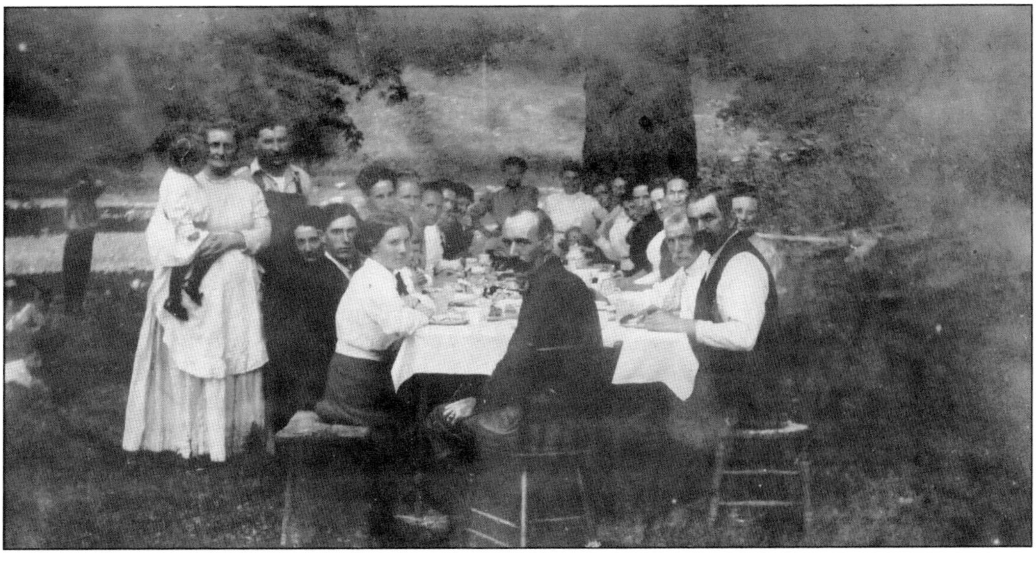

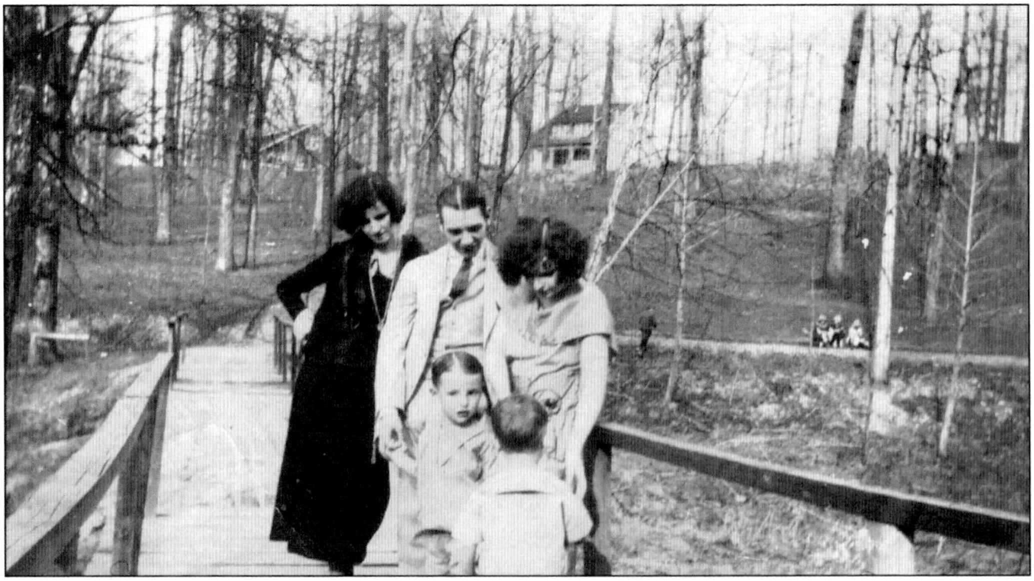

In 1925, a wooden bridge had taken the place of the covered one, and the water levels in the ponds had started to drop. In the background, on the hill, the Edgar Barber house can be seen. Barber was the man responsible for creating the city directories and the postcards of this era. The house, which is located at 148 Park Boulevard and is still standing today, has one of the best views of the park. (Jack Graham Jr.)

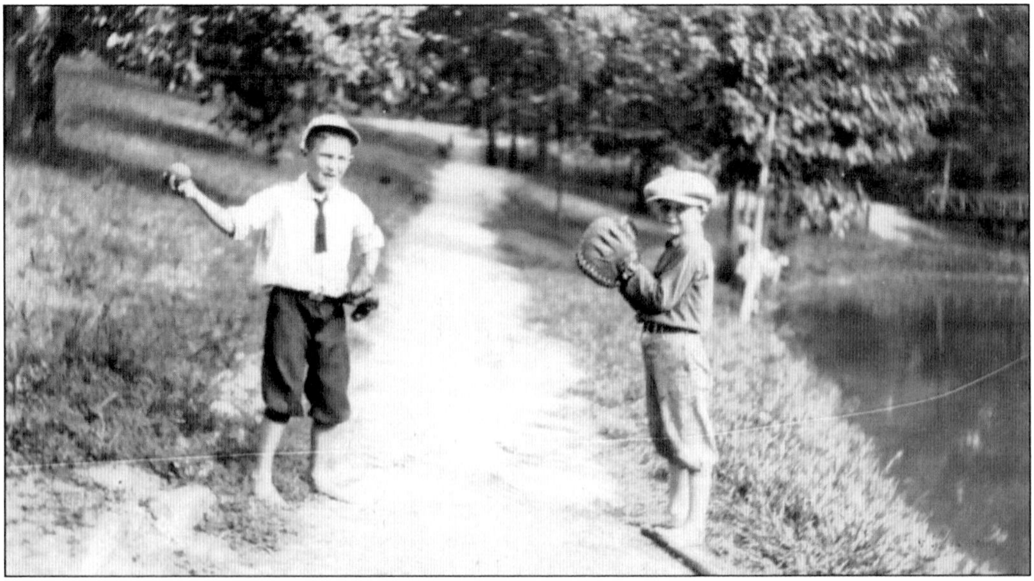

Walter Leonard, left, one of the oldest members of the neighborhood, remembers playing in the park with his friends the day the park was dedicated by the Daughters of the American Revolution. Walter was born on Gloria Avenue and then moved with his family to Acadia Avenue before building his own house on the former property of the Christian H. Fogle estate on Banner Avenue. (Walter Leonard.)

There are two sets of stairs on a large mound of dirt and rock near the corner of Park Boulevard and Cascade Avenue. It is believed that these were the steps used for accessing the pond in this area since all surrounding sides were too steep. Cascade Avenue may have been named for a cascade of water that fed the lake.

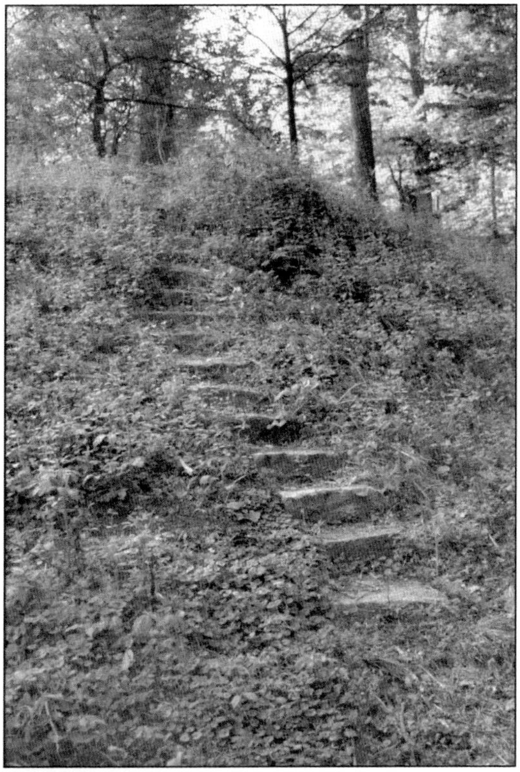

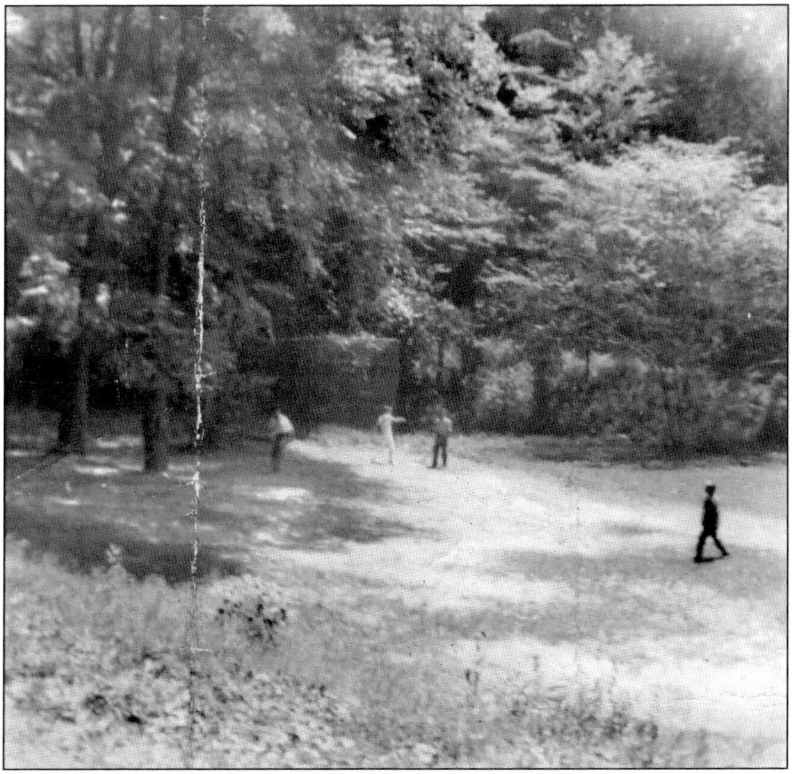

School groups used the park for meetings, parties, and celebrations. Neighbors remember hearing the Gray High School cheerleaders practicing their cheers, the yells of impromptu softball games, and children's laughter throughout the day and evening. Asked how a family living in a small bungalow could raise four boys without damaging anything, the resident said, "That was easy. The boys were always in the park." (Stacey Brendle.)

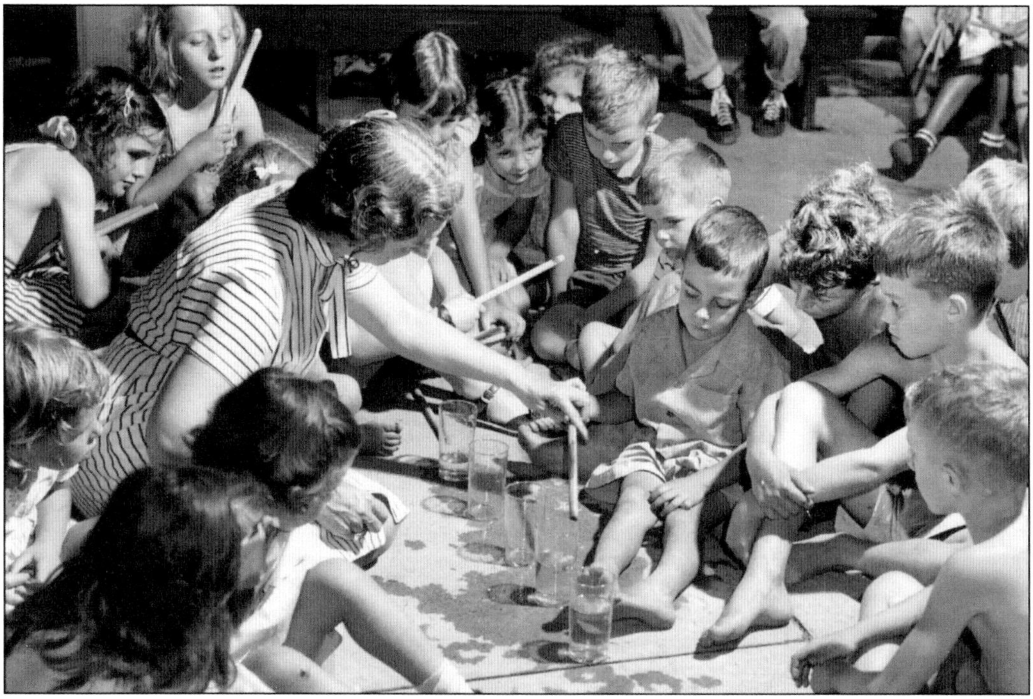

In the summers starting in the 1940s and lasting several decades, children congregated in the pavilions in Washington Park for summer activities. Dance, music, and other lessons were taught by various teachers who volunteered their time. In this picture, Katherine Detmold is teaching children about the different sounds glasses make depending on their water levels. (Reich family.)

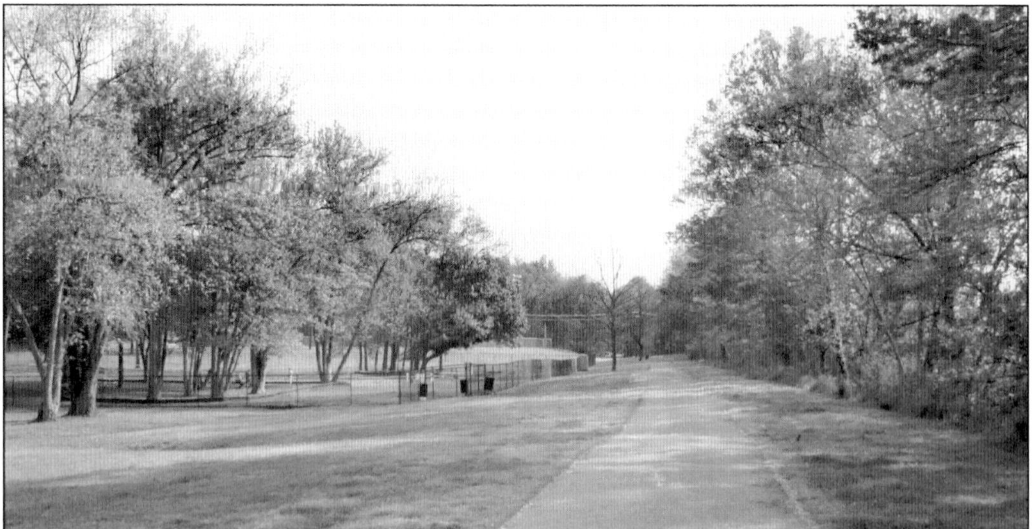

In May 2002, representatives from WOOF, the Winston Organization for Off-Leash Fields, met with the Washington Park Neighborhood Association (WPNA) board to introduce their organization and their proposal for a dog park. In June of that year, the director of Winston-Salem Parks and Recreations gave tentative approval, and in September, the WPNA officially endorsed the project. A fund-raiser was held to encourage public support, and in April 2003, the dog park was dedicated. (Washington Park Neighborhood Association.)

Four

Southside Baseball

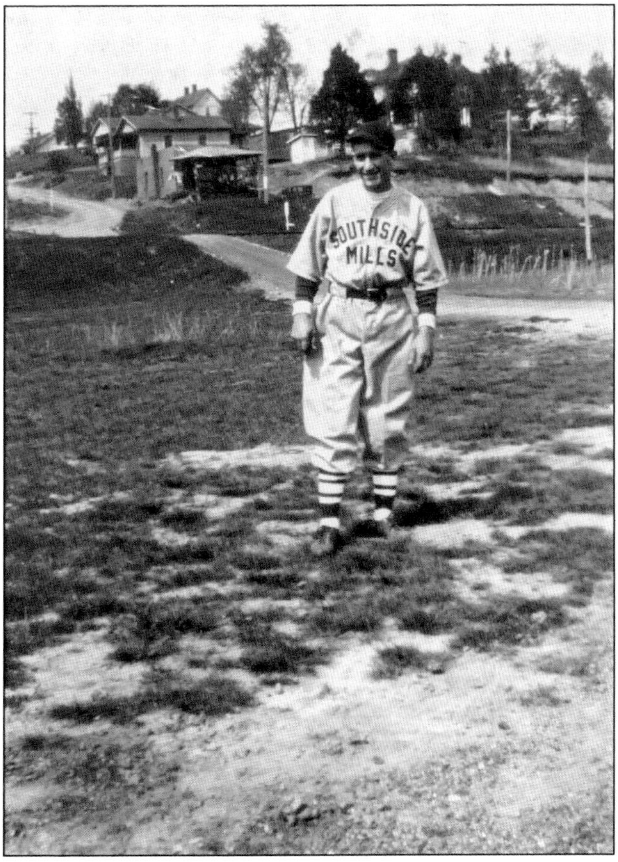

Baseball was a large pastime for many in Winston-Salem in the first half of the century. Industrial league teams were considered a step up from the town leagues, with the workers of the mills its most prominent players. These baseball teams provided entertainment for the communities, and their games were widely attended. Mill workers would turn out by the hundreds, if not thousands, to watch their team compete with a mill from a nearby town. The level of competition in these leagues was fierce, and companies were known to hire employees based on their baseball abilities alone. They were expected to carry the team to victory on the field instead of perform vigorously on the factory floor. Gene Hayes, pictured, played for R. J. Reynolds High School and then for Henry E. Fries's Southside Mills team. When Gene played for them, the mill had already been renamed Arista Mills. (Jean Hayes Mahaffey.)

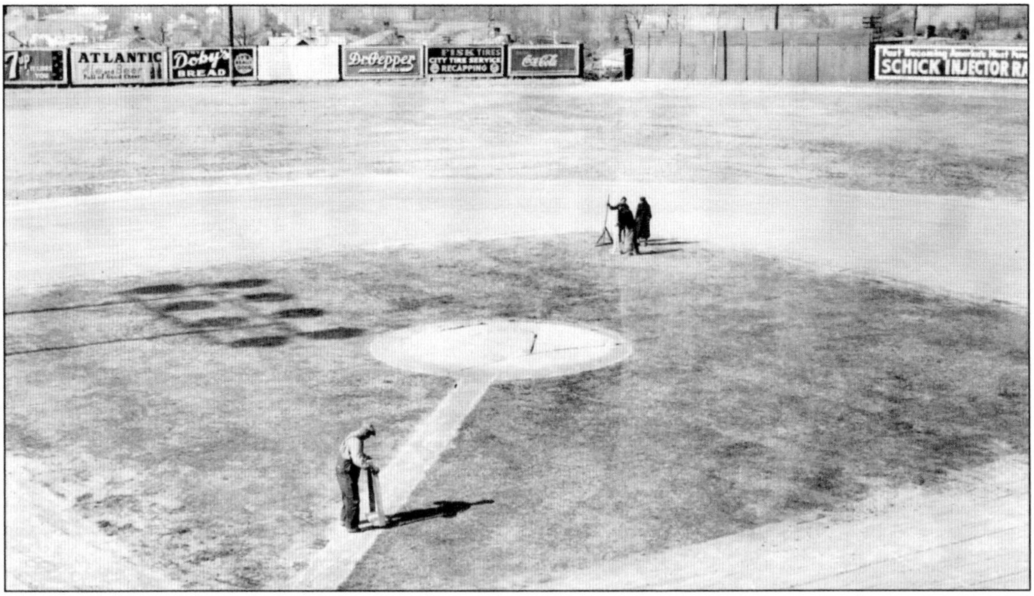

Professional baseball came to Winston-Salem in 1905, with early teams playing at Southside Ball Park, located where the North Carolina School of the Arts film school is located today. Team names and affiliations have changed over the years from the Twins, Cardinals, and Spirits to its current name, the Warthogs. Southside Ball Park burned in 1955 and a new park, named after the major league pitcher and Winston-Salem native Ernie Shore, was built on the north side of town. (Forsyth County Public Library Photograph Collection.)

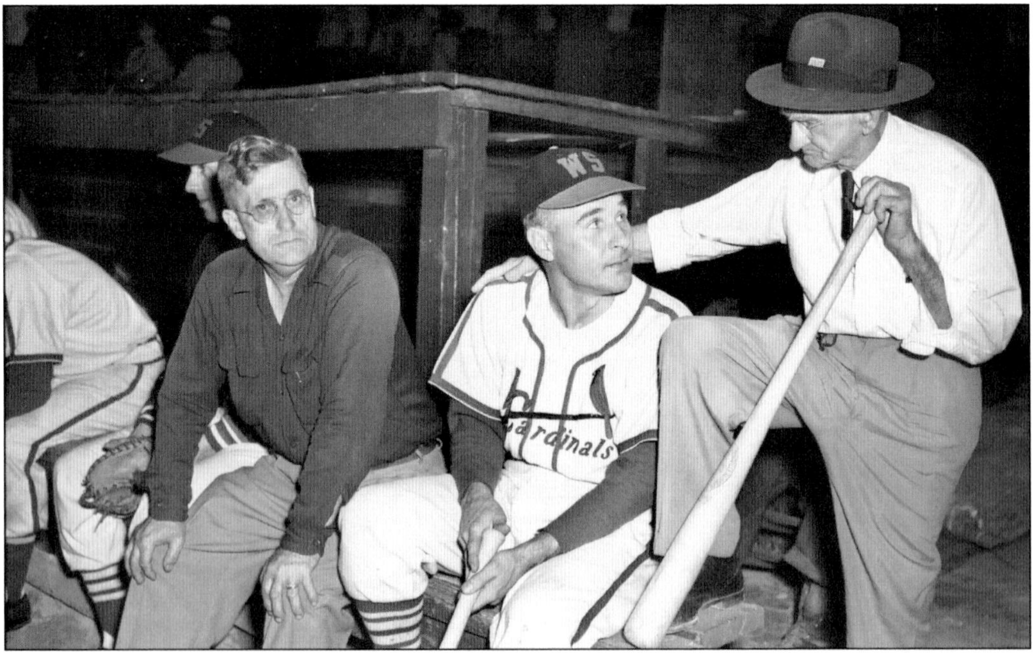

Lee Peterson (center), shown talking with J. A. Brewer (right), was a pitcher for the Winston-Salem Cardinals when they won the pennant in 1950. Washington Park resident Rodney Reich was a batboy and remembers the many games Peterson pitched, the games he won, and that he was one of the leading pitchers in the Carolina League. (Forsyth County Public Library Photograph Collection.)

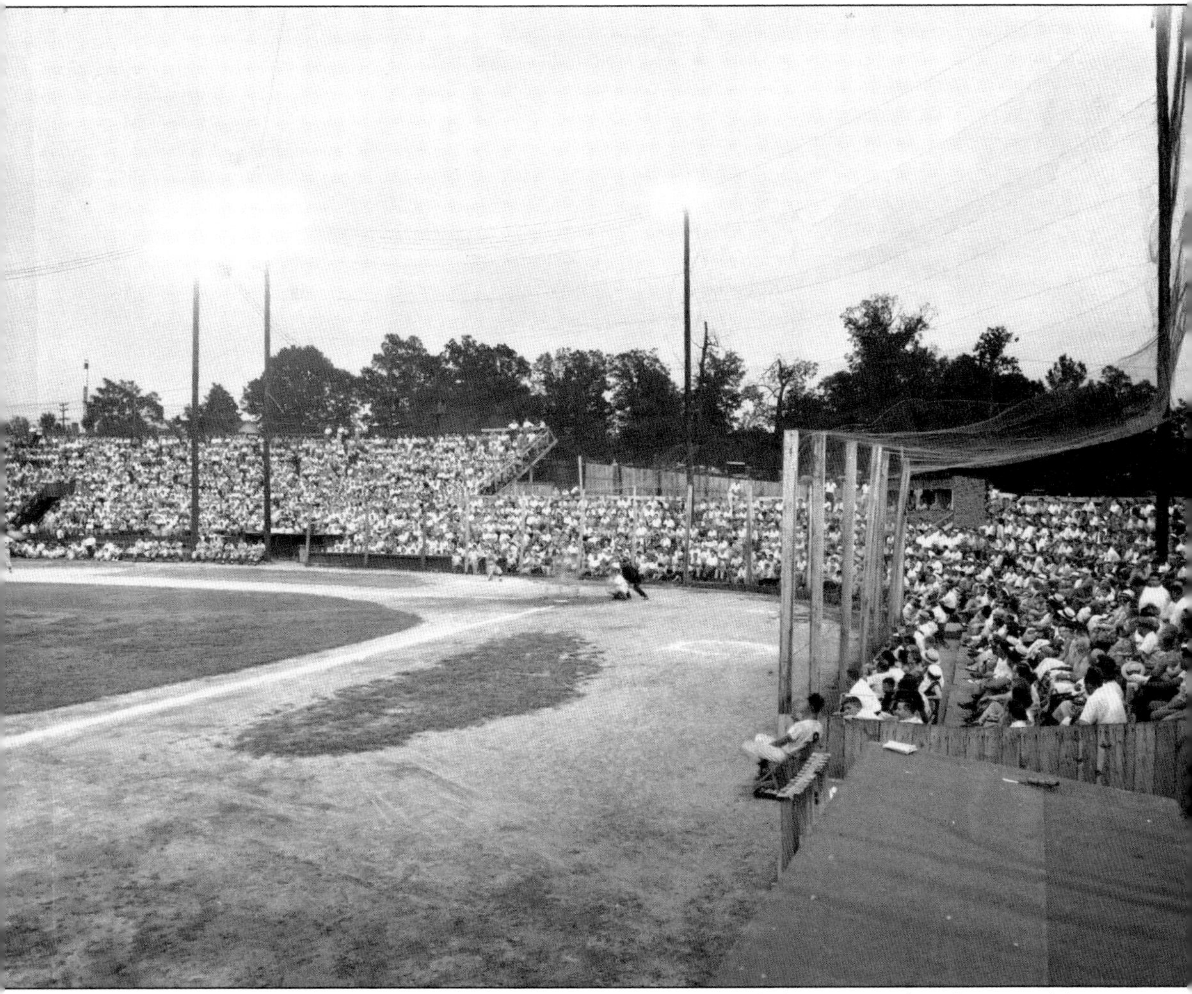

Baseball was a popular event, with night games drawing large crowds (as seen in this photograph). Nancy Shelton Bean recalled, "I told Dad how much I wanted to go to the ball game, and he took me to the very next game. The year was 1947. I remember going to the park and the seats were packed full of people. There were food stands that made the place smell good, and there was all kind of activity going on. It was a thrilling experience for a little girl. After that first game, I was hooked, and my dad, my mother, my sister and I went to every game afterwards. One time my Dad actually caught one of the Cardinal's baseballs that got hit into the stands. That was the ultimate treasure for me and I actually kept it for nearly forty years." (Forsyth County Public Library Photograph Collection.)

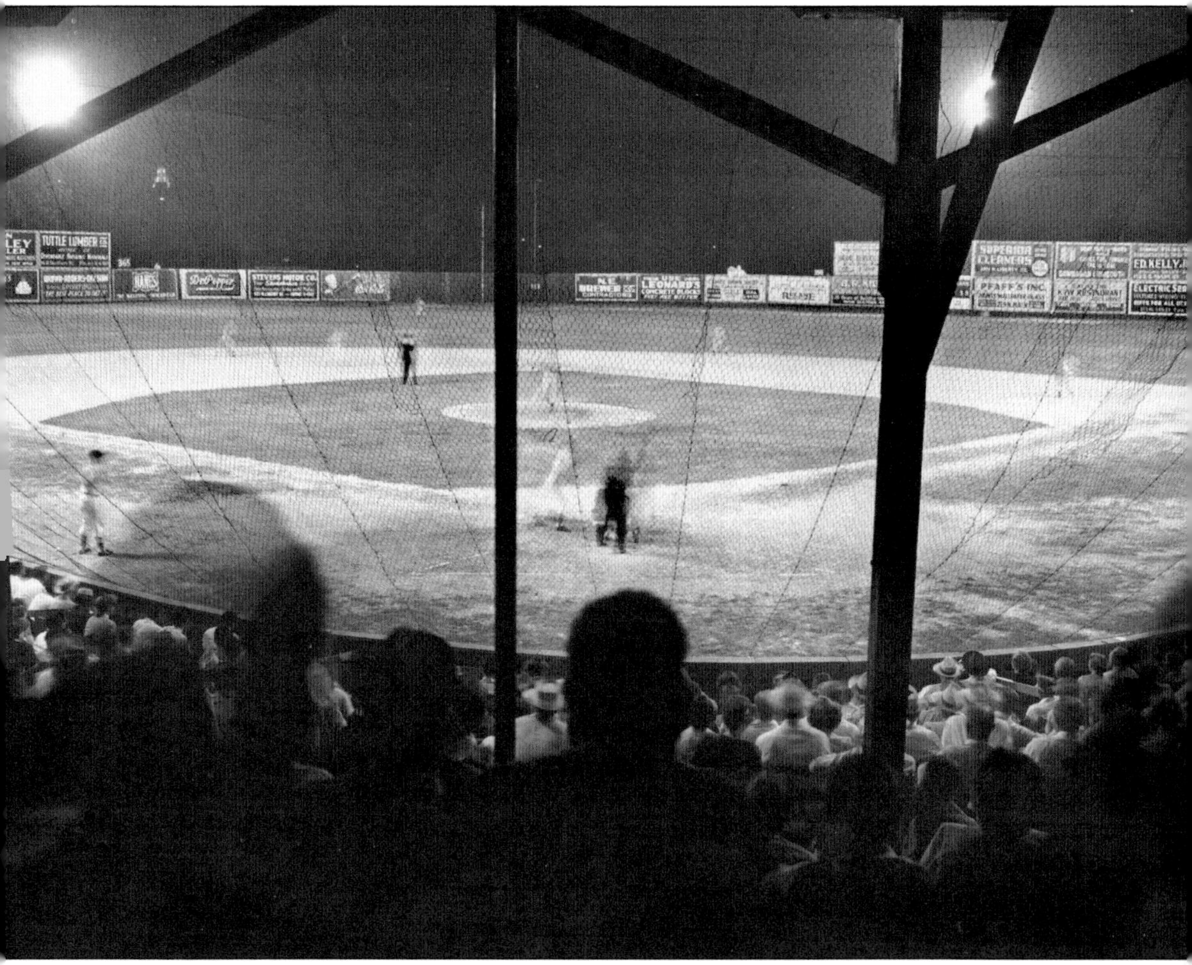

Gary Vernon stated, "In the seventh grade, George Milton was my homeroom teacher and he got a number of tickets for the class to go to a major-league exhibition game. The teams were on their way back from Florida spring training camps. The game was between the Yankees and the Dodgers so we got to see the great players at that time, Mickey Mantle, Yogi Berra, etc. Before I worked at the park, I can remember walking with my grandmother to evening games from our home behind Southside Baptist Church. My grandparents raised me, so that was a form of entertainment for them as well." In the distance, the lights for the R. J. Reynolds building can be seen. (Forsyth County Public Library Photograph Collection.)

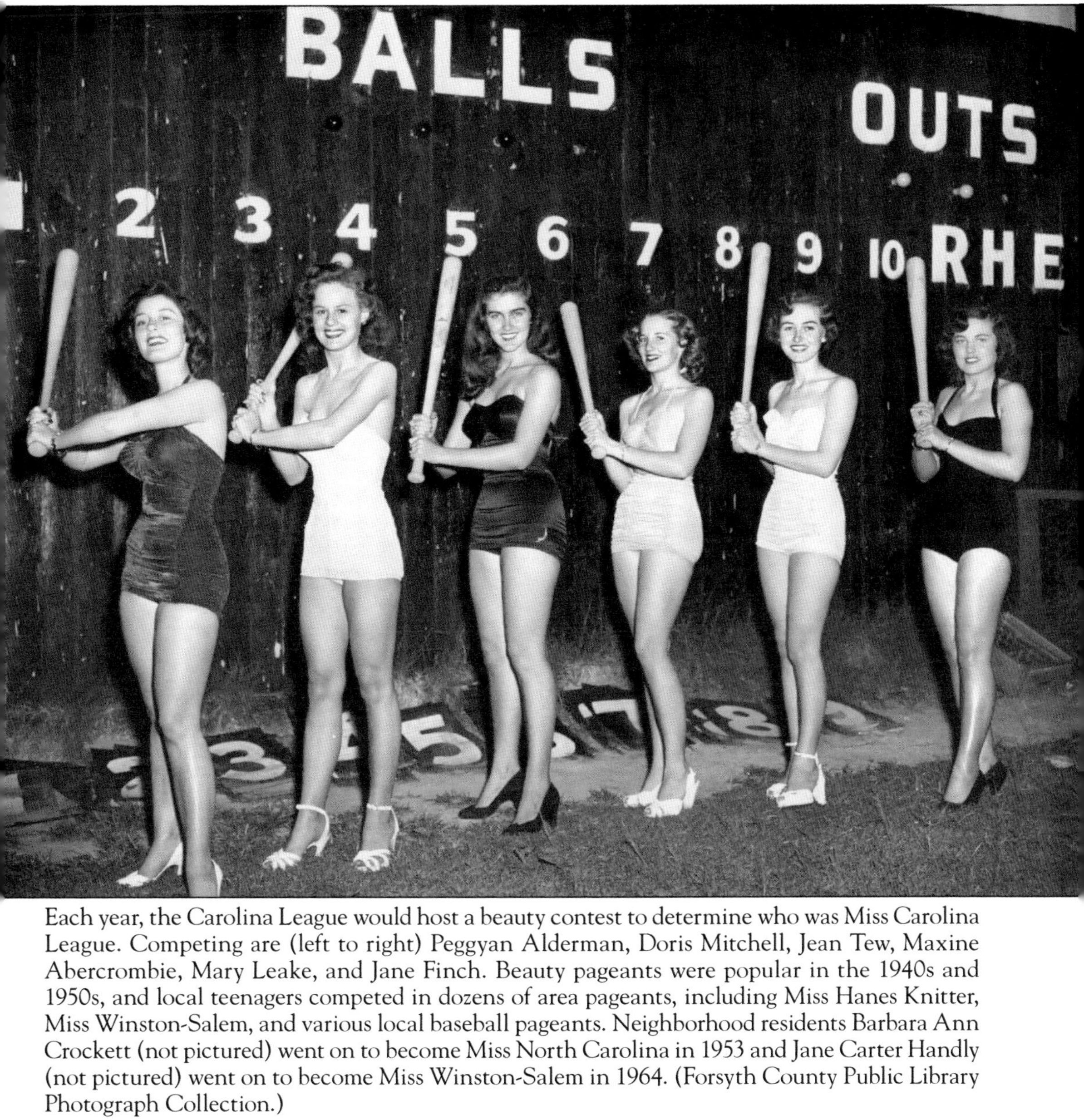

Each year, the Carolina League would host a beauty contest to determine who was Miss Carolina League. Competing are (left to right) Peggyan Alderman, Doris Mitchell, Jean Tew, Maxine Abercrombie, Mary Leake, and Jane Finch. Beauty pageants were popular in the 1940s and 1950s, and local teenagers competed in dozens of area pageants, including Miss Hanes Knitter, Miss Winston-Salem, and various local baseball pageants. Neighborhood residents Barbara Ann Crockett (not pictured) went on to become Miss North Carolina in 1953 and Jane Carter Handly (not pictured) went on to become Miss Winston-Salem in 1964. (Forsyth County Public Library Photograph Collection.)

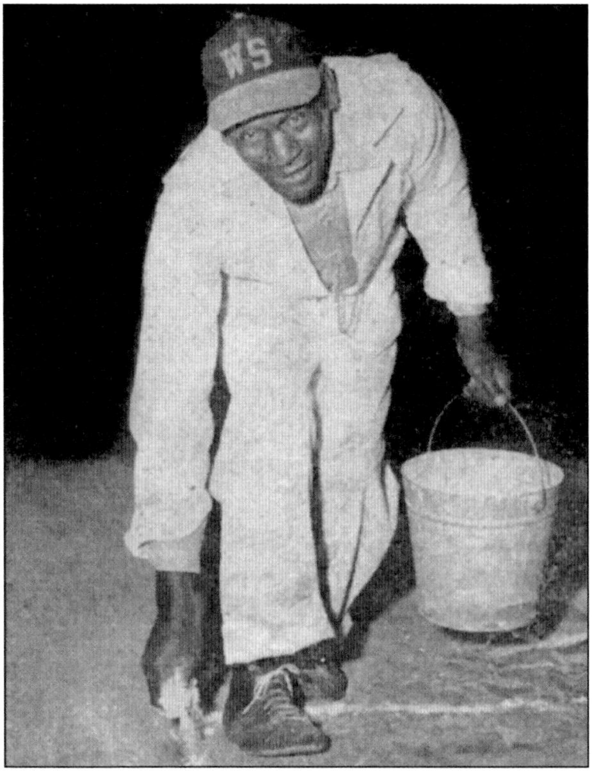

Frank Joyner was the Southside Ball Park groundskeeper for more than 25 years. In a *Twin-City Sentinel* article, he talked about May 1933, when lights were installed in the park and day games became rare. They also moved the fences in, cutting off more than 40 feet in the right field "so big left-handed hitters could train their guns for home runs." (Reich family.)

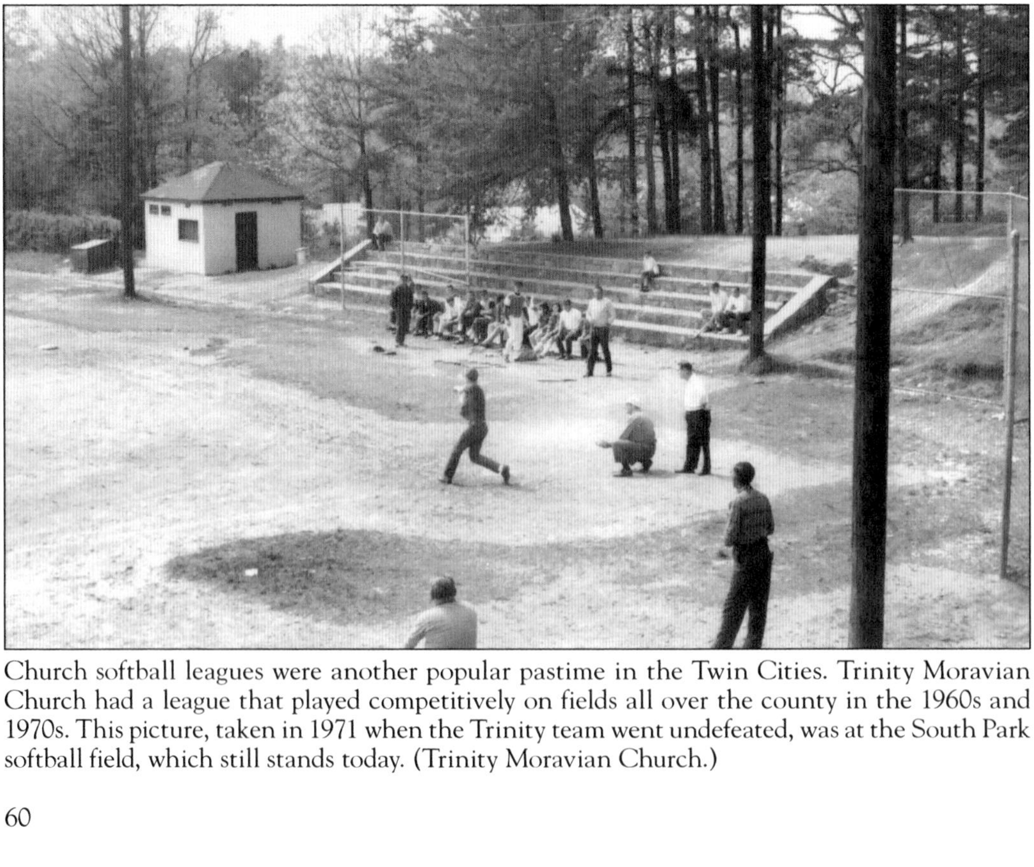

Church softball leagues were another popular pastime in the Twin Cities. Trinity Moravian Church had a league that played competitively on fields all over the county in the 1960s and 1970s. This picture, taken in 1971 when the Trinity team went undefeated, was at the South Park softball field, which still stands today. (Trinity Moravian Church.)

Five

CHURCH AND SCHOOL

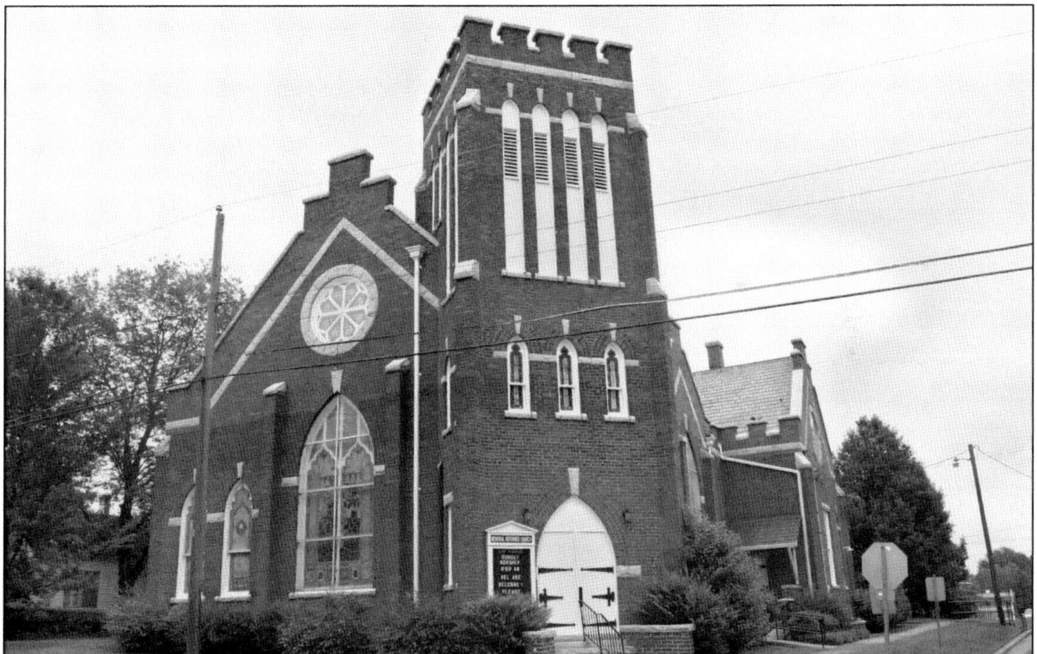

The Memorial Reformed Church is located at 236 Banner Avenue. In January 1915, the Sunday school was organized on the second floor of C. D. Couch's grocery store, on the corner of Hollyrood Street and Acadia Avenue. It was established as a congregation by nine members on May 2, 1915. Construction began in the fall of 1915 and was completed in 1920. The name was changed to Evangelical Reformed Church, and later to Memorial United Church of Christ before it reverted back to its original name. According to Walter Leonard, church was the gathering place for most people in the neighborhood and where they spent the majority of their time. His earliest memory is being in one of the pews with his head on his babysitter's lap, staring at the stained-glass windows while his mother played the organ and his father sang in the choir. (Memorial Reformed Church.)

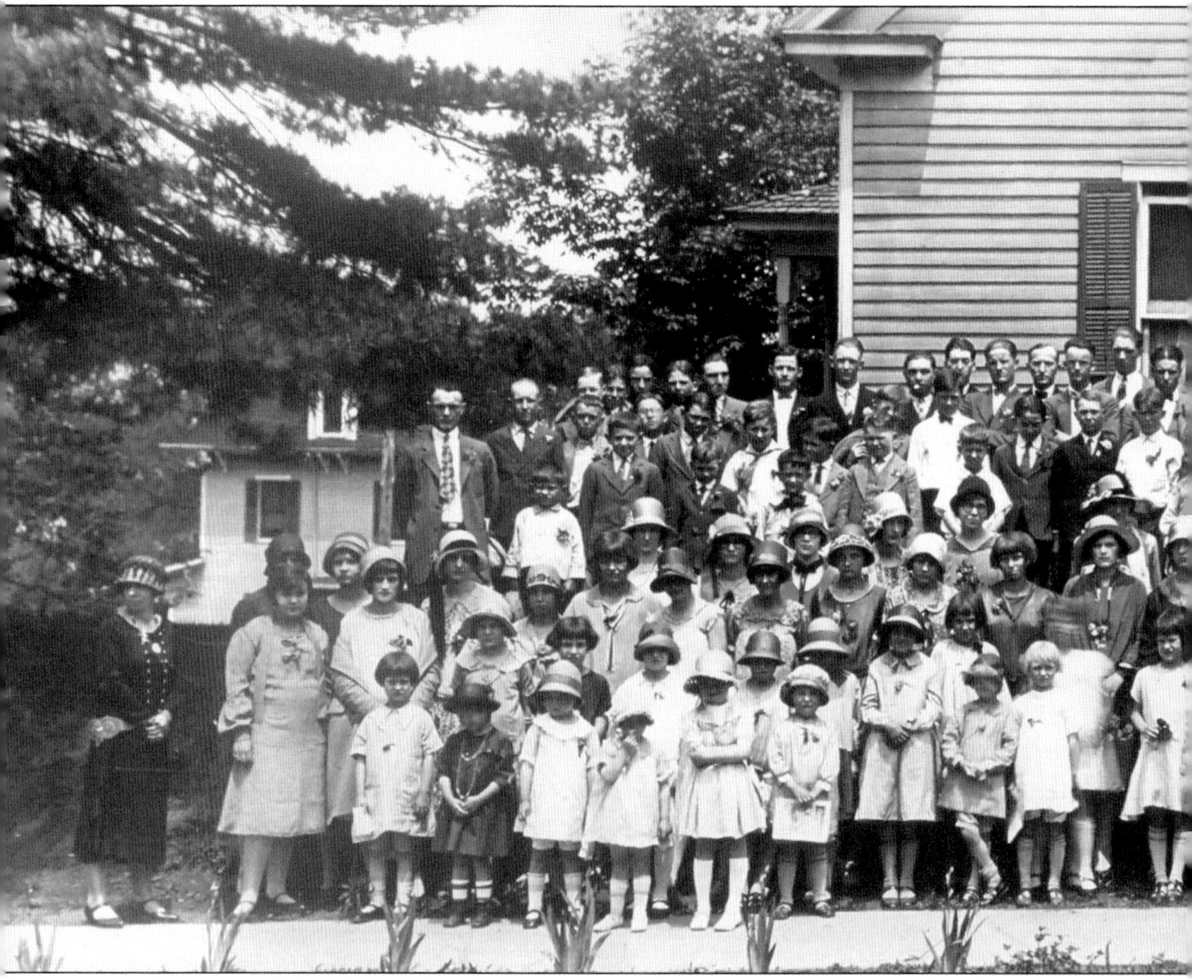

Walter Leonard is still a member of his childhood church. This photograph, taken in 1929, shows the entire neighborhood congregation standing before 229 West Banner Avenue, the house located across the street from Memorial Reformed Church. They selected this spot because of the sloping front yard. The woman and child holding hands standing in the first row on the right

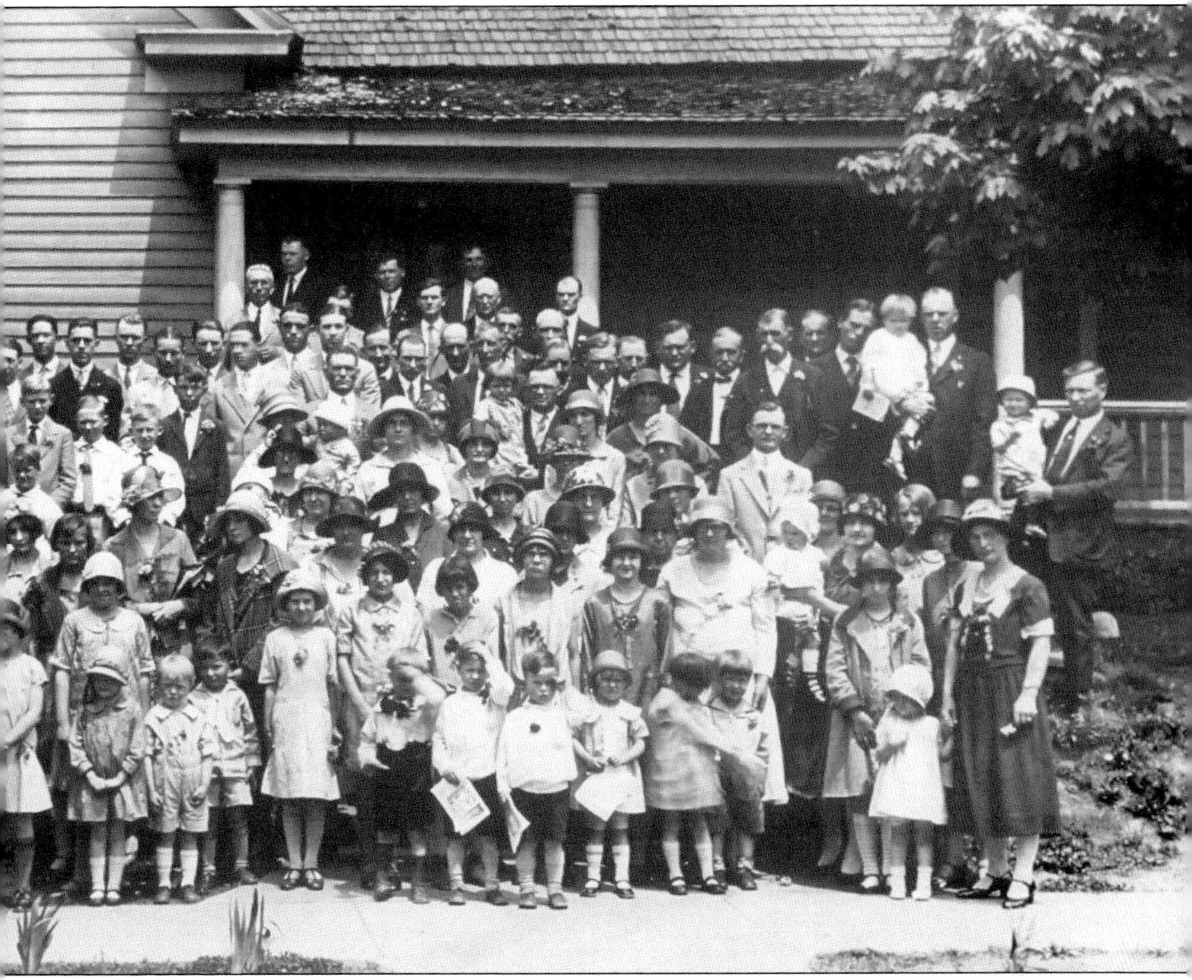

are Walter's mother, Clemmie, and his young sister Doris. They died in a car accident caused by a drunk driver on Stratford Road in the early 1930s. The bell tower in the church is dedicated to their memory. Walter is on the the fourth row, seventh from the left. He is standing slightly to the side, wearing a white shirt and tie. (Memorial Reformed Church.)

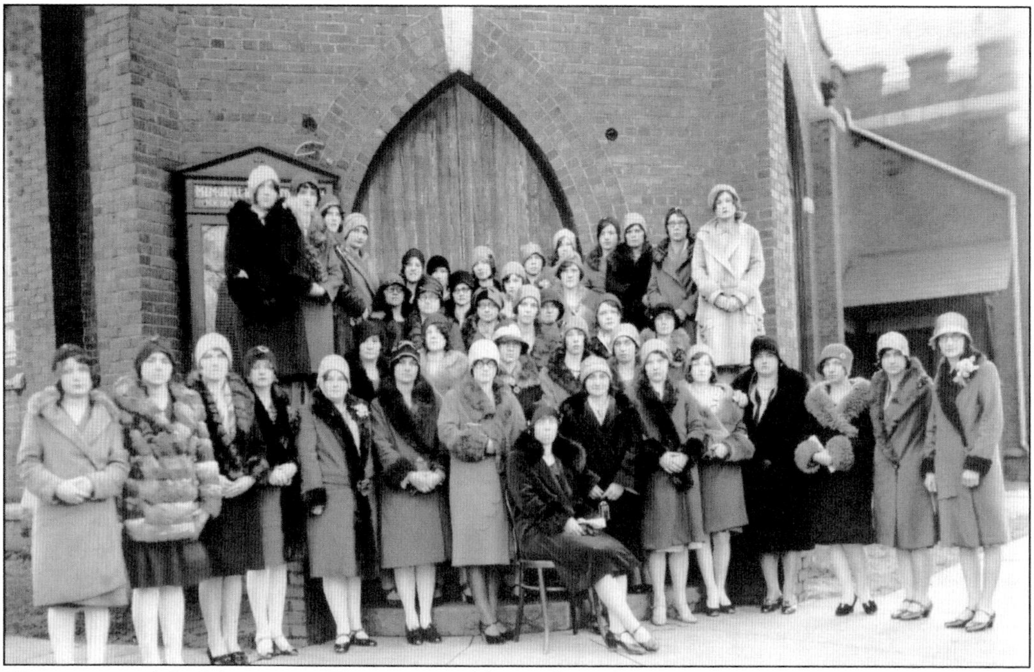

The women of the Missionary Women's Guild pose for a photographer outside the front entrance of Memorial Reformed Church. It's speculated that the woman sitting in the chair is Dr. Charles E. Schaeffer's wife and the leader of the guild. The church's exterior has not changed since this picture was taken in the early 1920s. (Memorial Reformed Church.)

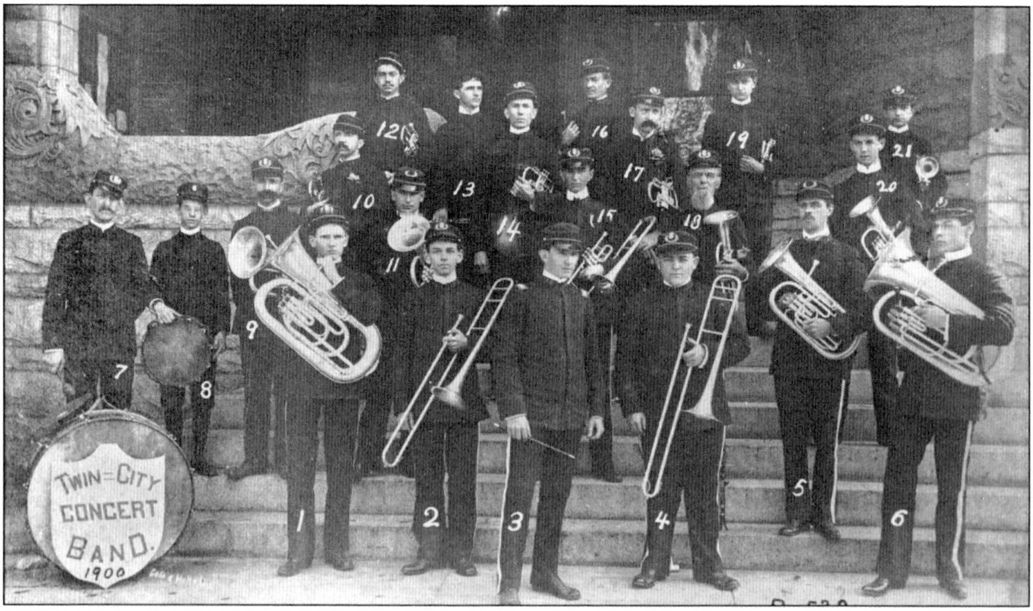

The Moravian Easter Band, shown in 1903, is a tradition that has been maintained for centuries. In the early days, band members copied the musical notes down in oilskin books. In the first row second from the left is Ralph Siewers, and the man second from the right in the first row is Fred Fogle. In the second row, third from the right is Ed .T. Mickey, Charles R. Fogle's partner in the Orinoco Company. (Forsyth County Public Library Photograph Collection.)

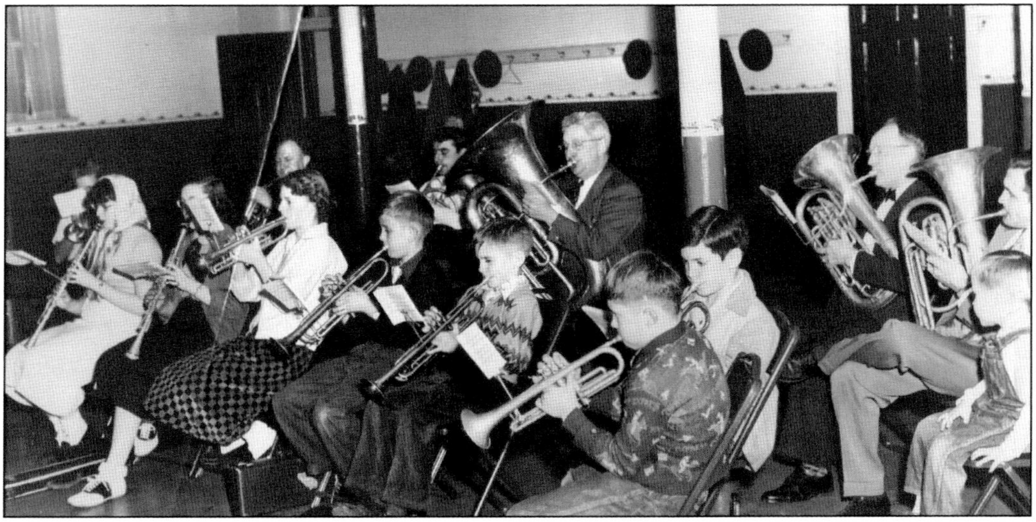

The Salem Band dates its beginnings to the founding of Salem in 1766, but its lineage extends to earlier times. The trombone choir, the forerunner of the church bands, had been an important instrumental organization in the Moravian Church since at least 1732. The first organized town band in Salem dates from the 1830s under the leadership of J. H. Leinbach and included 15 players. In 1872, the Salem Cornet Band was formed under the leadership of D. T. Crouse. Later, around 1898, this group and one that had been formed in the neighboring town of Winston merged into the Twin City Concert Band, which played at various functions. In the photograph above, members of the Trinity Moravian Church band practice for the Easter Sunrise service. This service attracts the greatest participation of members, from 43 players in 1898 to hundreds today. (Trinity Moravian Church.)

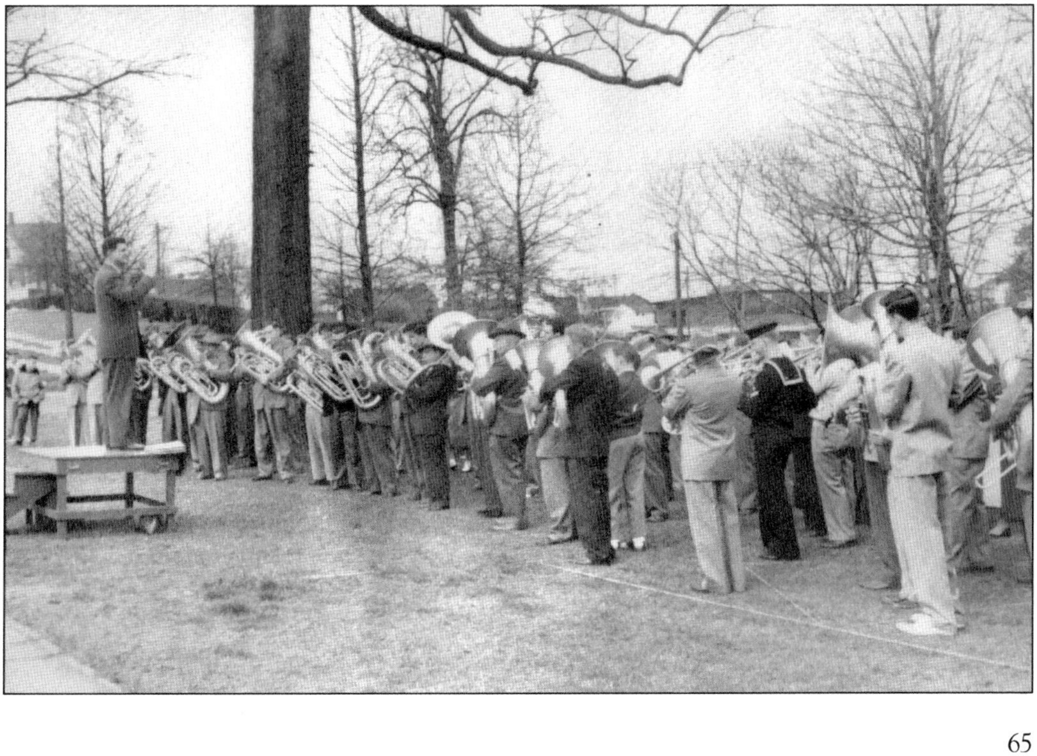

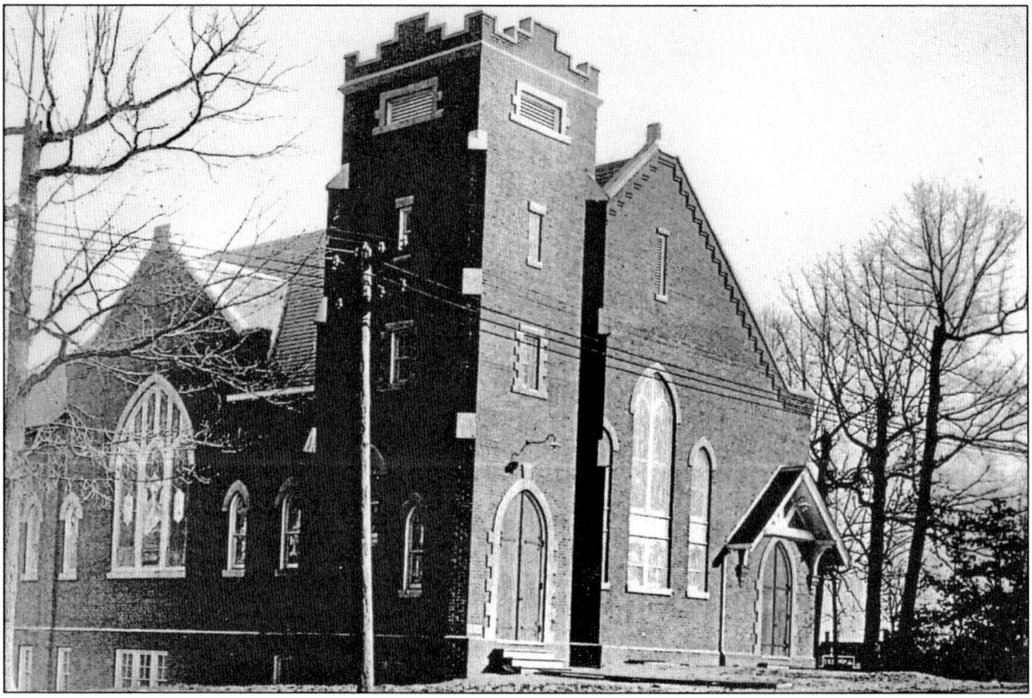

The beginning of Trinity Moravian Church took place in March 1886, when a group of ladies from the Home Moravian Church congregation began a Sunday school in a small, rented house at 327 Waughtown Street. This house became inadequate, and a chapel was built that same year on what is now called Chapel Street. Since the building was located midway between Salem and Waughtown in what is now the area of the North Carolina School of the Arts, it was called Centerville Chapel. In 1910, a committee of Moravians living in the area asked the central board to take steps to move the congregation to a new location on the trolley car line. In August 1911, work began on a new building on the Foster property on the corner of Sprague Street and Sunnyside Avenue (shown above). The Centerville congregation decided upon the name Trinity for a new church. A new Sunday school building (shown below) was completed in 1929. (Trinity Moravian Church.)

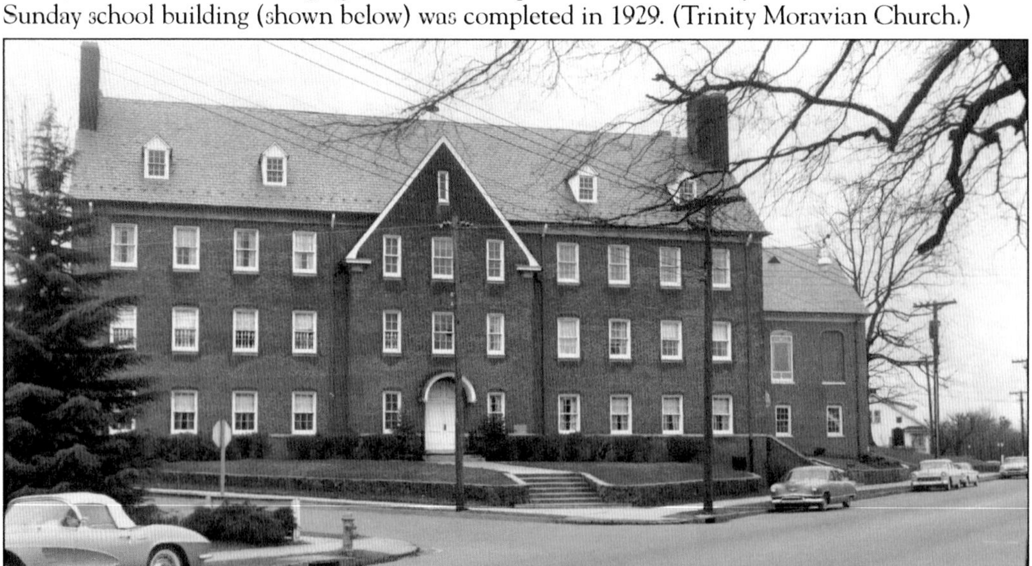

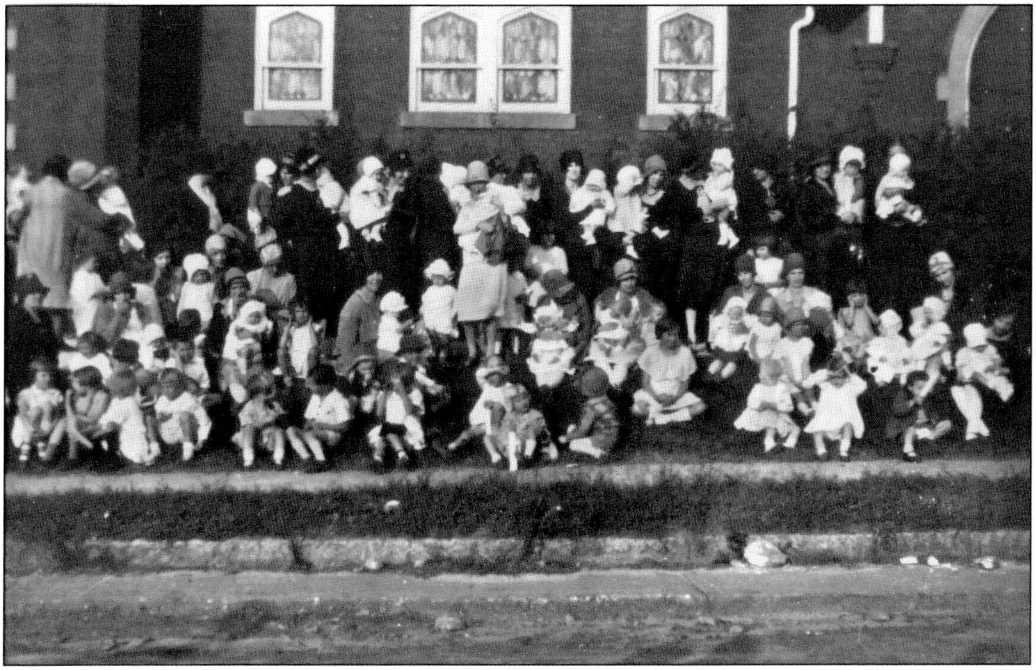

On July 14, 1912, Trinity congregation was organized by 96 charter members. In less than two decades, Trinity had 590 members and a strong commitment to benevolence in the community. Sunday school attendance was at an all-time high, as seen in the pictures above and below, and family-centric activities were a focal point outside of the regular Sunday service. Many Washington Park families walked the couple of blocks to attend Trinity's activities and now remember the impact this church had on their social life. (Trinity Moravian Church.)

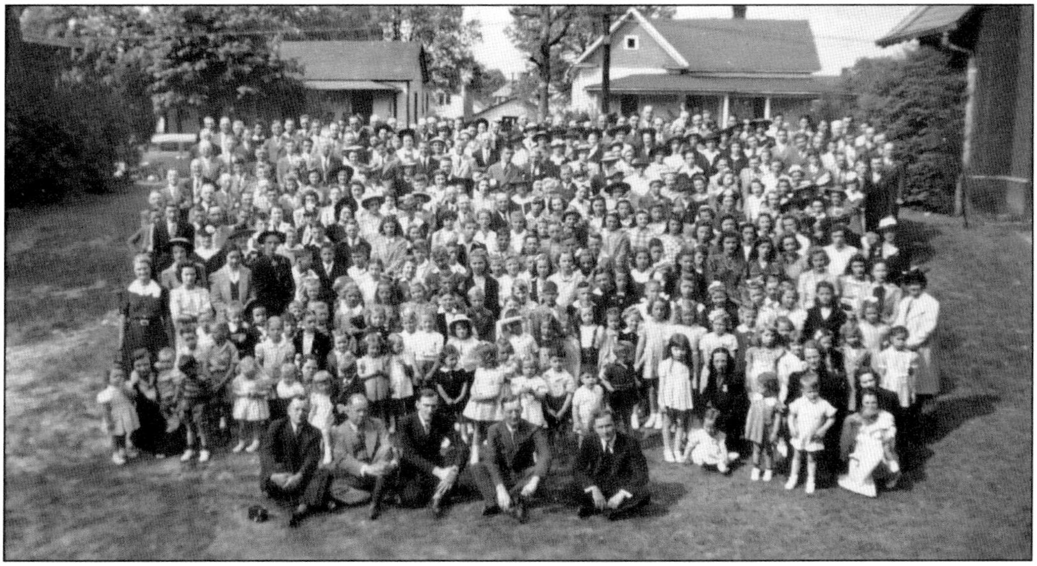

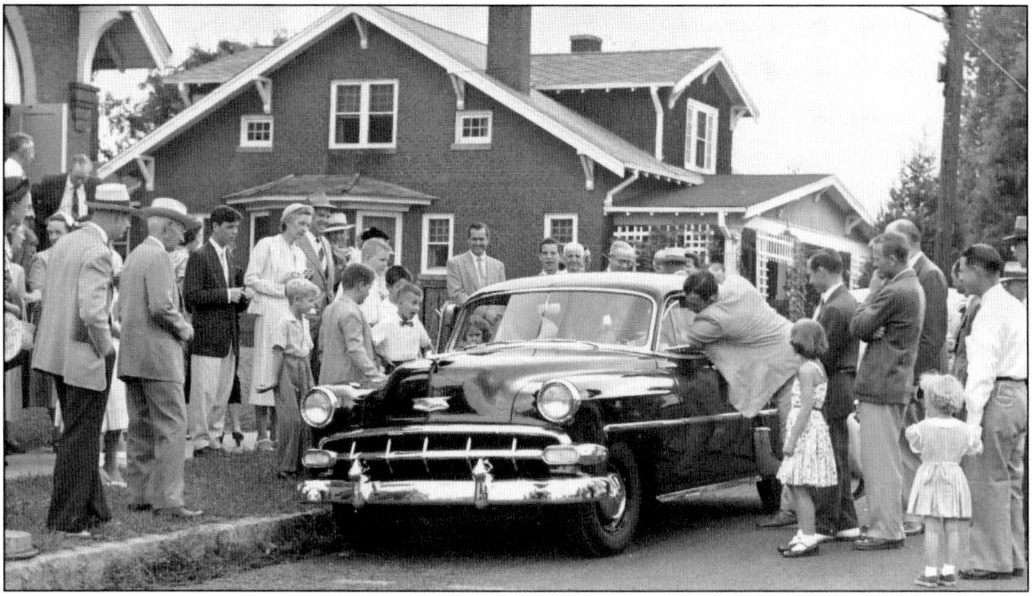

The Reverend Douglas L. Rights, shown in the driver's seat in both images, began his pastorate at Trinity in August 1919 and served for 37 years until his death on December 1, 1956. During his ministry at Trinity, a galley was added to the church, a parsonage was built in 1922, and a Christian Education Building was completed in 1929. Under his leadership, the Trinity congregation sponsored the establishment of two other Moravian congregations: Pine Chapel and New Eden. In 1947, the Moravian College and Theological Seminary recognized his achievements and awarded him an honorary doctor of divinity degree. On November 15, 1956, the Southern Province of the Moravian Church elected him bishop. He passed away on December 1, 1956. These photographs show Rights in a car his congregation presented him on August 29, 1954. (Trinity Moravian Church.)

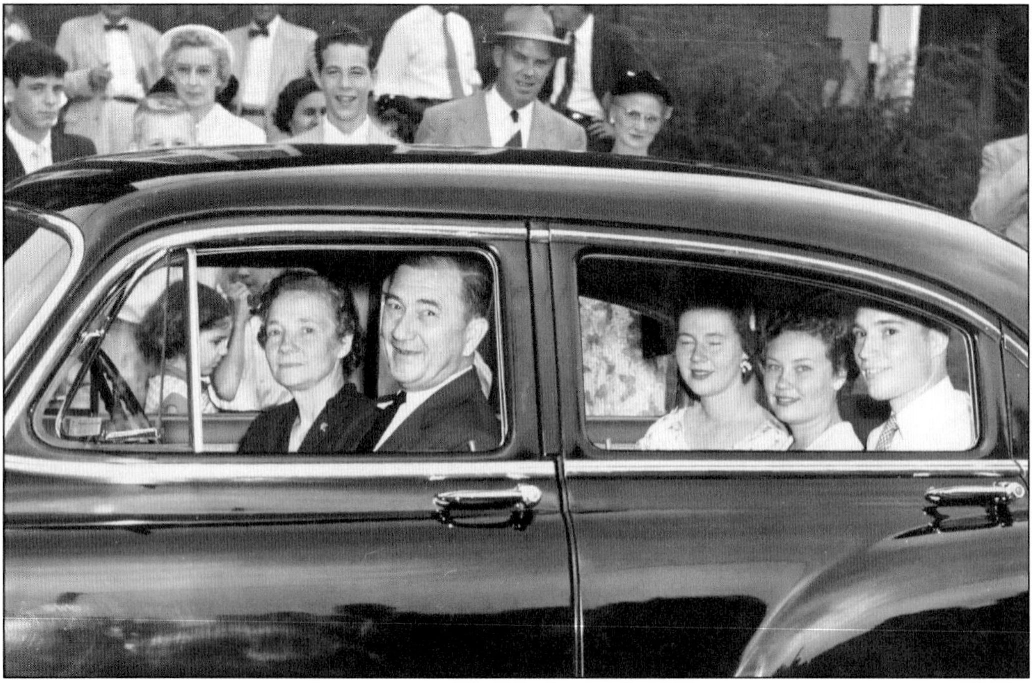

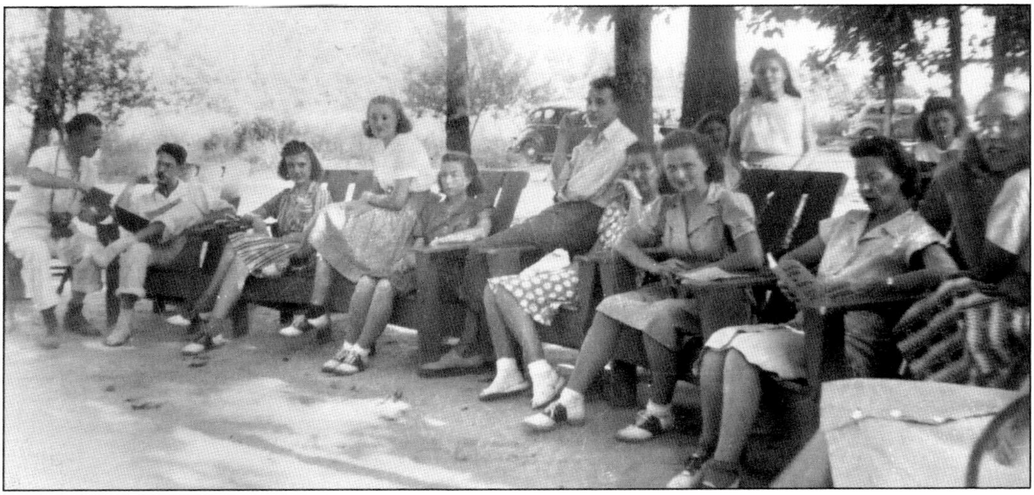

Church was a popular social outlet for teenagers and young adults. They would gather for outings that included ice cream suppers, potluck dinners, watermelon feasts, and songfests, where some people would play instruments and everybody would sing. Dr. Rights of Trinity Moravian Church gave land he owned south of Winston-Salem, down Highway 150 to the Kiwanis Club. A camp was built called Anikanati, meaning "happy hunting grounds," which many of the youth would visit. They would also gather at people's homes and at Trinity Church for music celebrations. Pictured below from left to right are Sammy Feldman, Terri Mabe, Sandra Shelton, Sharon Mabe, and Elizabeth Messick in the yard behind Trinity's education building. (Trinity Moravian Church.)

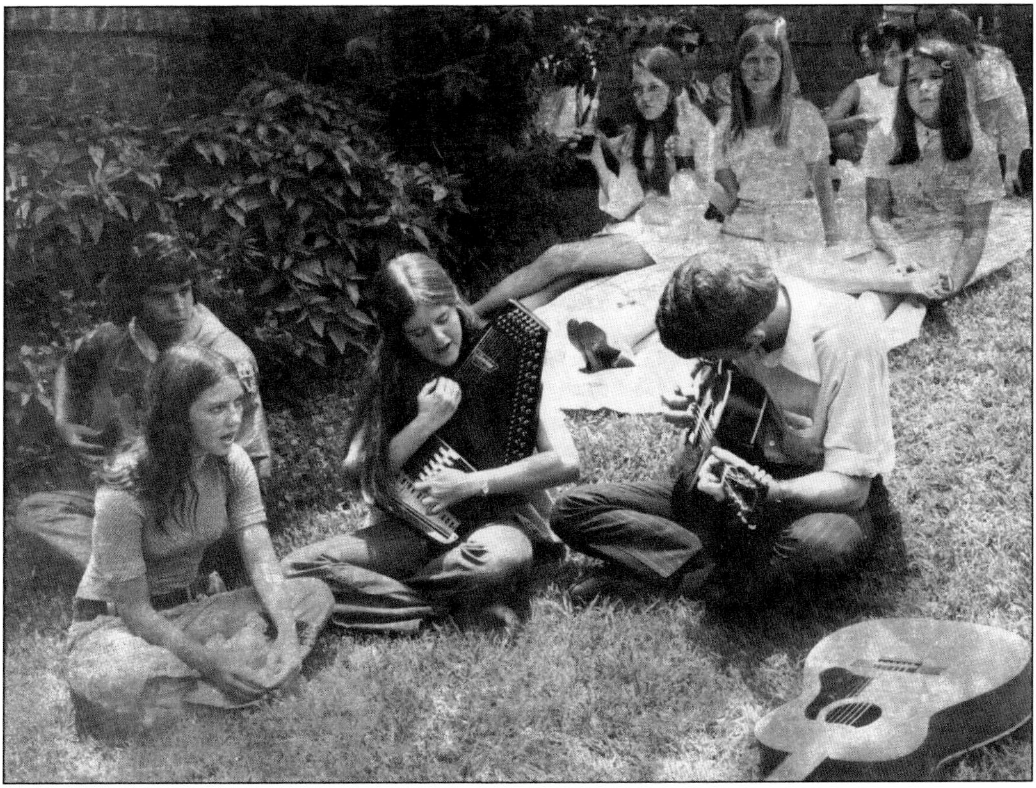

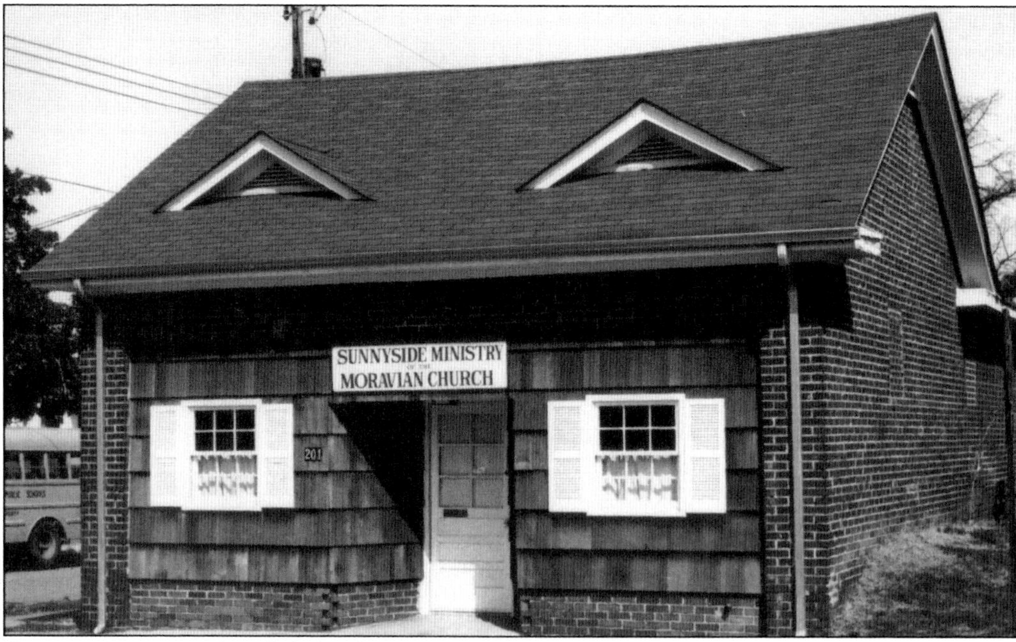

Trinity Moravian Church helped to initiate the Sunnyside Ministry project. This ministry, as described in a church bulletin, "will be in the people business, seeking to meet the hurts of people, materially and spiritually, in the Sunnyside area of Waughtown." Today it helps neighbors avoid life-threatening situations brought on by financial crises. (Trinity Moravian Church.)

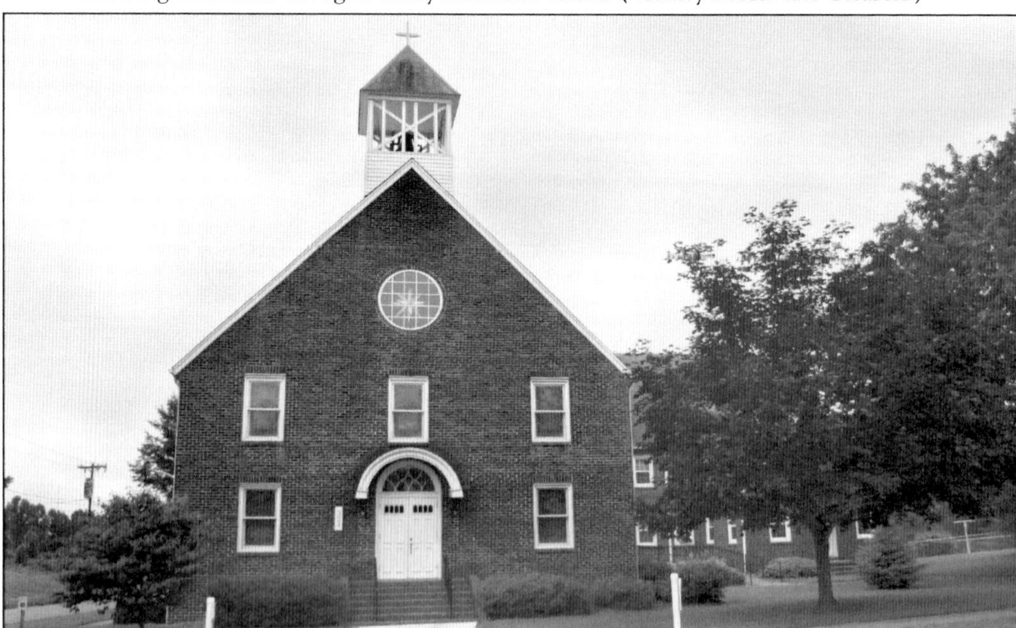

When Henry E. Fries built a cotton mill in the Southside of Salem in 1896, the need arose for a Sunday school and chapel for the workers and their families (shown here). The Sunday school grew so quickly that a meetinghouse was built in 1904 and given the name Pine Chapel. On November 16, 1924, Pine Chapel was organized as a branch under Trinity Moravian Church. (Trinity Moravian Church.)

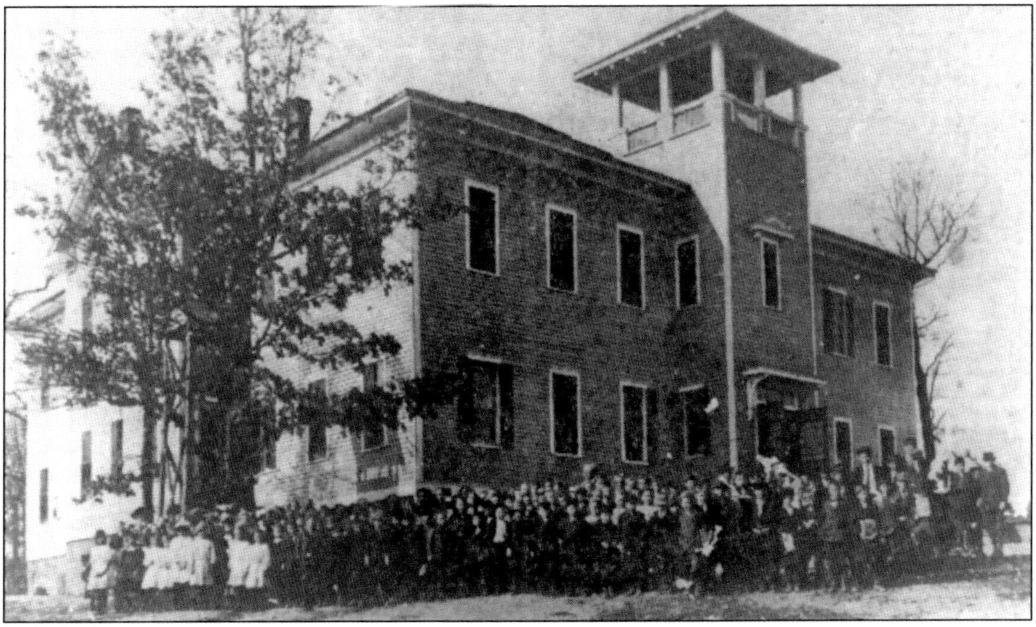

Centerville Street, now Waughtown Street, was so called because it was located between Salem and Waughtown. It was the first macadamized road in Forsyth County, created around 1890 because there existed such an impossible barrier of mud that construction engineer Charlie A. Reynolds went to the county commissioners and requested the use of convicts to break stone and place it on the road. This enabled people to expand beyond the Salem boundaries, which eventually led to the formation of Centerville Church, and shortly thereafter Centerville School (shown above). Neighborhood churches provided the early education to its residents through Sunday school lessons and elementary studies (shown below). This building, once located on Chapel Street, has been torn down, and the property is now part of the North Carolina School of the Arts. (Above, Forsyth County Public Library Photograph Collection; below, Trinity Moravian Church.)

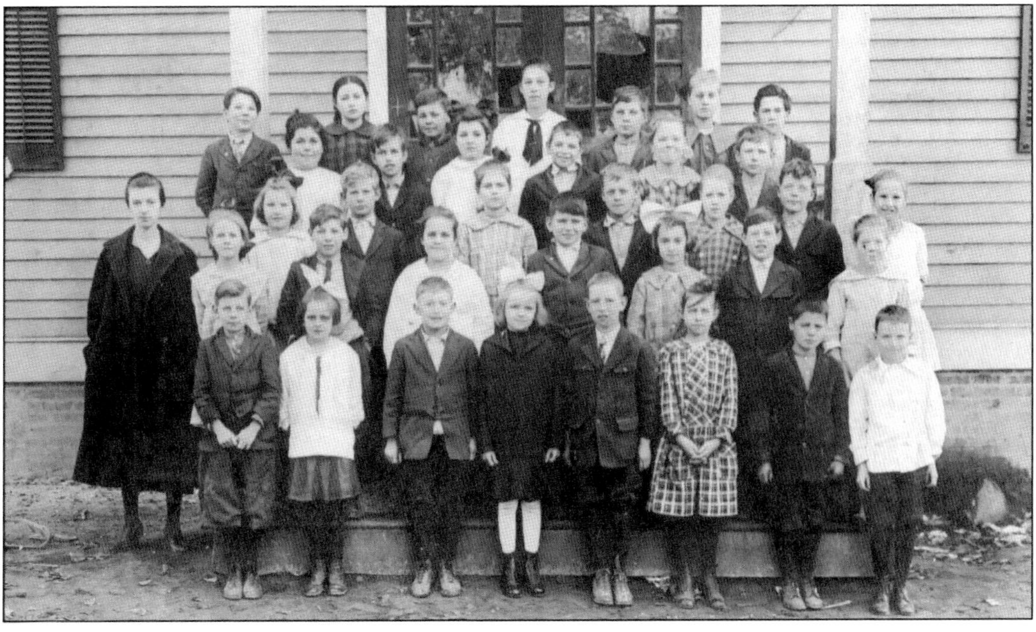

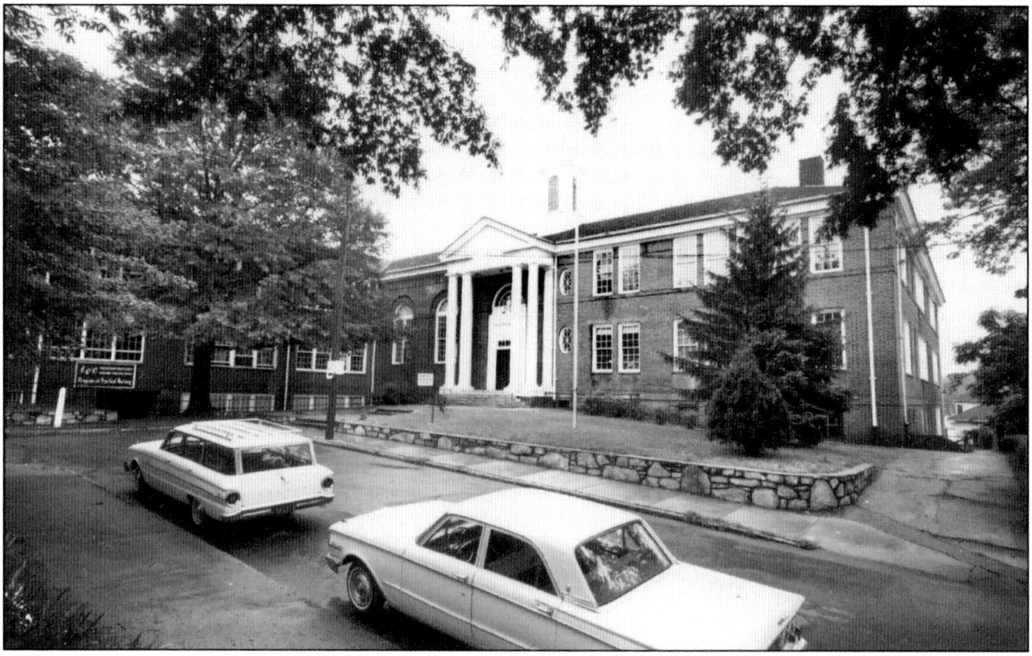

Central Graded School was located in Salem on Race and Church Streets next to St. Phillips Church and was the main elementary school for the Washington Park children. Many remember walking down South Main Street and crossing in the tunnel built under the Salem Avenue to arrive at the school. They also remember the fields flooding and not being able to play in the playground for weeks on end. When Old Salem Foundation began renovating the area to turn it into a historic designation, they bought and tore down all nonhistorical dwellings in the area. The school building, shown above and below, was demolished between 1976 and 1977, and the property was planted with grass and fruit trees. (Above, Forsyth County Public Library Photograph Collection; below, Old Salem Museums and Gardens.)

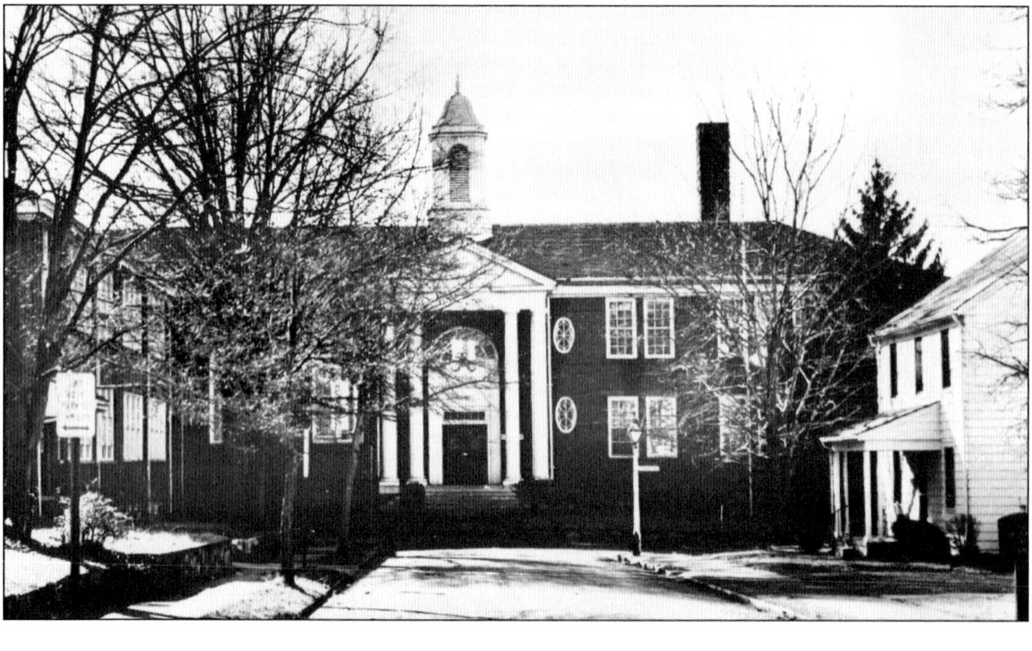

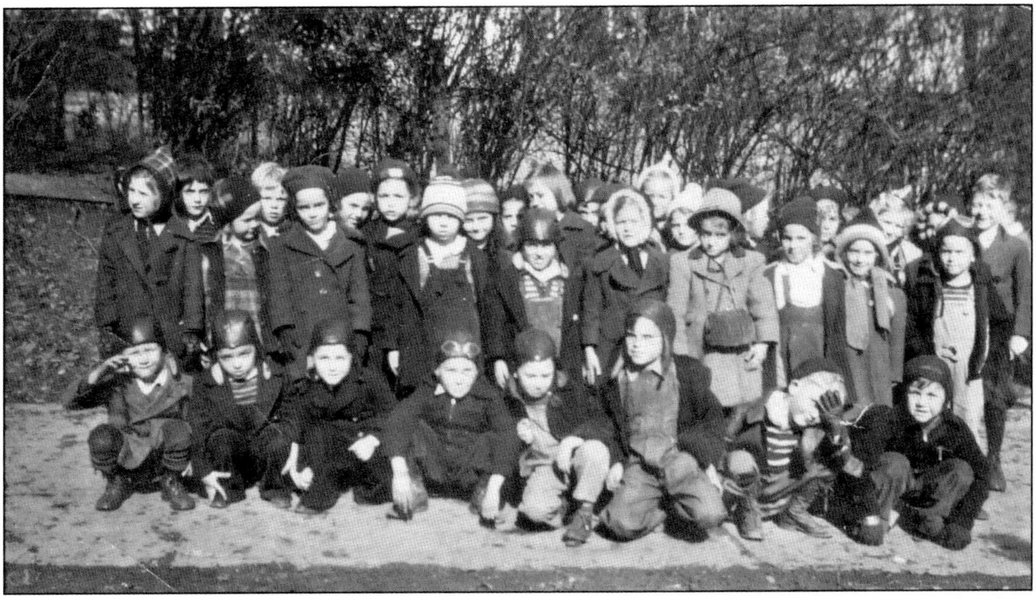

When Jean Hayes lived on Shawnee Street, she used to walk a couple of blocks to school at Central Elementary. The boys, influenced by World War II, wore leather flight hats and donned aviator goggles, as shown on the heads of some of her classmates in her first-grade class picture. Jean is on the second row, fifth from the right. (Jean Hayes Mahaffey.)

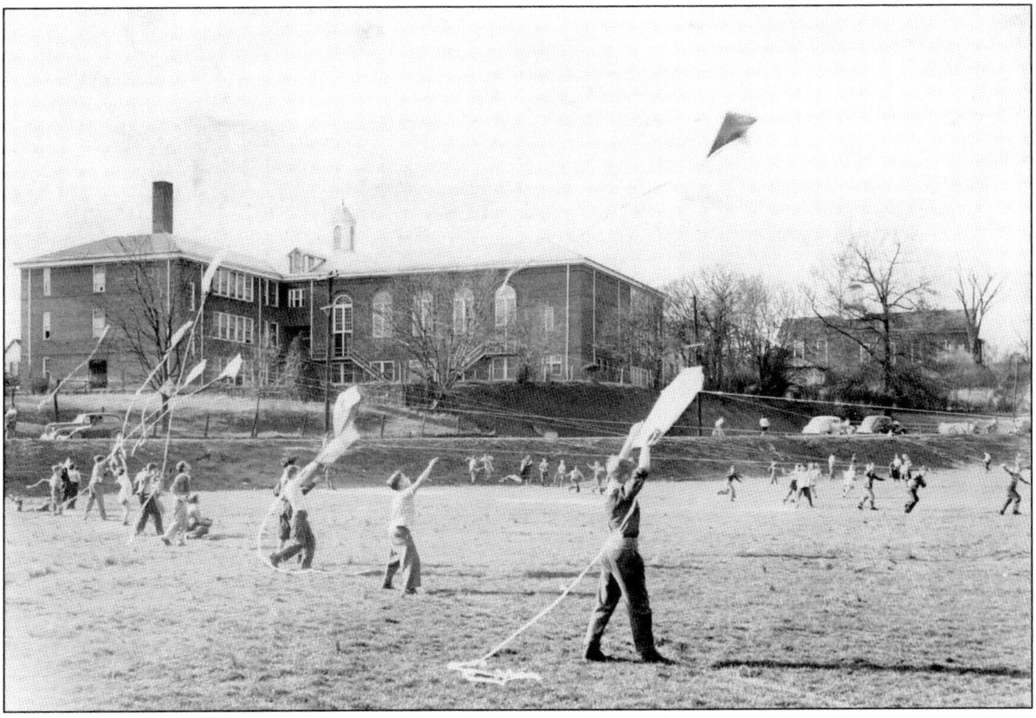

Schoolchildren around the city would make kites to fly in the annual kite-flying competition held in the fields behind Central Elementary School. This field is now used by Salem College and Academy as their athletic fields, and a portion along Salem Creek serves as part of the Southeast Greenway. (Forsyth County Public Library Photograph Collection.)

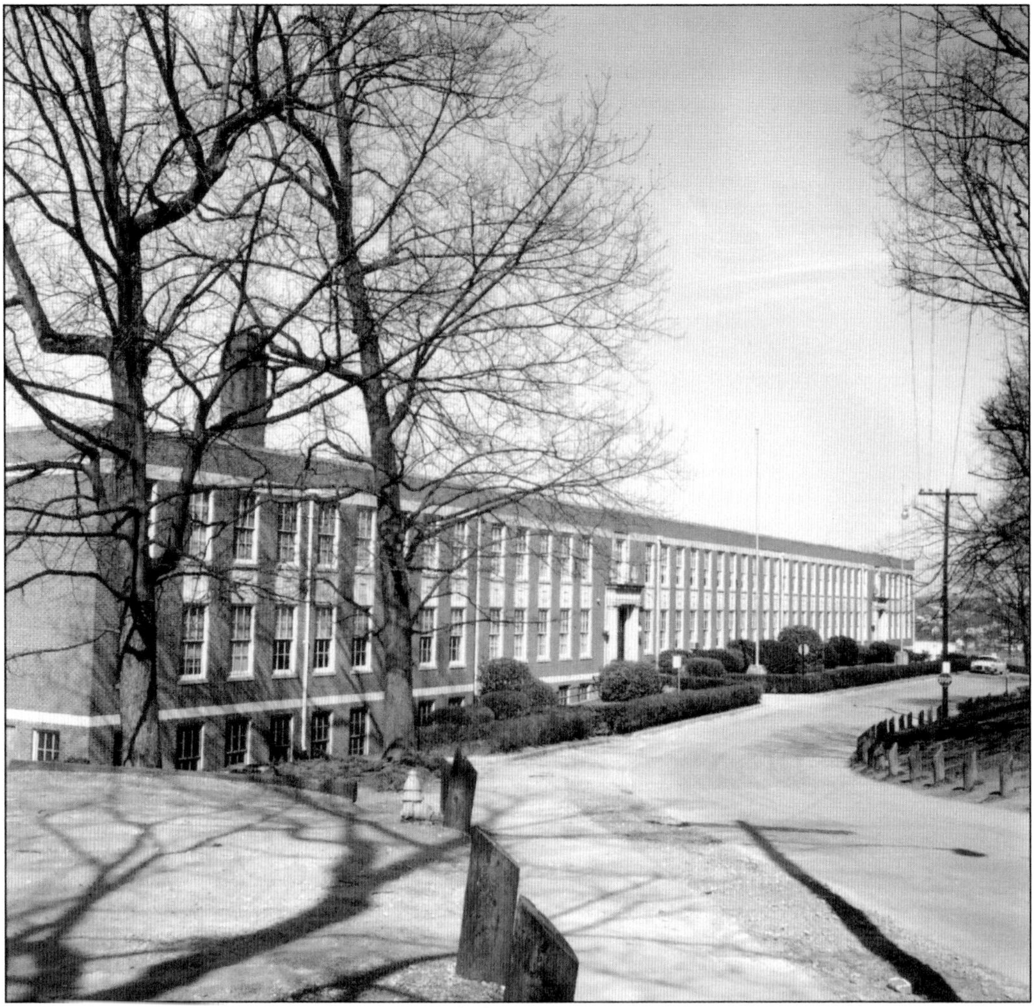

The James A. Gray High School was founded in 1930 as South Junior High School and was one of the first junior highs schools in Winston-Salem. It included sixth, seventh, and eighth grades and became a high school in 1935, when its named changed to South High School. In 1939, the name was again changed to James A. Gray High School, honoring one of Winston-Salem's citizen benefactors. Around this same time, North High School became John W. Hanes High School, rounding out the three all-white high schools named Reynolds, Gray, and Hanes. In 1941, the south end of the Gray High School building was expanded to provide space for the science laboratory, the band room, two lavatories, the machine shop, and five more classrooms. By 1957, over 1,000 students, including the eighth grade, attended this school. (Forsyth County Public Library Photograph Collection.)

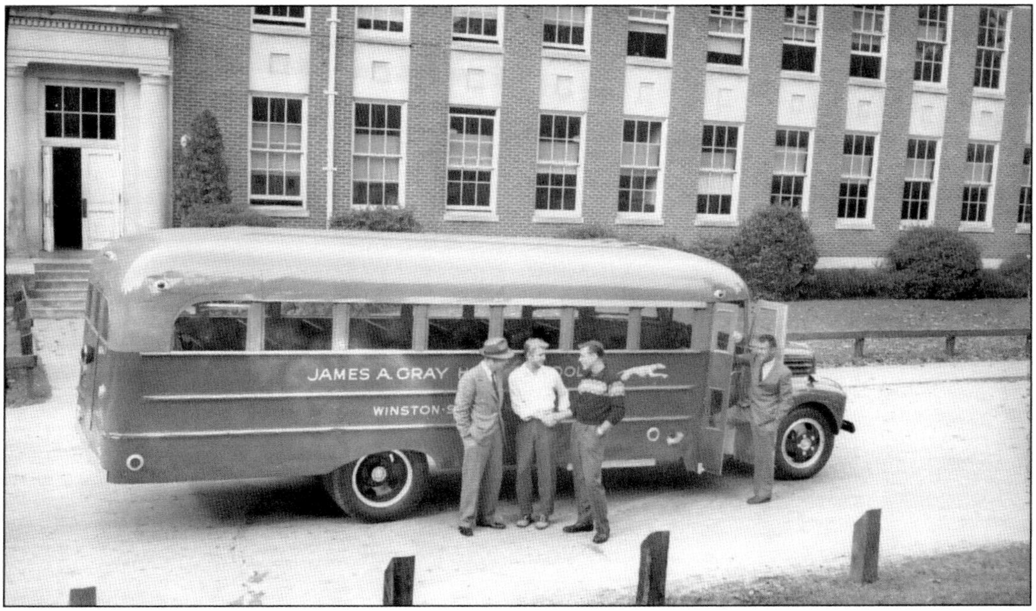

Many of the teenagers who attended Gray were able to walk to school, take the city bus (shown below), or drive their own car. Most of the students lived in the Washington Park area, the Waughtown area, Konnoak Hills, and beyond. According to Sherry Dagenhardt Griggs, class of 1964, "Unless students were involved in after school activities, they didn't hang around after school let out. The other bus (shown above) was used for school activities. The players rode this bus to football games, baseball games, etc. After 1960–1961, the activity bus no longer carried the name of the school on the side, but rather Winston-Salem Forsyth County." (Above, Forsyth County Public Library Photograph Collection; below, Sherry Dagenhardt Griggs.)

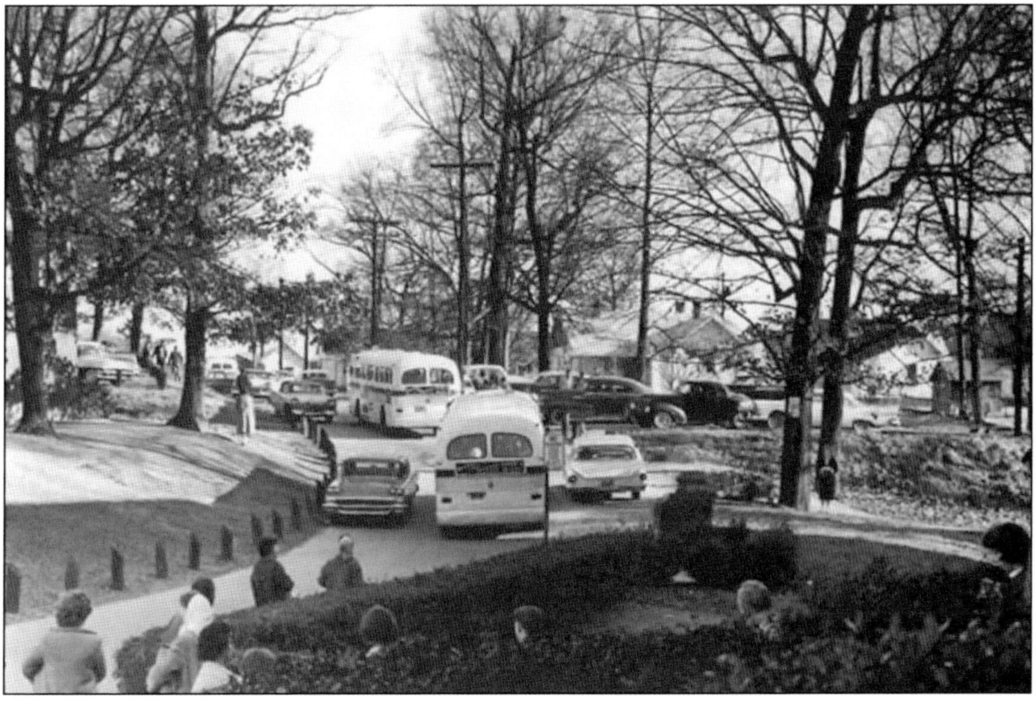

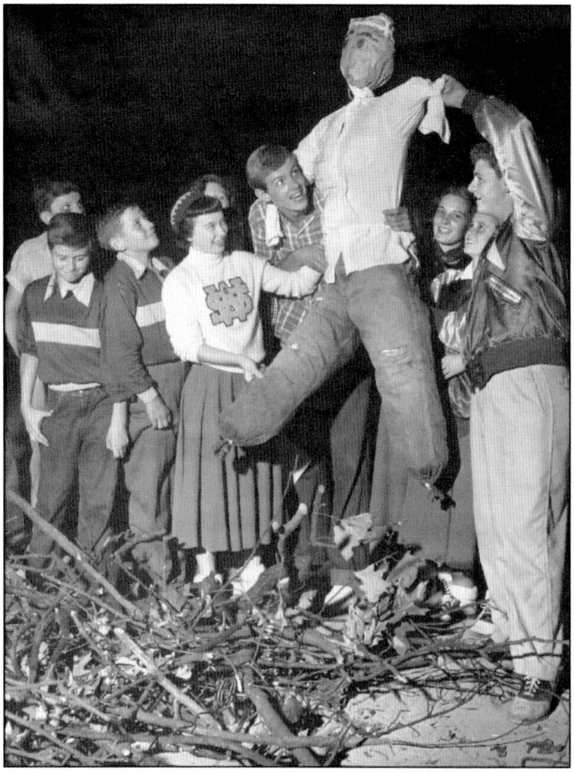

According to Sherry Dagenhardt Griggs, homecoming was always a big deal. The pep rallies, such as the one in this photograph, were "ear shattering, and a huge bonfire was always a crowd pleaser. The spirit of the school was great and we pretty much stuck together. There was a homecoming dance after the game. It was also a more formal time, especially for how you dressed. Guys were not allowed to wear jeans, so khakis were the standard of the day. Girls wore skirts or dresses with hose, no slacks allowed. Even in the freezing weather if we went to a football game, we wore tailored wool slacks and a matching sweater topped off with a heavy coat and gloves. No sweats, jeans, etc. I remember my senior year when I sponsored someone for homecoming. I wore a very nice suit and a hat along with gloves. And this was pretty much how everyone was dressed." (Above, Forsyth County Public Library Photograph Collection; below, Sherry Dagenhardt Griggs.)

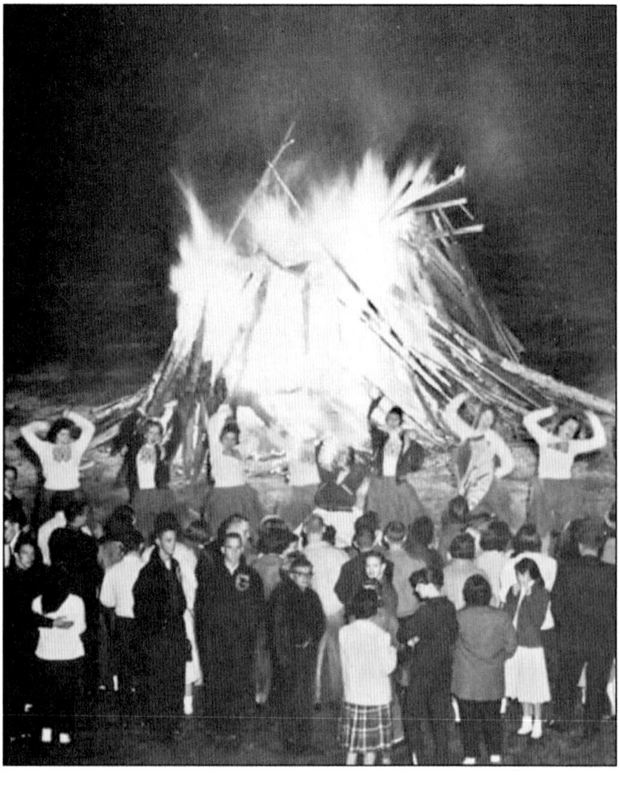

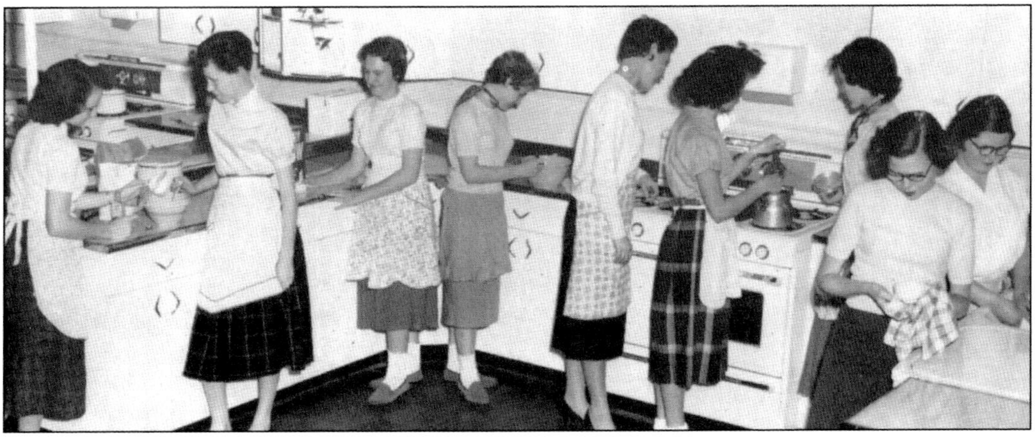

Reka Rich, home economics instructor at Gray High School, helps students practice in one of the new kitchens in 1951 (above). Machine shop class was directed by G. D. Sexton (shown below), and students attended either the morning or the evening class. The morning class was allowed a Coca-Cola break at 10:00 a.m. "Home Economics was something all the girls took, mostly in the sophomore or junior year," said Sherry Dagenhardt Griggs. "I had Mrs. Bruce for Home Economics. We actually learned to lay out a pattern, cut and assemble a garment. There was a book we were required to study to write out balanced menus and even got to cook on occasion. It was strictly a girls' thing, no boys allowed." (Frank Frye.)

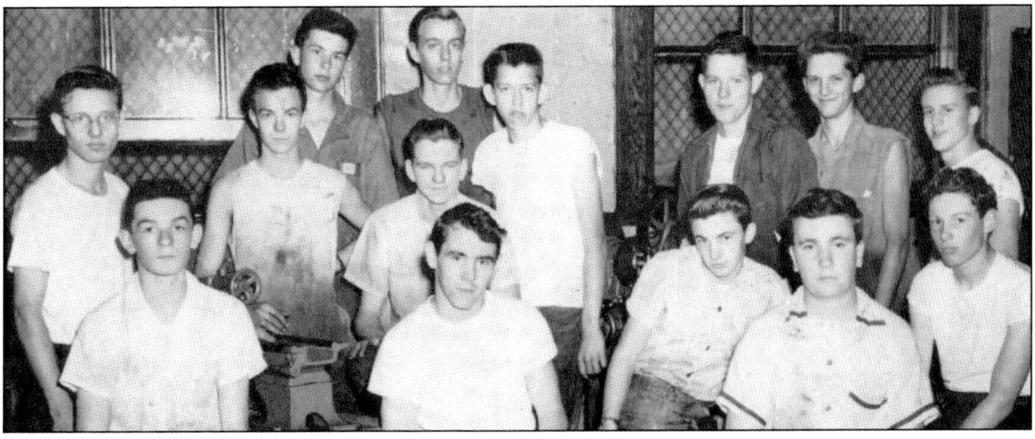

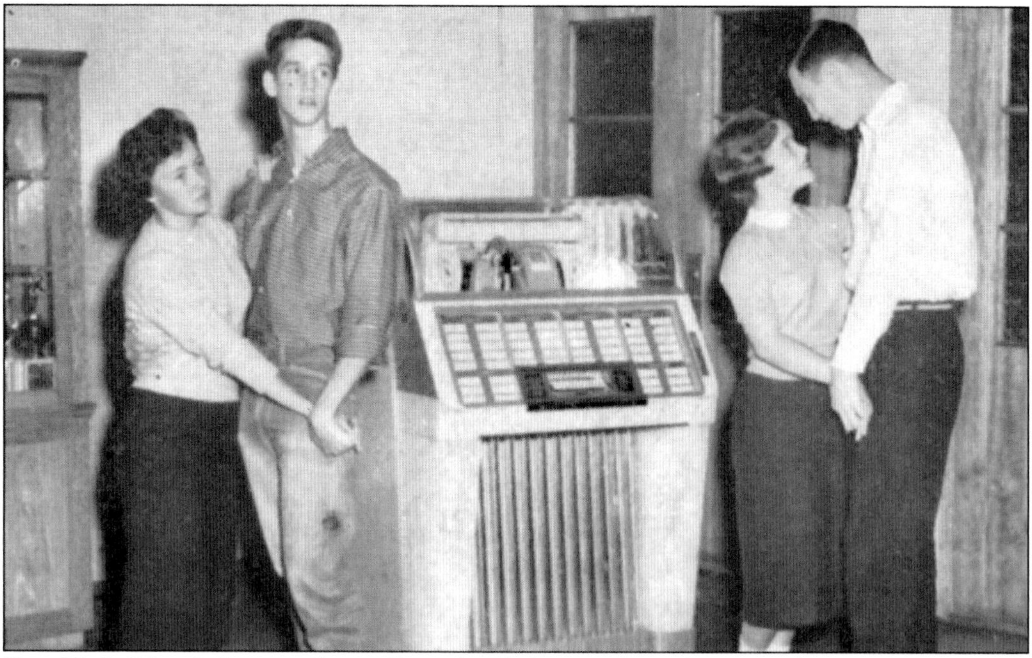

Gray High School alumnae Sherry Dagenhardt Griggs, class of 1964, said, "One thing that we did then, that would never be allowed now is that we danced during school. We had a 20 minute break for a snack in the mornings, where we could purchase things in the cafeteria. Our lunch was about 45 minutes long and you could go through the lunch line and eat in 20 minutes. So you went across the drive to the gym. Here we had a jukebox and you could shag away the last of your lunch period." Shown above in 1951 (left to right), Jo Ann Posey, Jack Byrd, Ann Morris, and Buddy Dorset dance in the boys' gymnasium. Shown below (from left to right), Millie Holt, Janet Fansler, and Ronnie Brown decorate the gym for a Halloween dance. (Frank Frye.)

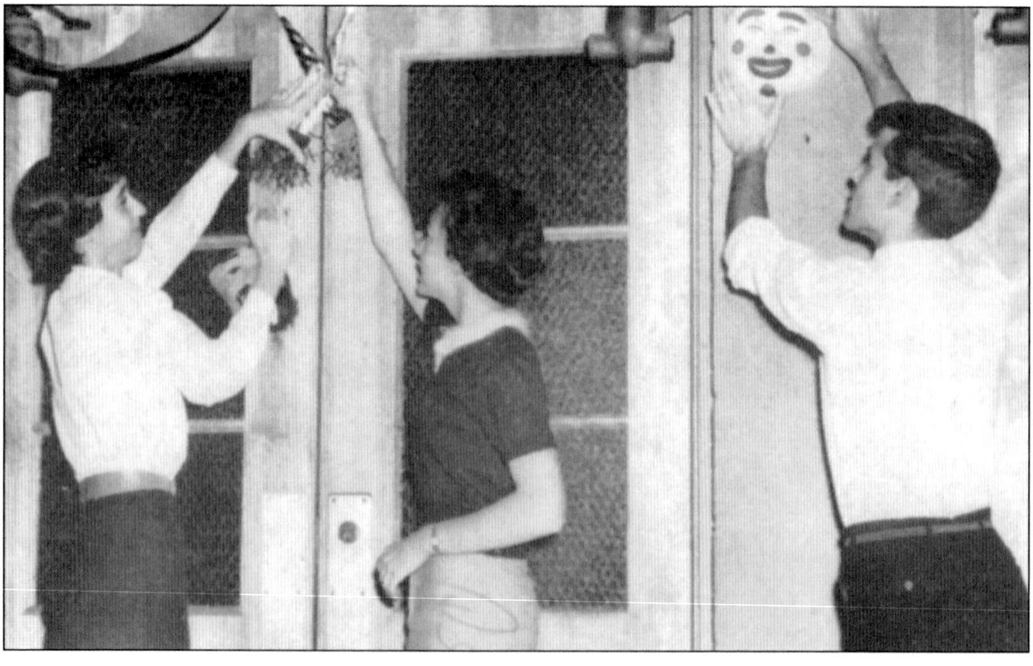

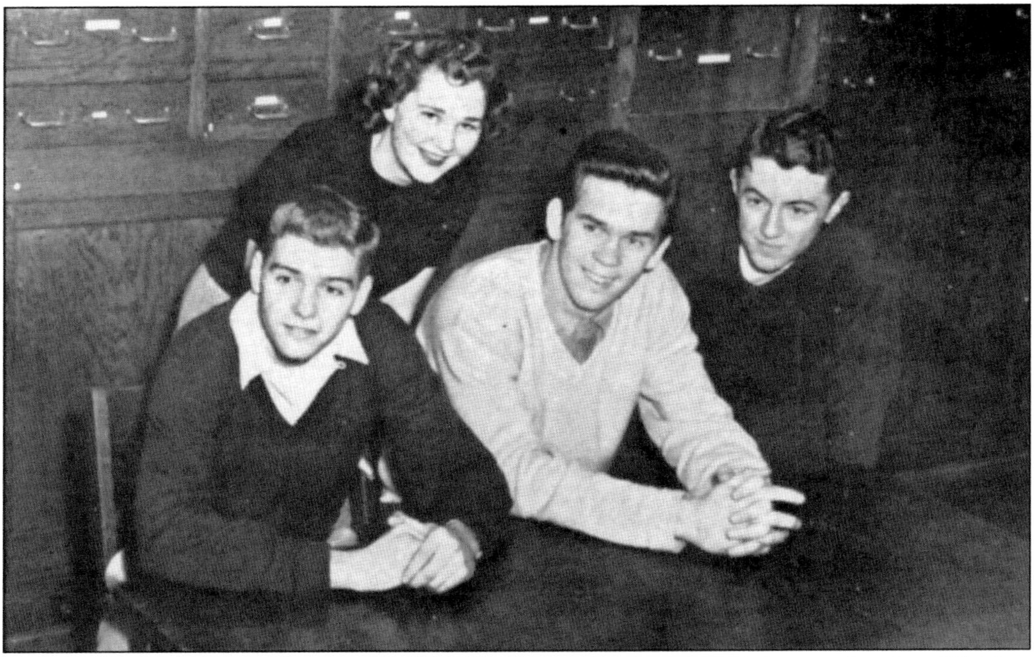

The junior class officers for Gray High School in 1951 were, from left to right, Ray Whitley, vice president; Pat Pierce, secretary; Richard Sharpe, president; and Rodney Reich, treasurer. (Rodney Reich.)

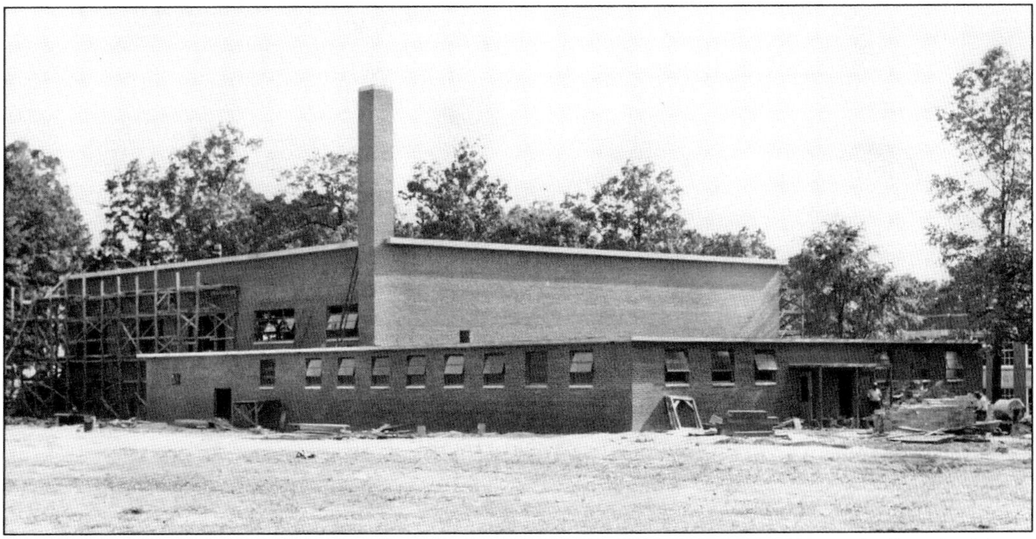

Gray High School built a new boys' gymnasium in 1950–1951 to house the popular boys' athletic teams. Students remember sitting on the wooden, pull-out bleachers and cheering on the Greyhounds. They also remember the backboards with "No Smoking" signs painted on them for fear that someone would drop a cigarette into the bleachers and start a fire. (Forsyth County Public Library Photograph Collection.)

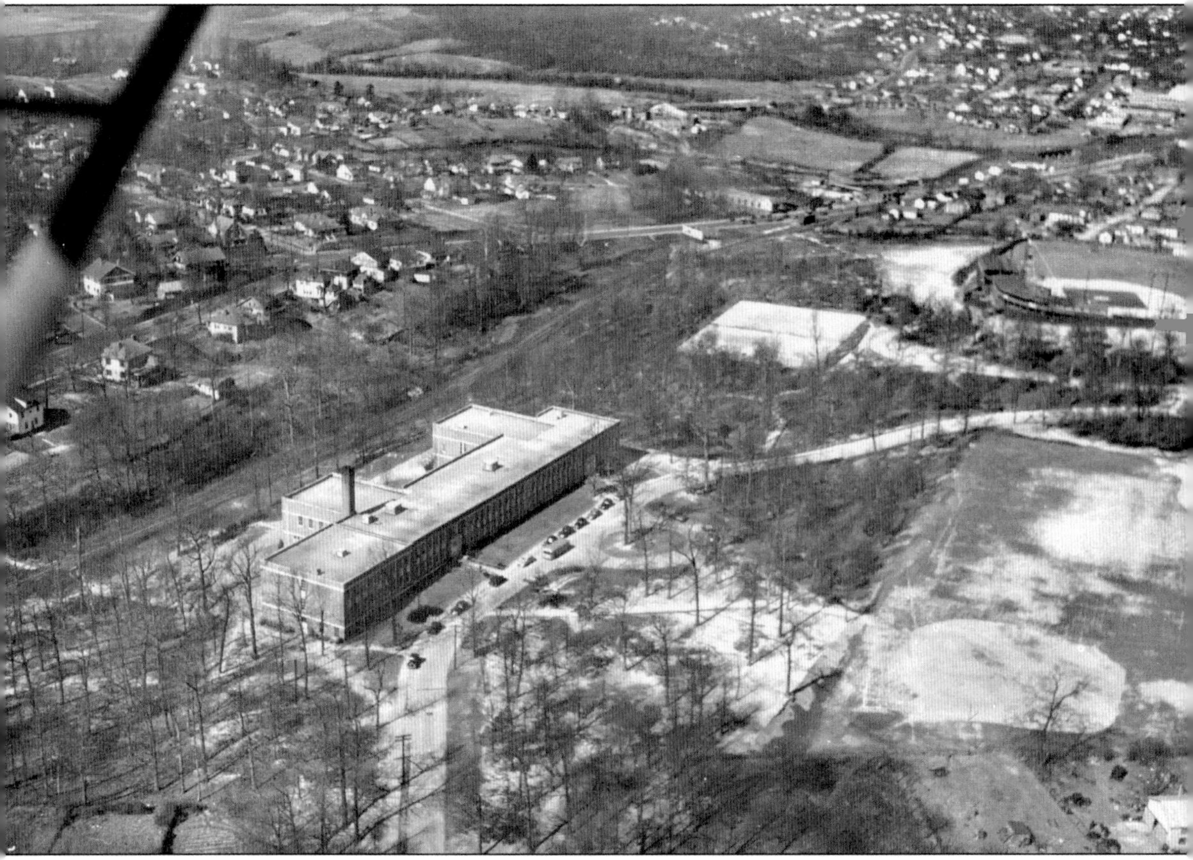

This aerial photograph of Gray High School, taken in 1940, shows the school before the addition of the boys' gymnasium. In the top right corner is the South Side Ball Park. South Main Street and Waughtown are both visible, as are the railroad tracks that run behind Gray High School, separating it from the Washington Park neighborhood. The land in the upper left corner was developed into shopping malls, car dealerships, and restaurants along Peter's Creek Parkway. The homes and businesses that once stood along South Main Street, just over Salem Creek, have been removed, and it's now fields, tennis courts, and small businesses. (Forsyth County Public Library Photograph Collection.)

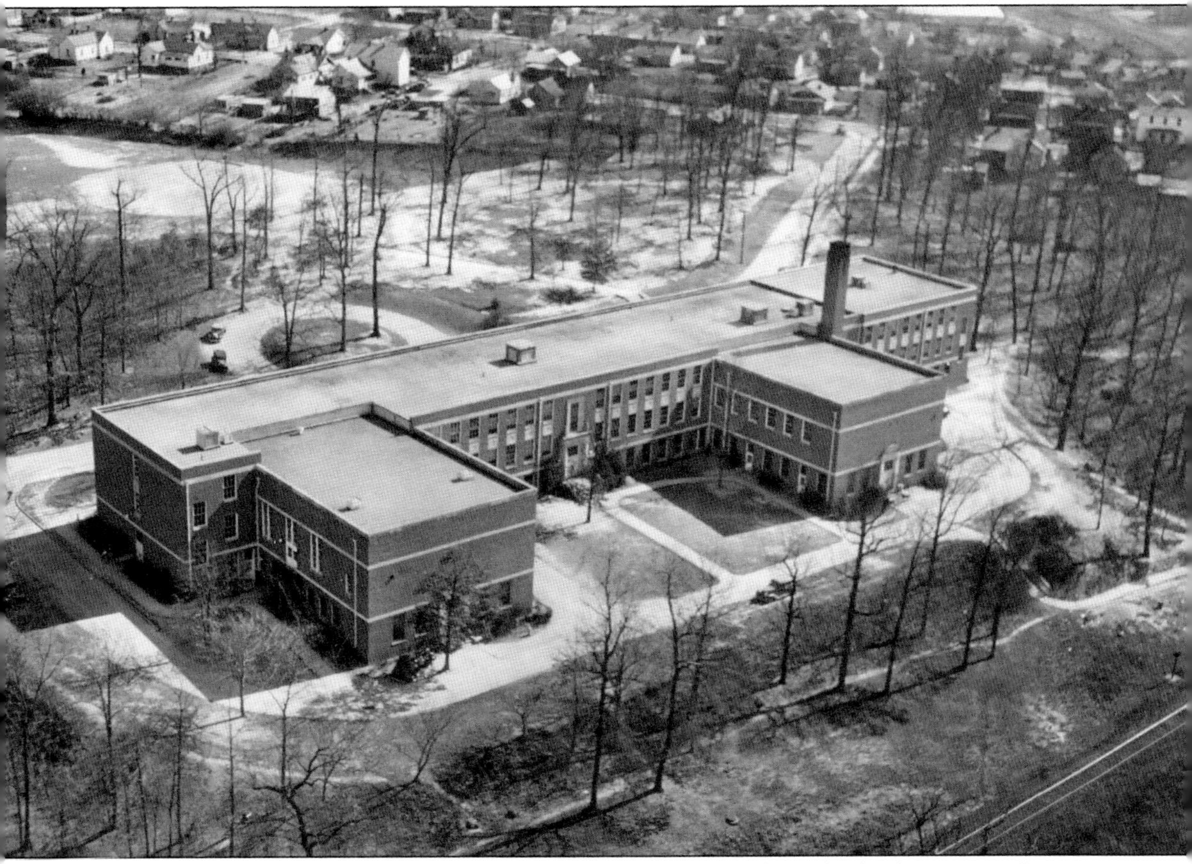

This aerial shot of Gray High School, taken in 1940, shows Gray from the back entrance facing southeast. The homes in Sunnyside are still standing and haven't been replaced by the North Carolina School of the Arts housing complex, Center Stage, yet. (Forsyth County Public Library Photograph Collection.)

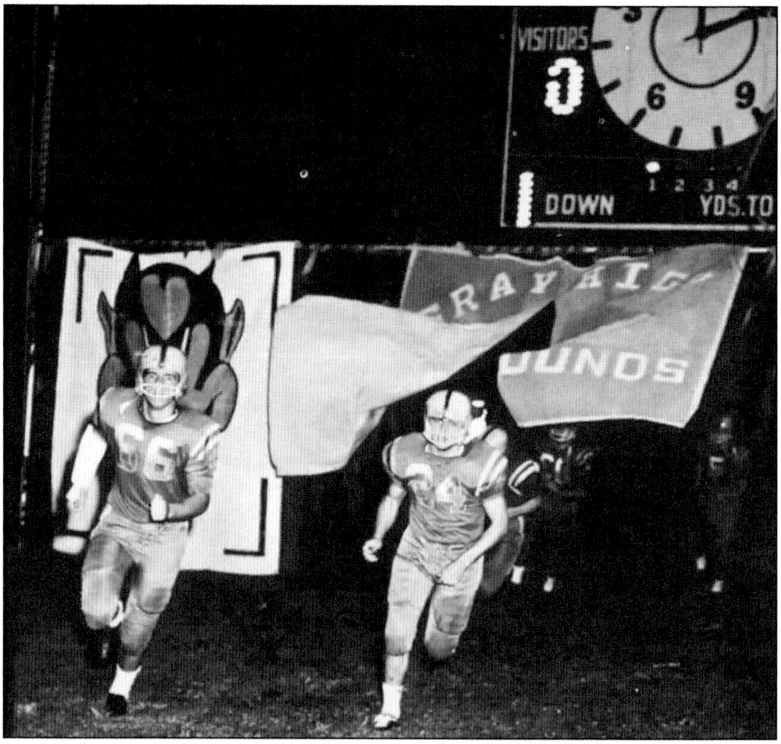

Like baseball games at South Side Ball Park, Gray High School football games were a family event. Neighbors remember walking or driving to Bowman Gray Stadium to cheer on their team, and everybody they knew attended. They remember how the players would tear through the paper sign announcing them onto the field and how everybody went wild with excitement. (Sherry Dagenhardt Griggs.)

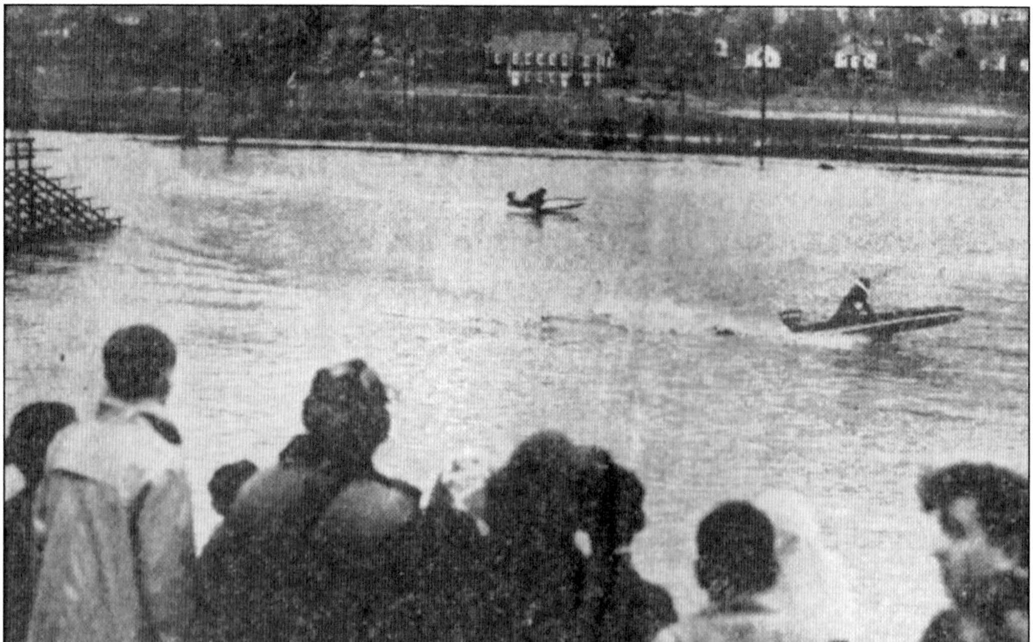

Salem Creek is notorious for flooding during bad storms. The low-lying areas around the Salem Athletic Park and Happy Hills Park turn into shallow lakes, which normally recede after a day. In years past, before the Salem Lake dam was built, the flooding would turn the fields of Central Elementary School into fun boating areas. (Reich family.)

Six

Washington Park's Citizens

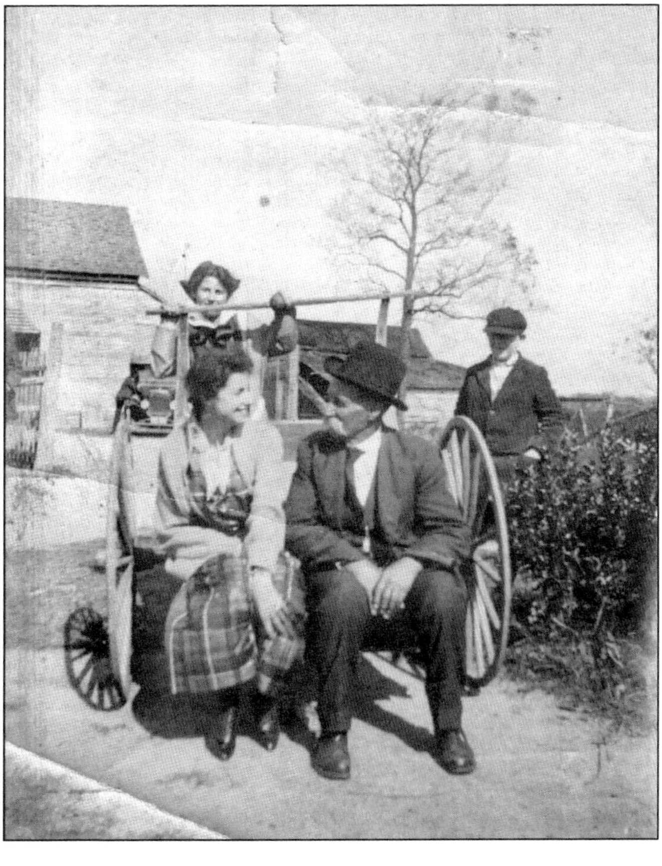

The land above Salem was once considered too steep for farming and was as used as hunting grounds for wild game and fowl. Some pioneering families chose to try their hand at farming the land and built homesteads above the ridge overlooking Salem. The Sniders (pictured here) bought land along Sprague Street and farmed wheat and corn, among other crops, as well as raising cattle, hogs, and chickens. During the latter part of the 19th century and the first part of the 20th century, work was still organized along familial lines. Women were tasked with running the household, including milking the cows, producing the butter, spinning yarn and keeping ahead of the domestic chores. The men tilled the fields and managed the day-to-day chores of running a farm. (Jack Graham Jr.)

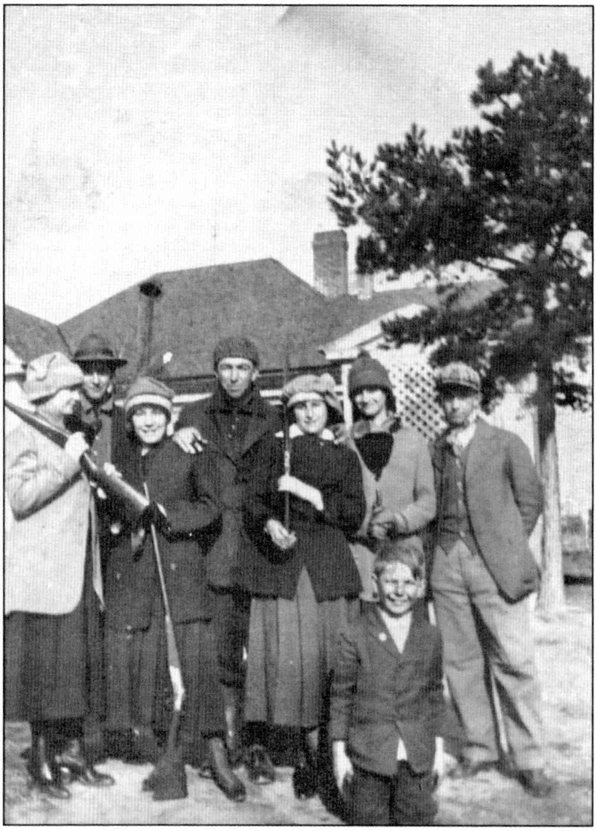

The lands south of Salem were hunting grounds through the early 1930s. This picture, taken on the Snider farm on Sprague Street, shows family members and their friends before they embarked on a hunting expedition for deer and fowl. (Jack Graham Jr.)

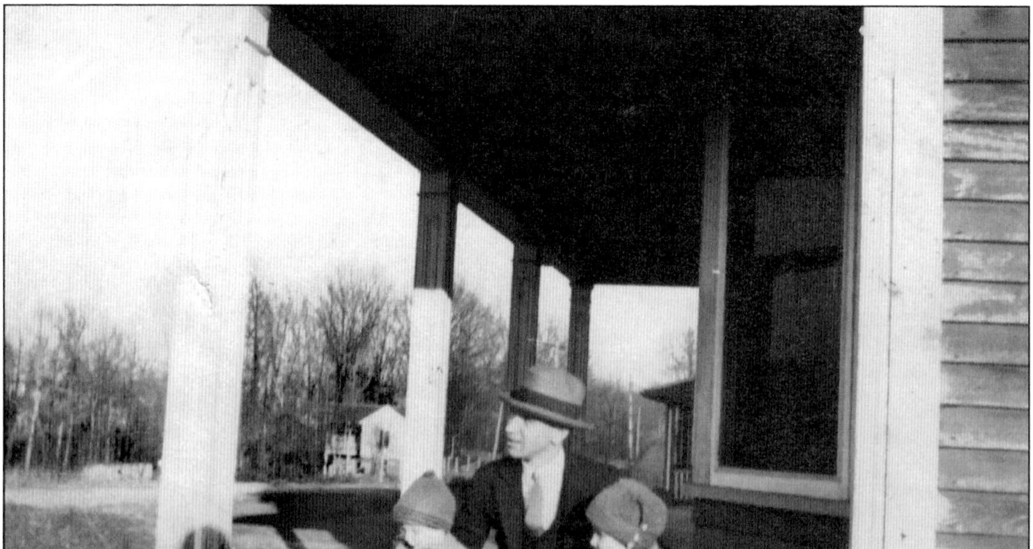

When June Snider married Merle Whitney, her parents bought the newlyweds a house in the new neighborhood of Washington Park. Their house, built on a lot behind the Christian Fogle farm, was one of three houses, including the Fogles' caretaker's house (shown in the background). The house, located at 606 West Barnes Avenue, is still occupied today. (Jack Graham Jr.)

Wagons were popular gifts for Christmas in 1923. The land to the west of Banner Avenue wasn't developed, as it had been farmland for the Fogle family and wild fields during the early years of the neighborhood. It would be another 25 or more years before homes would dot this landscape. (Jack Graham Jr.)

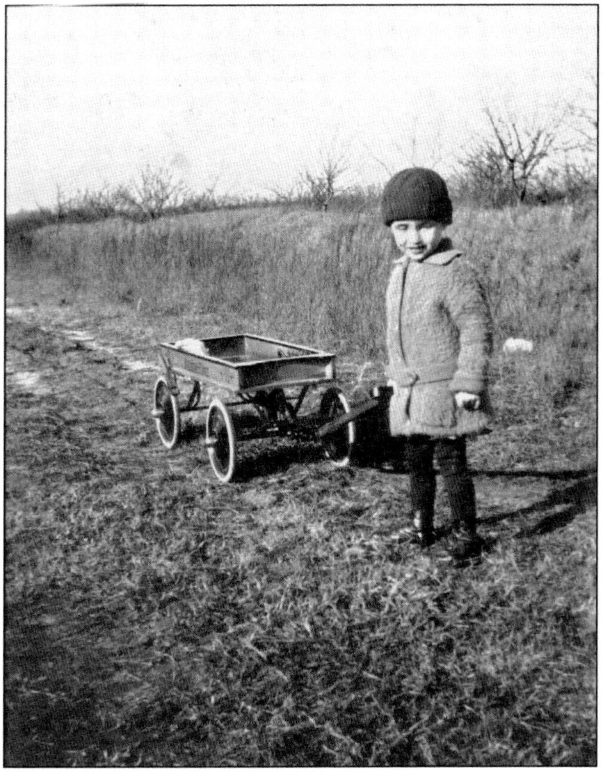

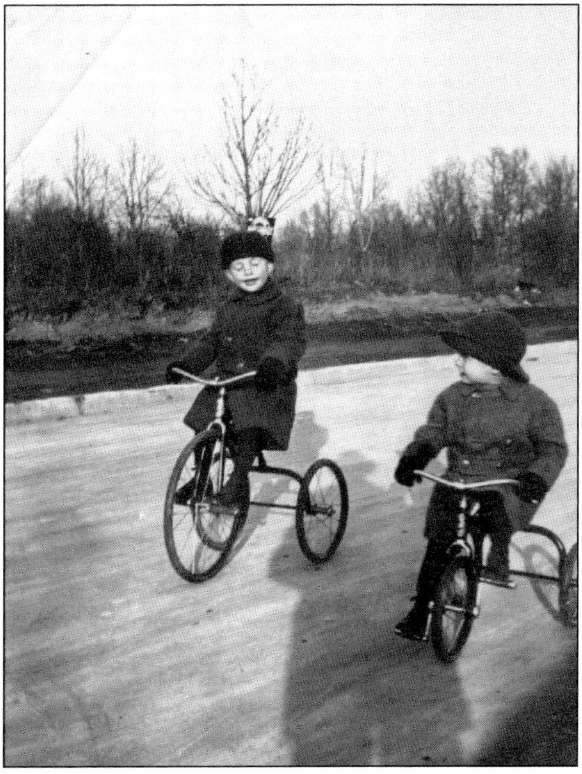

Merle Whitney Jr. and his younger brother Hoyt ride their new bicycles in front of their home at 606 West Banner Avenue. All the roads in the neighborhood were dirt for the first 40 years. Macadamized roads were built on some streets, and then paved roadways became the norm. (Jack Graham Jr.)

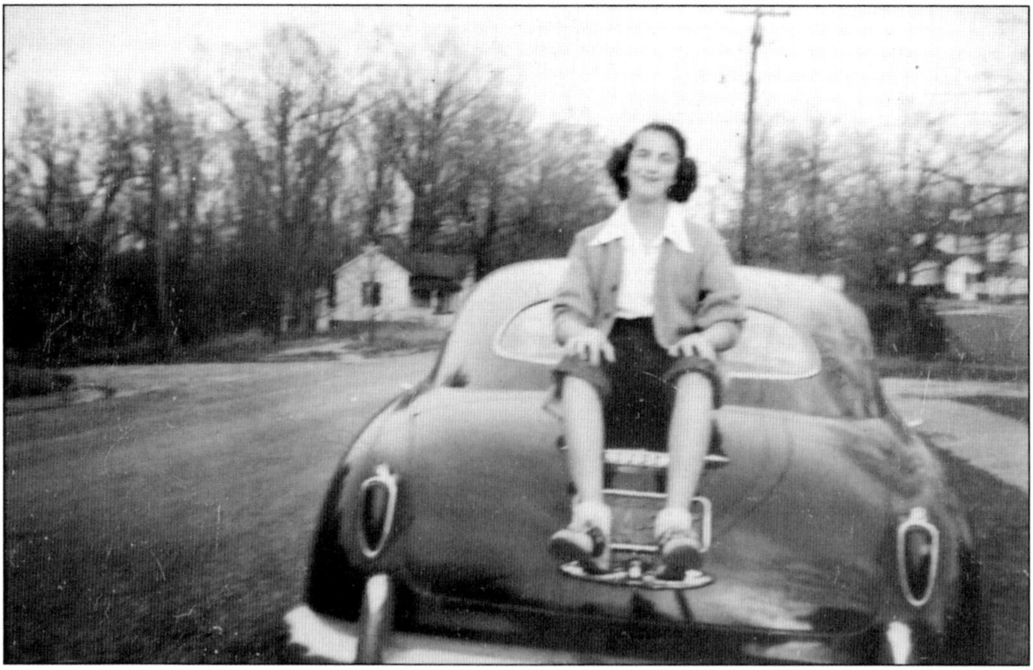

Once automobiles became popular, streetcars became obsolete. Families gravitated toward the convenience of having their own transportation, and the wealthier residents bought additional cars for their children. Hanging out, cruising, and parking were all pastimes that neighbors recalled sharing around the streets bordering the park. Janie Whitney Dooley, shown here, sits on her can in front of her parents' house at 606 West Banner Avenue. (Jack Graham Jr.)

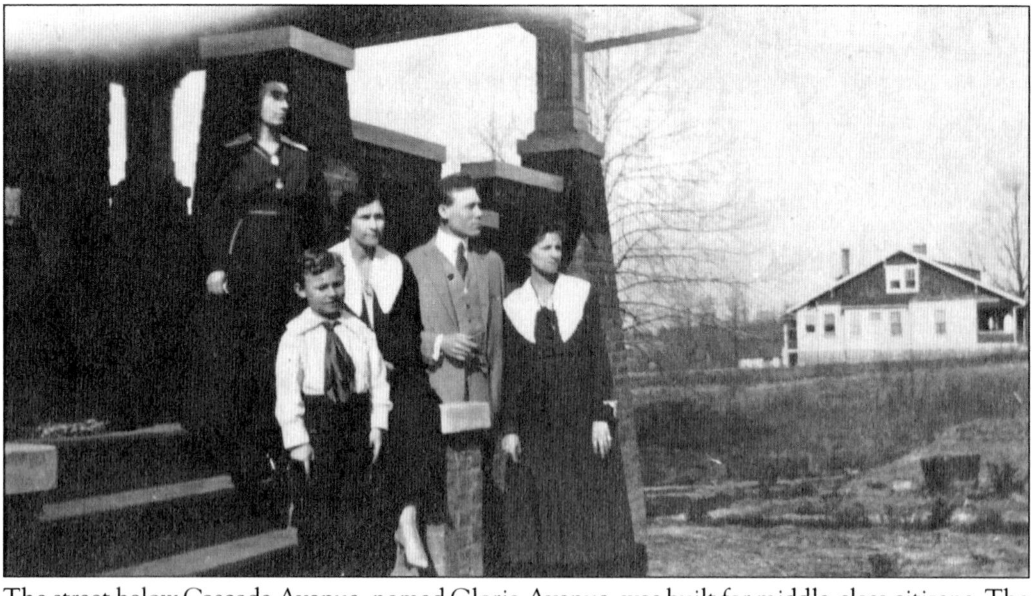

The street below Cascade Avenue, named Gloria Avenue, was built for middle-class citizens. The family pictured here *c.* 1917 might be some of the residents of 205 Gloria Avenue. The man and the woman on the right are Merle and June Whitney, who lived at 606 Banner Avenue. The three houses between 205 Gloria Avenue and the one shown in the distance would not be built until 1920. Broad Street is a dirt road that can barely be seen. (Jack Graham Jr.)

Merle Whitney Sr. (in the back) and a friend sled along Banner Avenue on January 5, 1926. In the distance, the John L. Gilmer house on Cascade Avenue can be seen over the treetops. The Whitney family almost bought this house, but June Whitney didn't want "to live in the woods," as the area surrounding that house had yet to be landscaped. (Jack Graham Jr.)

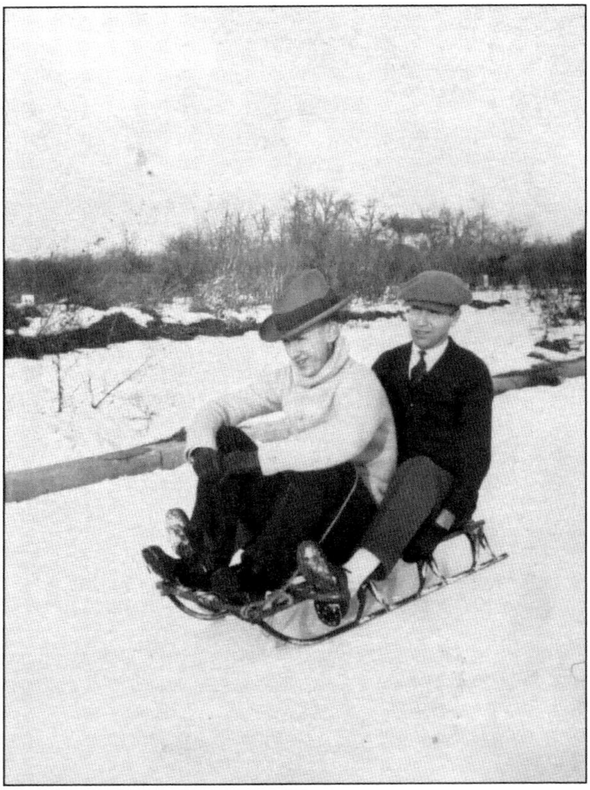

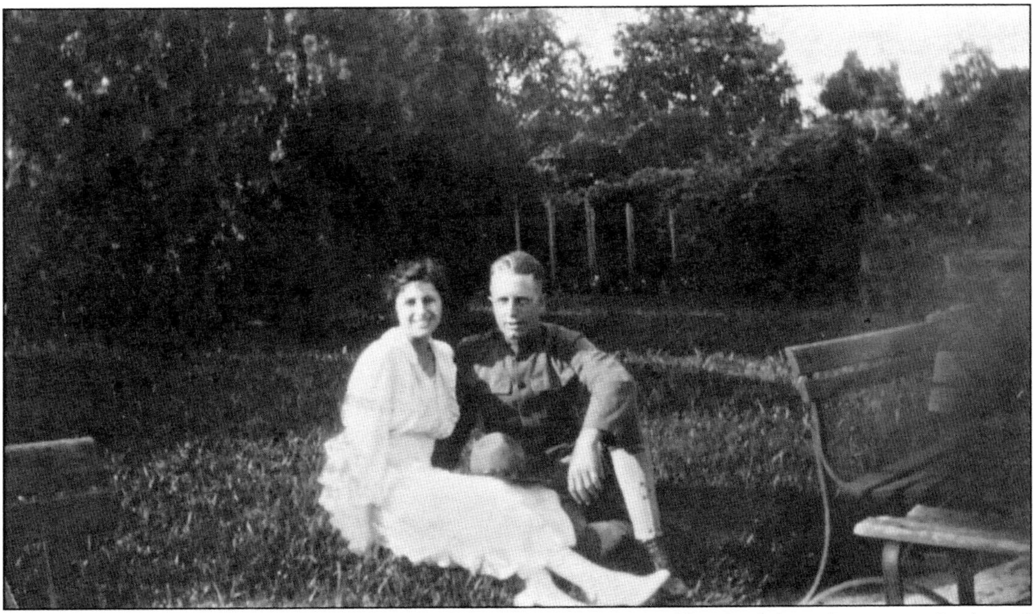

Many men and women viewed marriages as matches sanctioned by God, but they were also based on affection. In some homes, marriages were selected based on social status and goals. That was not the case for Merle Whitney. While he served in World War I, his love for his future wife, June, didn't wane. When the war ended, he returned to Winston-Salem and married her in 1920. (Jack Graham Jr.)

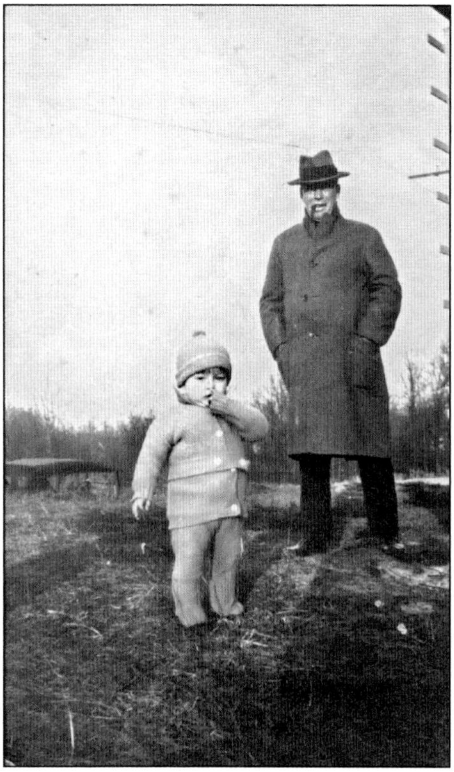

Merle Whitney Sr. built many companies and is best known for establishing the barbershop in the Robert E. Lee Hotel; he also established barber schools on Trade Street, Silas Creek Parkway, in the state of Kentucky, in Charlotte, North Carolina, and on military bases; plus the Whitney Furniture Company, which he gave to his sons to run. The top of his new Packard can been seen parked in front of his house at 606 West Banner Avenue. (Jack Graham Jr.)

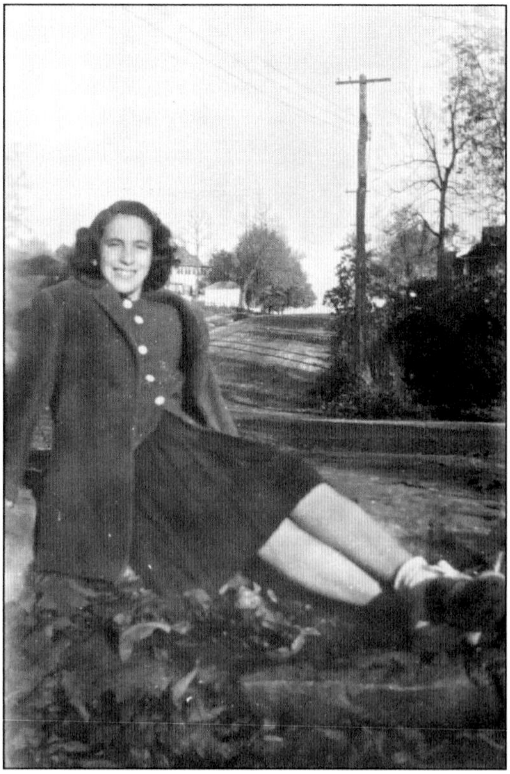

Washington Park played a central theme in the social life of its residents. Janice Whitney Dooley posed for a friend at the park entrance on Vintage Avenue. Above her is the Miller House, located at 42 Park Boulevard, and their orchard, which descended toward the park. The Millers' maid's home is still standing in the backyard. (Jack Graham Jr.)

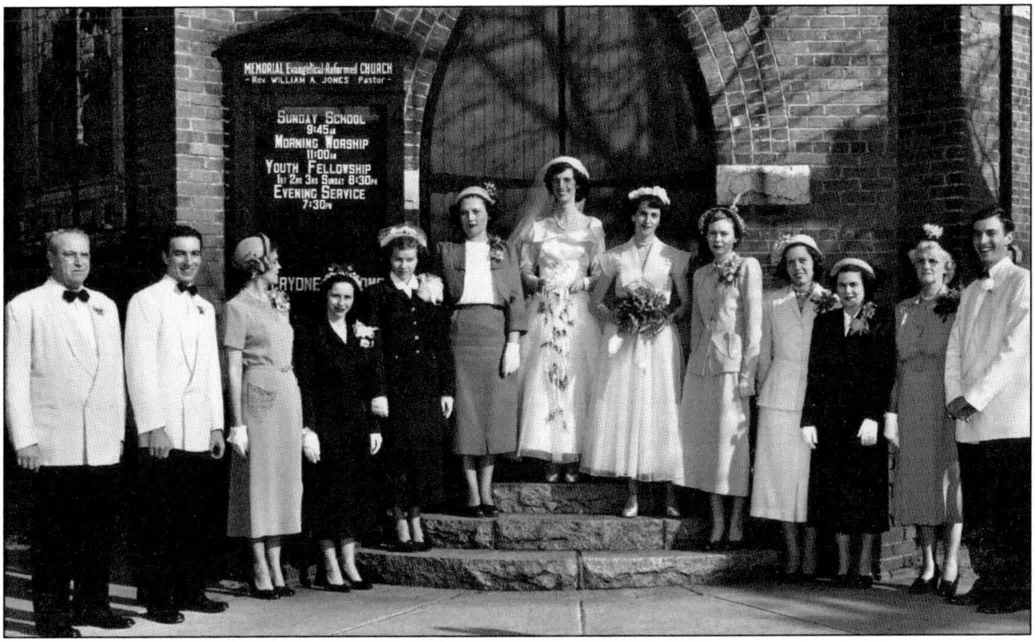

Norma Whitney, the daughter of Merle Sr. and June Whitney, married Jack H. Graham on Monday, April 10, 1950, at the Memorial Reformed Church on the corner of Hollyrood Street and Banner Avenue. The small neighborhood church was the focal point for many residents' social lives, including picnics, activities, and gatherings in the evenings. Many of the residents were married here. (Jack Graham Jr.)

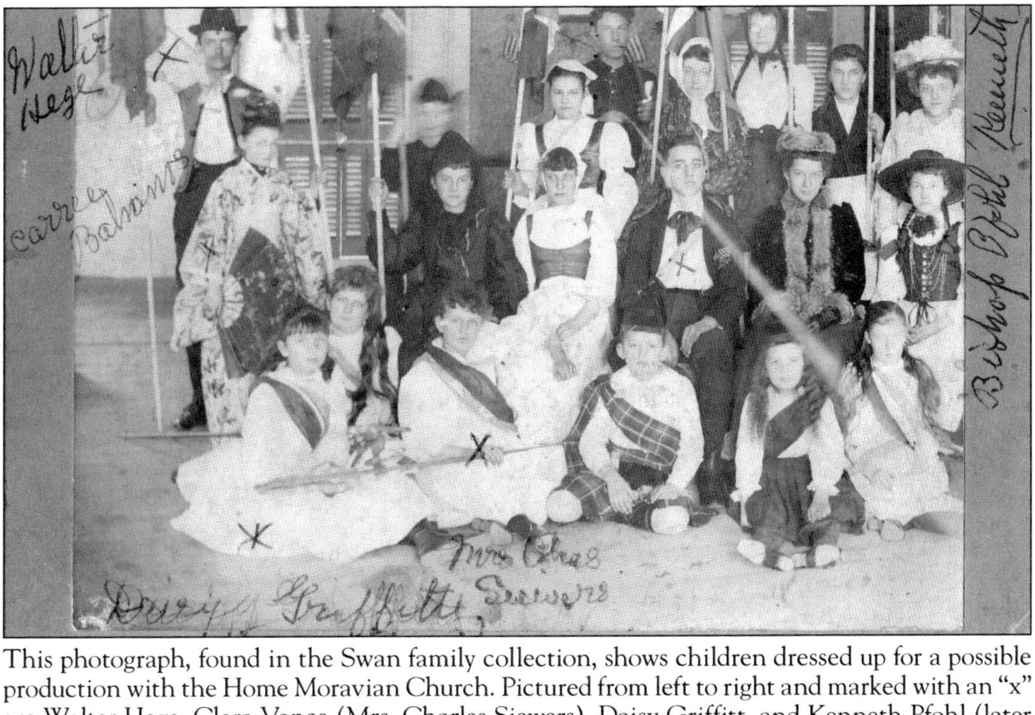

This photograph, found in the Swan family collection, shows children dressed up for a possible production with the Home Moravian Church. Pictured from left to right and marked with an "x" are Walter Hege, Clara Vance (Mrs. Charles Siewers), Daisy Griffitt, and Kenneth Pfohl (later in life Bishop Pfohl). The date of the photograph is unknown. (Swan family.)

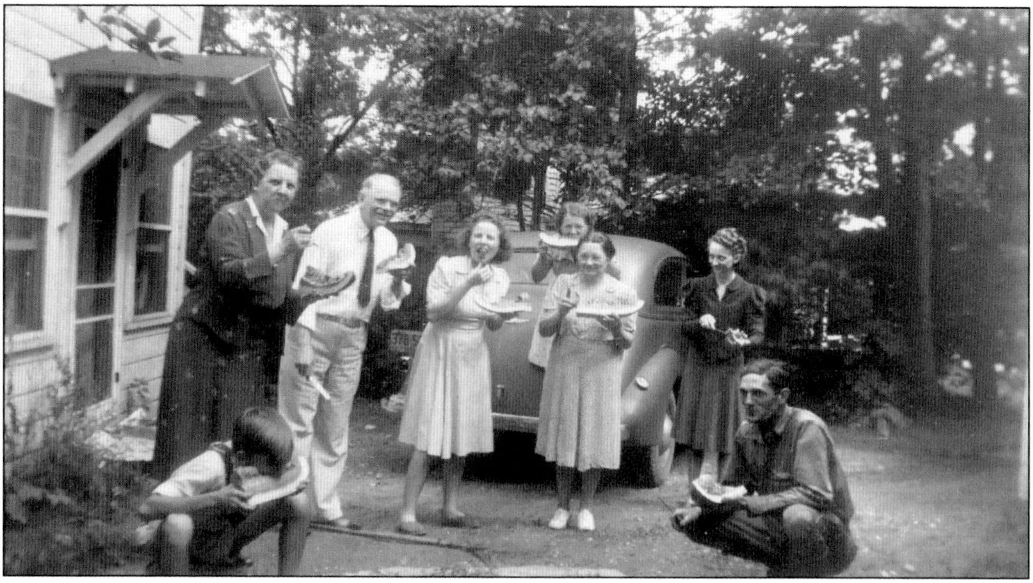

Although money was scarce and entertainment had to be created, many still found ways to take much-needed vacations. The Barrow family, shown above, took a vacation in August 1924 to Sparta, North Carolina, to get away from the heat. Sparta is located in the northwestern corner of the state. (Swan family.)

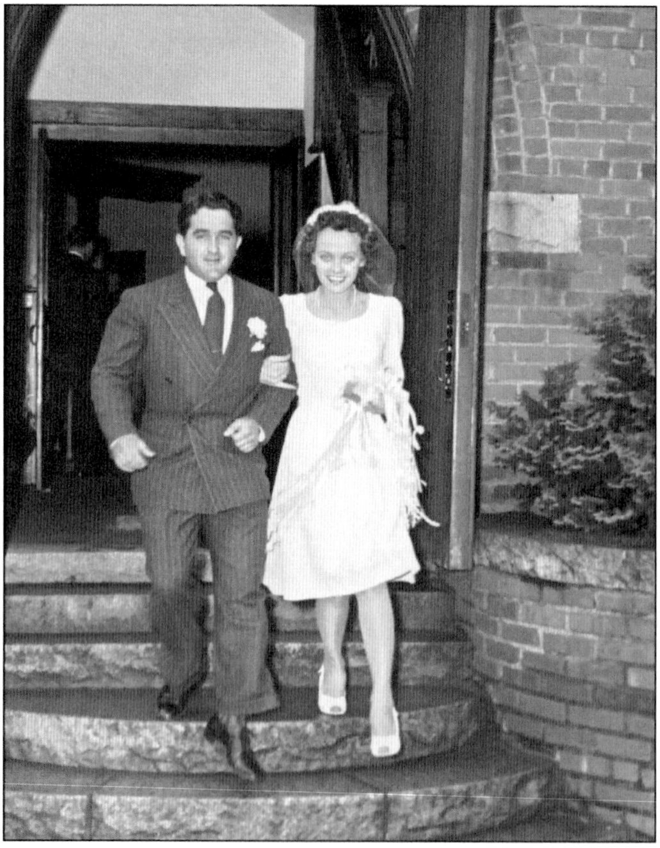

Ralph Leonard of Acadia Avenue married Helen Ledbetter of Sprague Street on May 26, 1946, at the Memorial Reformed Church on Banner Avenue. Ralph Leonard is the younger brother of Walter Leonard, and they are the sons of the founder of Quality Oil Company and Leonard Oil Company. Ralph and Helen built a house on Banner Avenue, down the street from Walter. His daughter Beverly lives there today. (Beverly Leonard Paszkowski.)

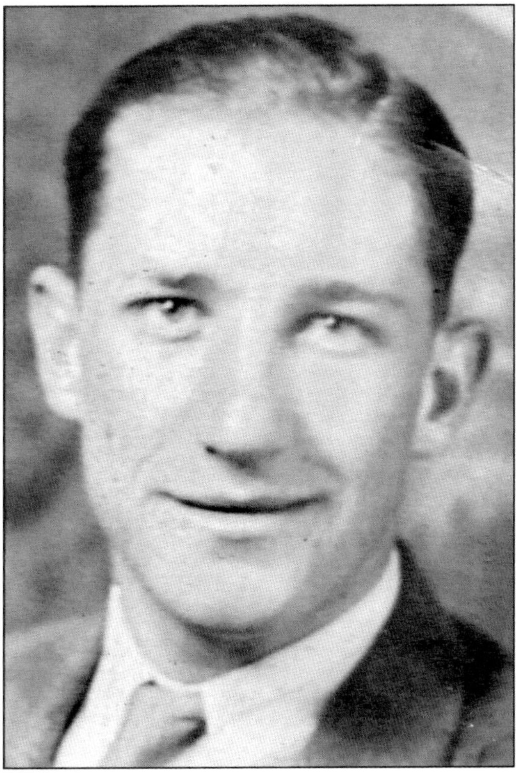

Eugene "Gene" R. Hayes saw a beautiful girl sitting on her aunt's porch on the corner of Shawnee and Broad Streets in late July 1932 and walked up to her. A week later, they ran off to York, South Carolina, and got married. Gene's new wife, Grace Herold Borders, had turned 14 on July 31, 1932, and, like Gene, believed in love at first sight. The couple gave birth to their first daughter, Jean, on July 3, 1933 and their second daughter, Barbara, two years later while living in their one-bedroom home on Shawnee Street. Gene said the only repercussion he suffered from getting married when they did was he could no longer play baseball for R. J. Reynolds High School. Their love endured, and their marriage lasted for 68 years until Grace passed away in 2002. (Jean Hayes Mahaffey.)

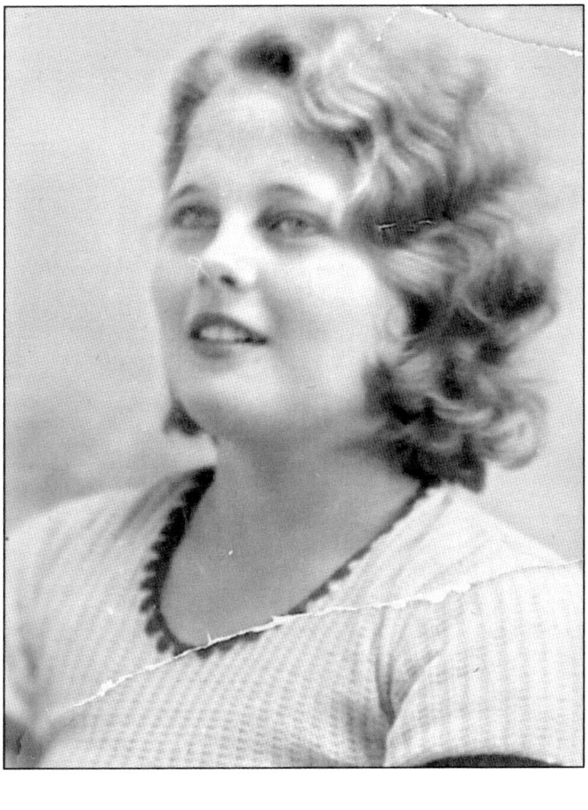

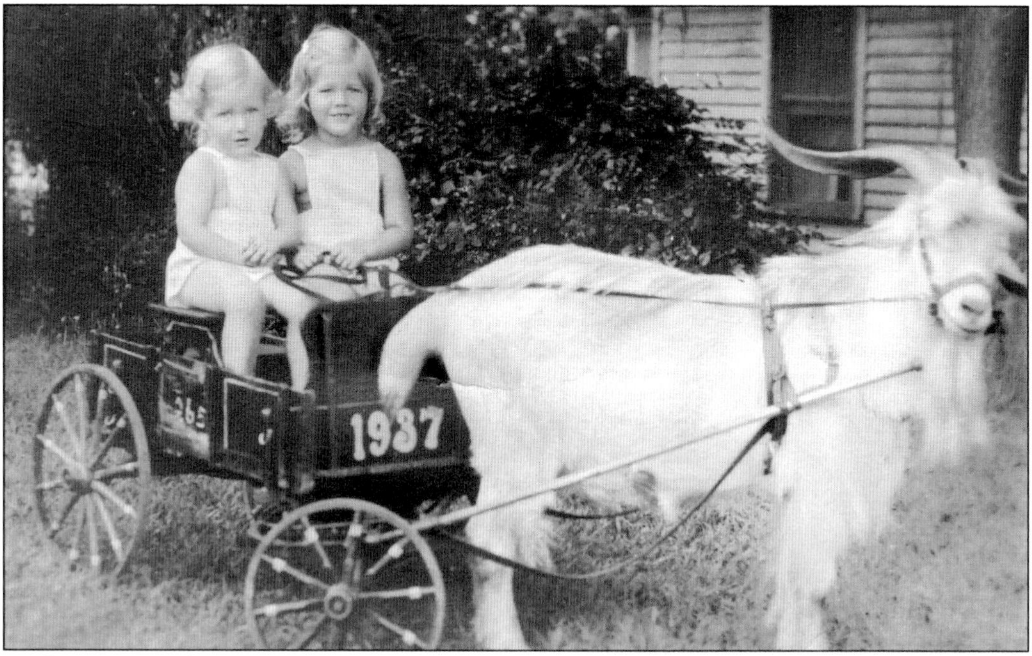

In the 1920s and 1930s, it was not uncommon for photographers to come around and offer goat rides to children and take their picture. The photographers came to the Washington Park neighborhood in 1937 and snapped this photograph of Barbara (left) and Jean Hayes in front of their house on Shawnee Street. (Jean Hayes Mahaffey.)

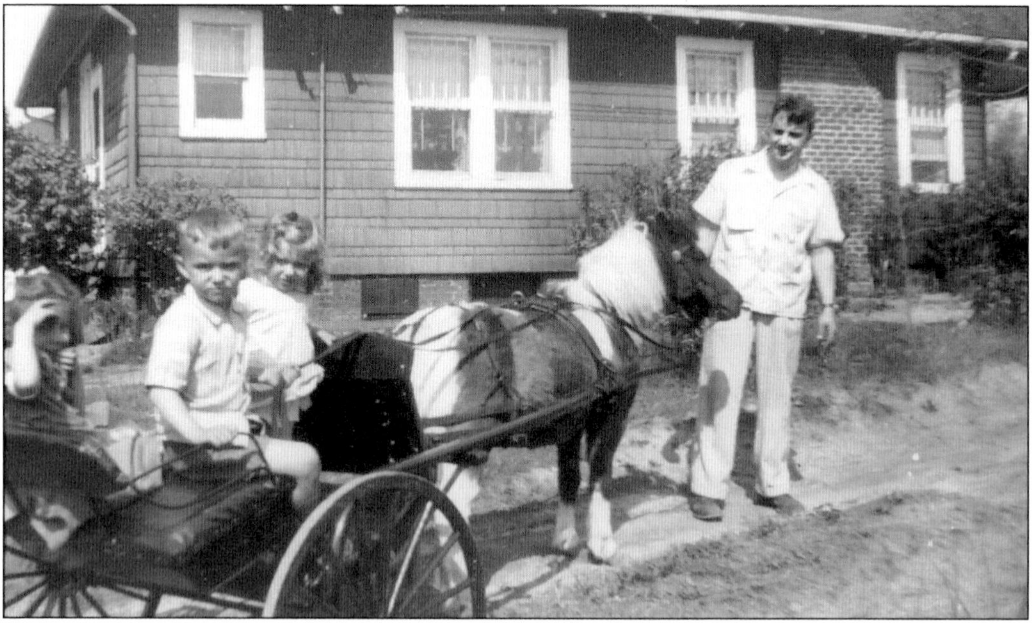

Earnest L. Frazier, who lived at 315 Gloria Avenue, had a cart and a small covered wagon. He was part owner of the Blue Bird Cab Company, and on the weekends, he would take the neighborhood kids on rides around Washington Park. He'd take the children to Reynolds Park, where they'd play in the swimming pool. They'd bring a picnic lunch and stay all day. Pictured are Rodney Reich and friends beside Rodney's house at 312 Vintage Avenue. (Rodney Reich.)

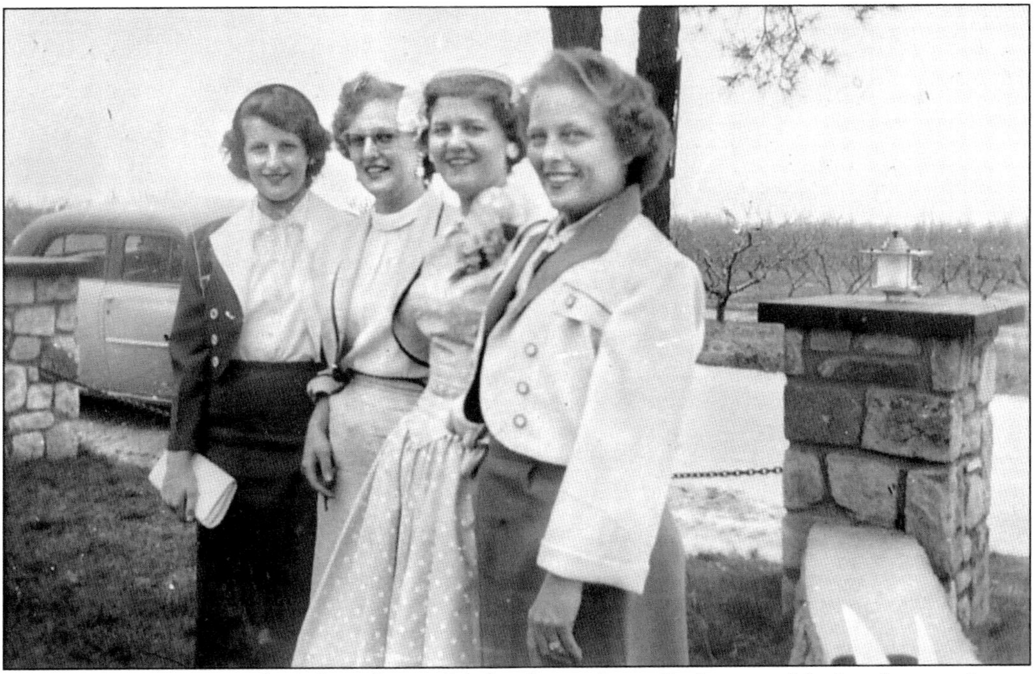

Gene and Grace Hayes had three beautiful daughters, Jean, Barbara, and Judy, after moving to a larger home off Konnoak Drive. The girls remember the expansive fields, the goat farm they managed, and that their home was the gathering spot for all the local teenagers. The women, pictured on Easter, from left to right are Judy, Barbara, Jean, and Grace. (Jean Hayes Mahaffey.)

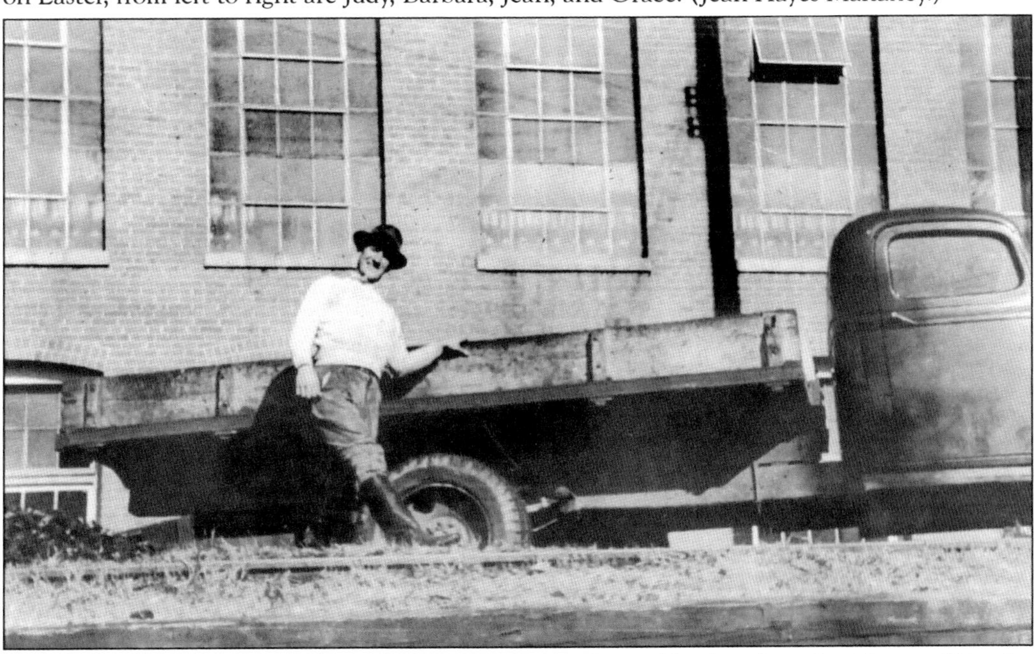

Gene Hayes, like many people in the Washington Park neighborhood, worked for a mill in the Southside. Gene was a dye-room foreman with Arista Mills, and he drove a truck for Plemmons and Irving and for Haigwoods before forming his own company, Hayes Heating and Air. (Jean Hayes Mahaffey.)

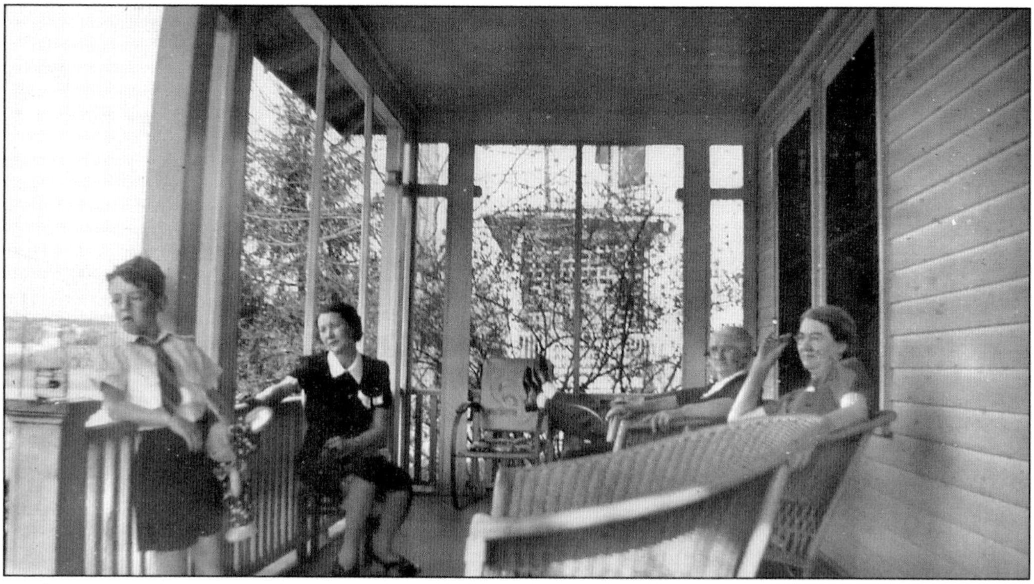

Rodney Reich's grandparents lived in the first house on the corner of South Main Street and Vintage Avenue. Many evenings were spent on their front porch, talking to the neighbors and visiting with family. In 1947, a church was built across the street, but before then, it was a vacant field, perfect for playing ball with the neighborhood kids. (Rodney Reich.)

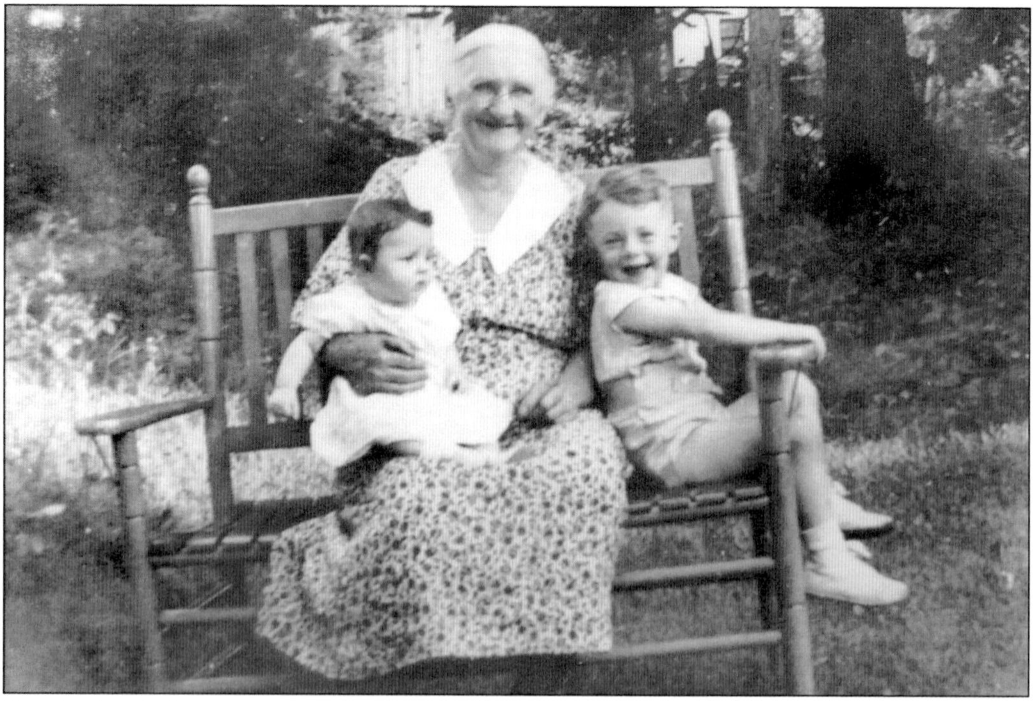

Families lived close to one another, many in the same neighborhood, and spent their Sundays visiting. Others, like Rodney and Rita Reich, pictured with their Grandma Reich, lived down the street and spent their time going back and forth between the houses. Rodney's grandfather drove a bus for Greyhound Bus Lines, located three blocks over, on the corner of Marshall Street and Salem Avenue. (Rodney Reich.)

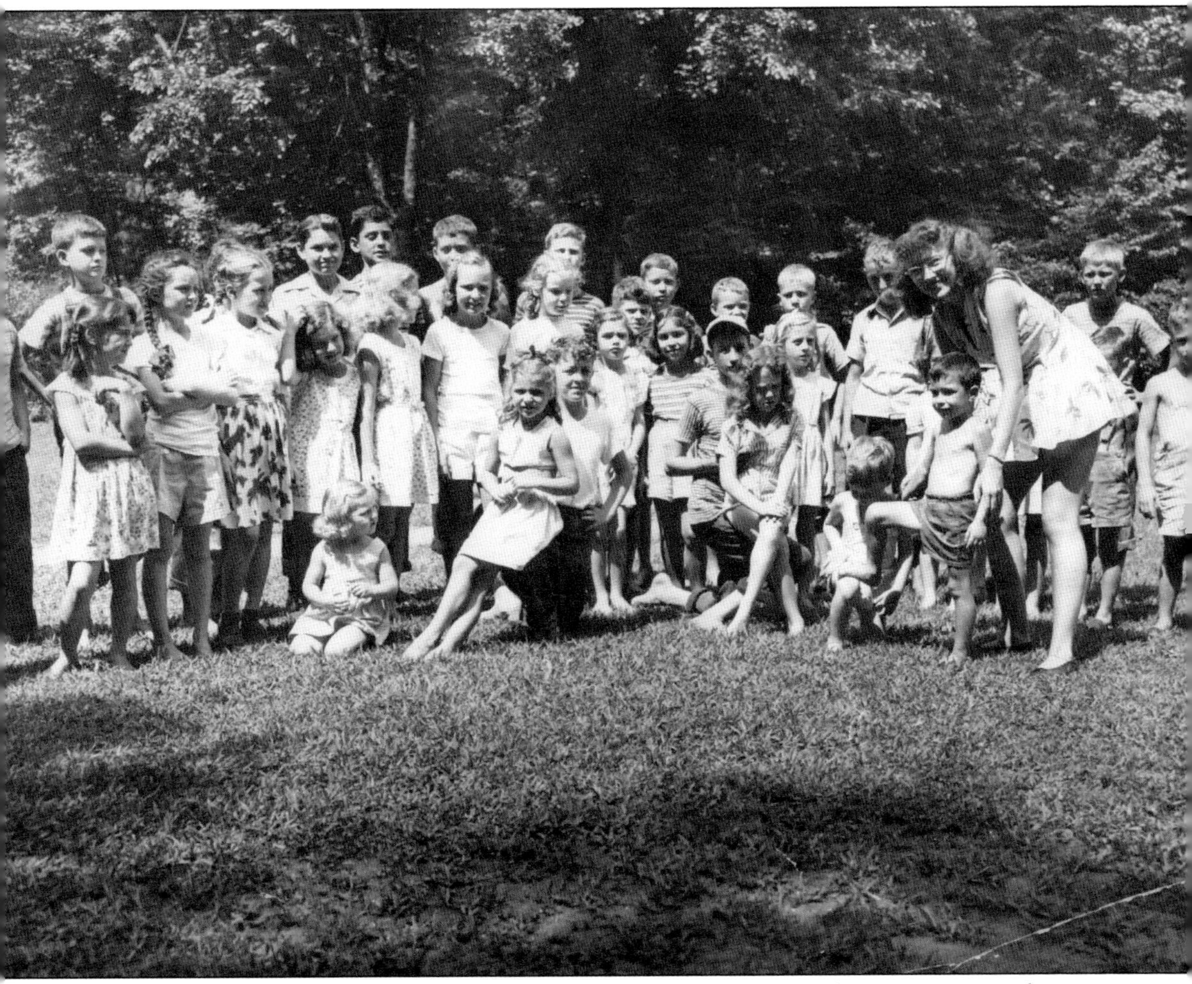

Frances Barrow taught dance to the neighborhood children during the summer months in Washington Park. She moved to the neighborhood when she was nine years old, attended Central Elementary and Gray High Schools, and then opened a dance school on Burke Street. After 20 years, she moved her school over to South Main Street by the North Carolina School of the Arts and taught many more years. Frances is known for her high kicks and her lively stories. (Rodney Reich.)

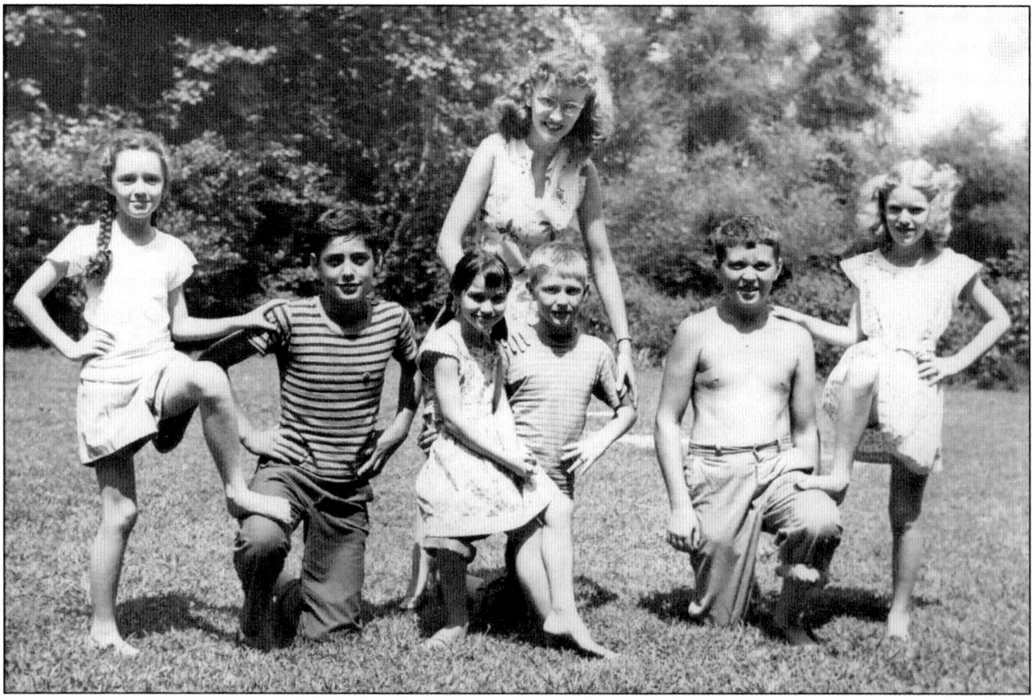

After an afternoon of learning dance moves from their teacher, Frances Barrow (standing in the back), the kids posed for photographer Frank Jones in 1947. They are (from left to right) Rita Reich, Raymond Turner, Mary Tesh, Howard Rayhelp, Ernest Yokley, and Eleanor Fishel. (Rodney Reich.)

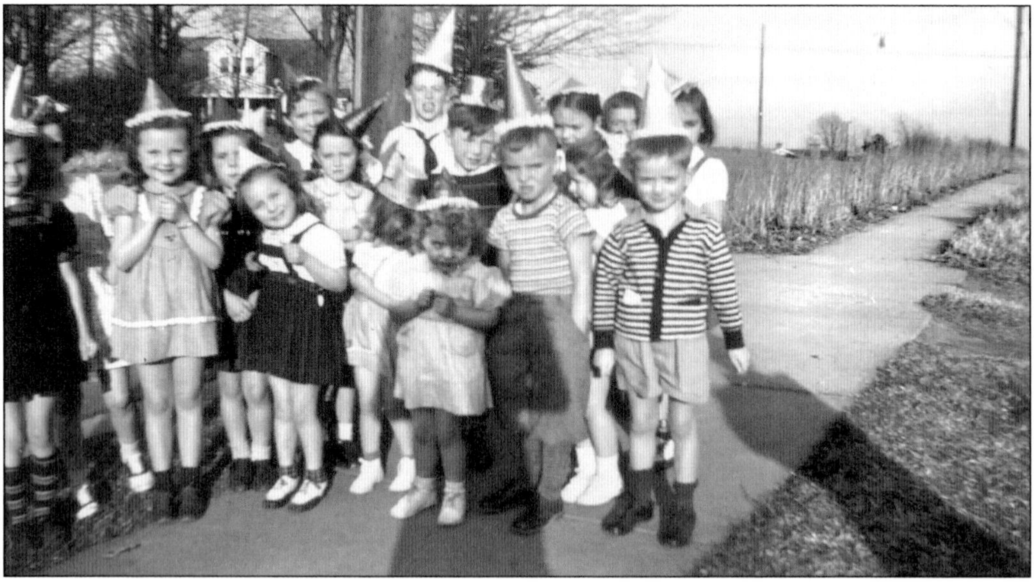

Birthday parties were celebrated with all the children in the Washington Park neighborhood. This picture, celebrating either Rodney or Rita Reich's birthday, was taken in front of their house at 312 Vintage Avenue, which at the time was the first house on the avenue (it intersected with Park Boulevard). Rodney remembers flying kites and playing in the fields next to his house before the ranch homes were built. (Rodney Reich.)

Frank Jones, a photographer for the *Winston-Salem Journal*, took a number of photographs of the summer activities in Washington Park over the course of an afternoon. Among them was this photograph of Tommy Pitts and Judy Frazier, which ended up in the personal collection of their former neighbor Rodney Reich. Frank Jones was known to all the neighborhood children as "that man that always was around with his camera." (Rodney Reich.)

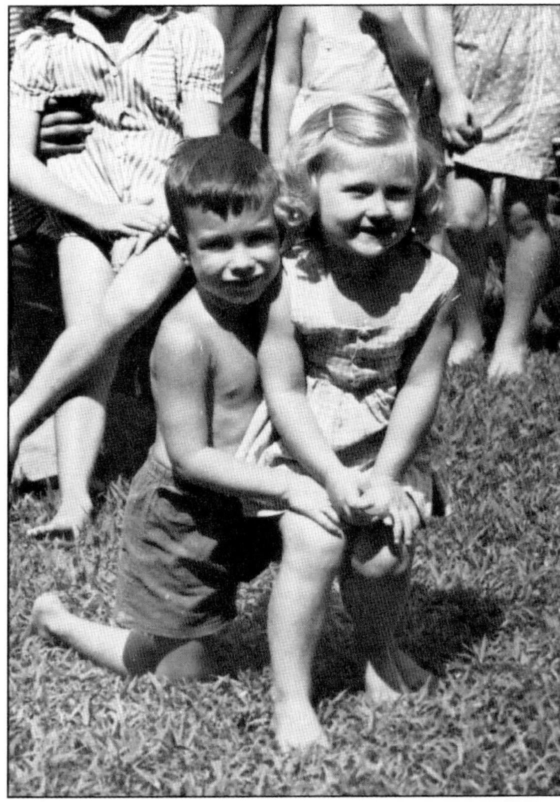

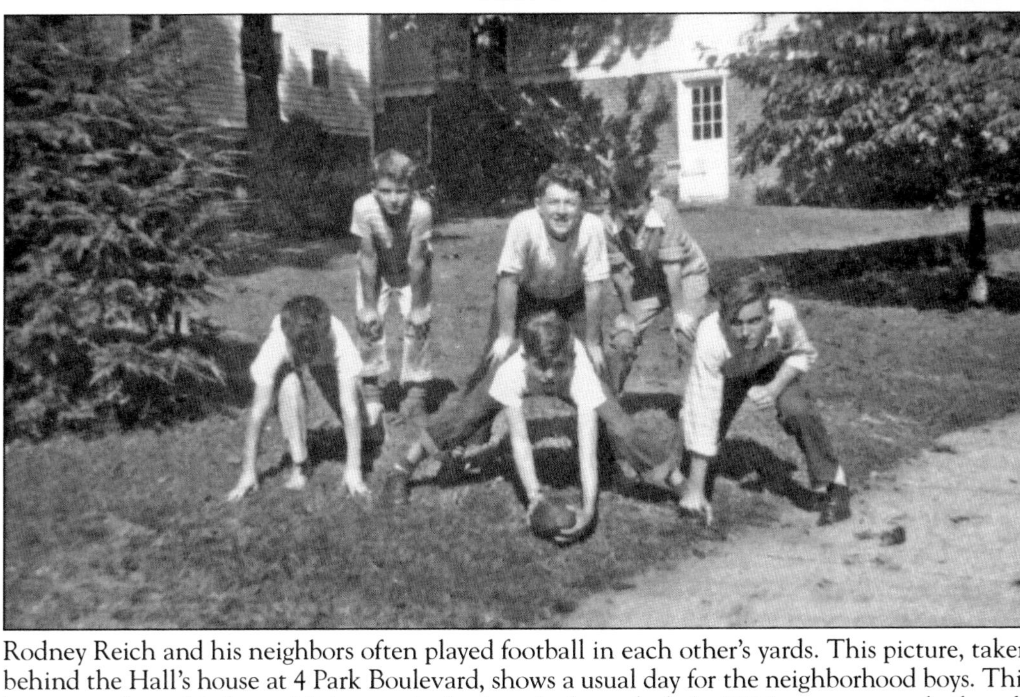

Rodney Reich and his neighbors often played football in each other's yards. This picture, taken behind the Hall's house at 4 Park Boulevard, shows a usual day for the neighborhood boys. This house now has a kitchen addition on the back and a large deck. In 2004, a garage was built to fit the bungalow style and period of the home. (Rodney Reich.)

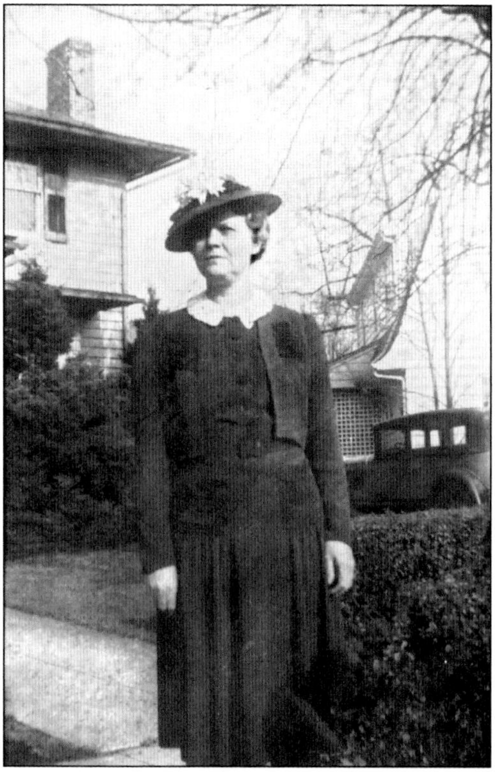

Mabel S. Barrow, shown here in front of her home, married J. Durham Barrow and built a house at 7 Gloria Avenue in 1928. Their relatives lived around them and on neighboring streets. Durham Barrow was a clerk at R. J. Reynolds Tobacco Company. After he died, Mabel's sister came to live with her. Frances Barrow, her niece, remembers playing with her cousin Antoinette, Mabel's daughter, and always getting into "fun" trouble. (Swan family.)

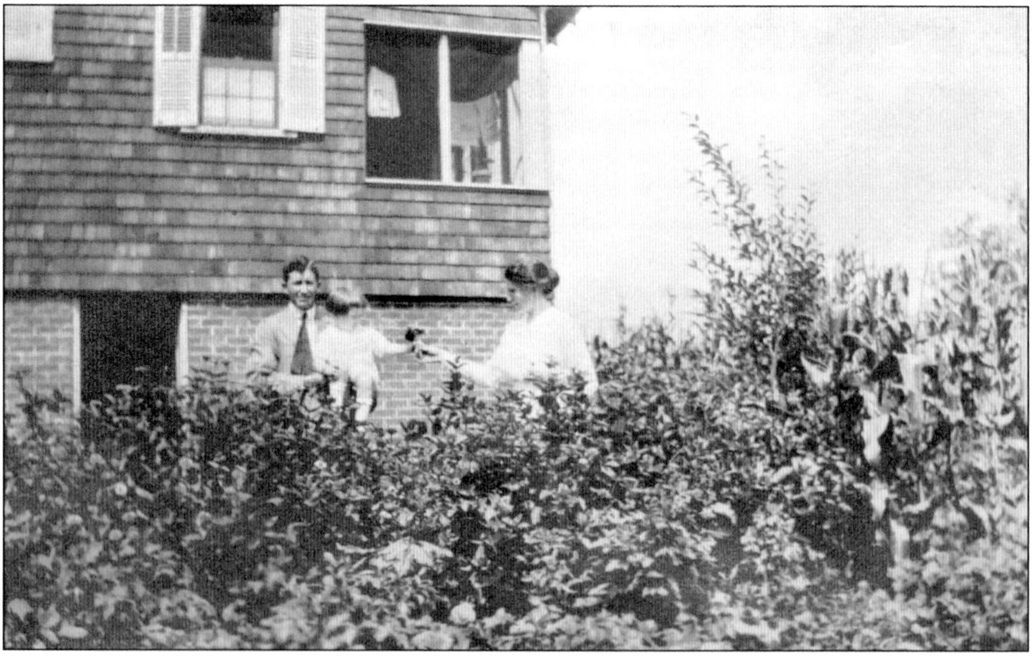

This family, believed to be Magnus Mattison and his wife, Florence, stands beside their home at 60 Park Boulevard. He was a traveling salesman and lived here after L. C. Stinson. The house was built by their neighbor William F. Miller and the Fogle Brothers and is the same house pictured on page 45. (Butter and Balint Birkas.)

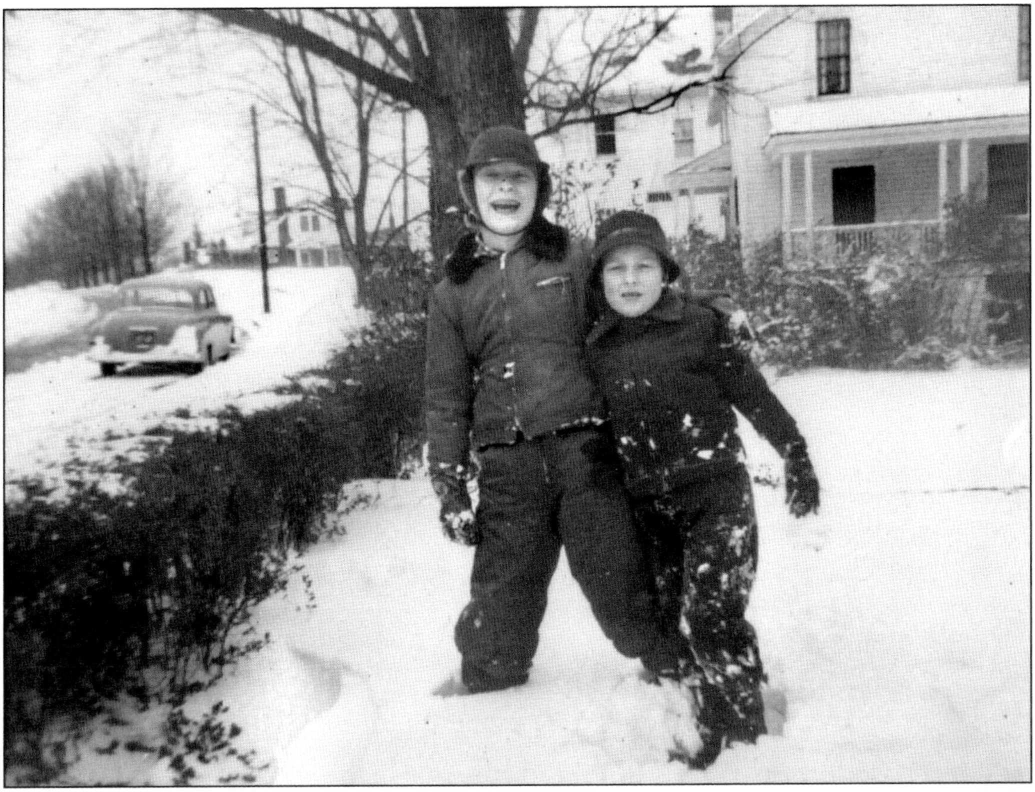

Back when the winters in Winston-Salem yielded snow, the city used to close off the gently rolling streets of Washington Park for sledding. Children, along with their parents, would head over to Doune Street and sled the three-block distance to the bottom. Other streets were used for sledding, too. The hill on Banner Avenue, up by the "Banner Manor," as Christian Fogle's farm at 514 West Banner Avenue is nicknamed, has been used for sledding for over 80 years. Pictured are the Swan children (above) as they play in their front yard on Park Boulevard. The house in the foreground (above) was reportedly the barn on the Fleshman estate, moved from the corner of Park Boulevard and Gloria Avenue. The family photograph (bottom) was taken next to the park on Banner Avenue. (Above, Swan family; below, Memorial Reformed Church.)

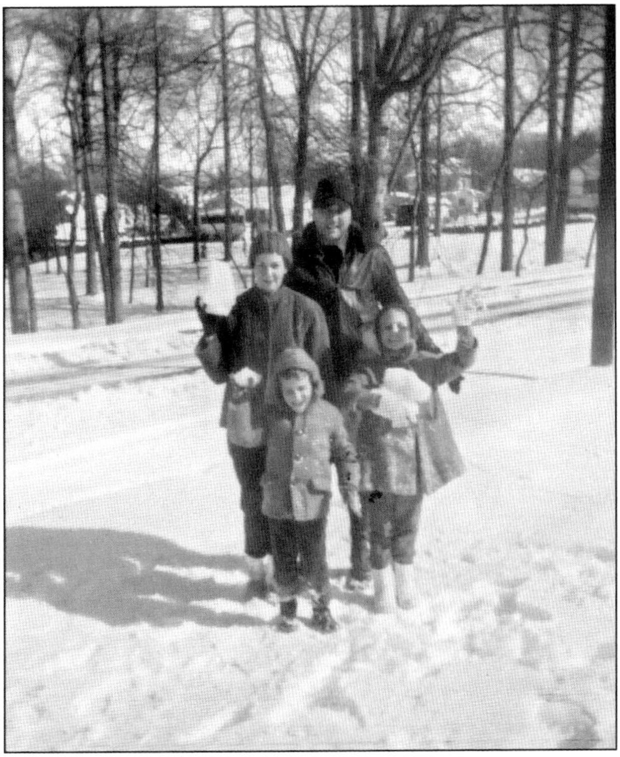

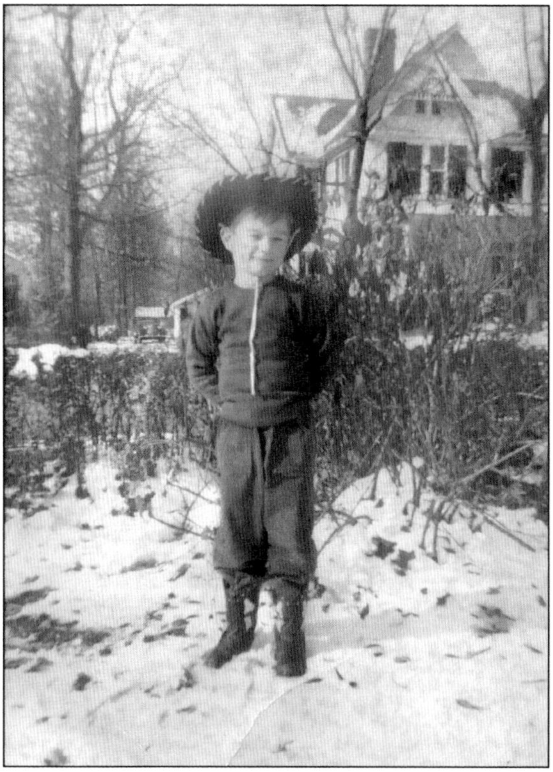

Long before video games and computers, children passed their time by playing cowboys and Indians, and it didn't matter if it was 20 degrees and snowing, or 90 degrees and humid. Chester Swan, pictured on his front lawn on Park Boulevard, was no exception. The house in the background is the Eller Davis home, located at 14 Park Boulevard, moved from the corner of Cascade Avenue and Broad Street in 1918. (Swan family.)

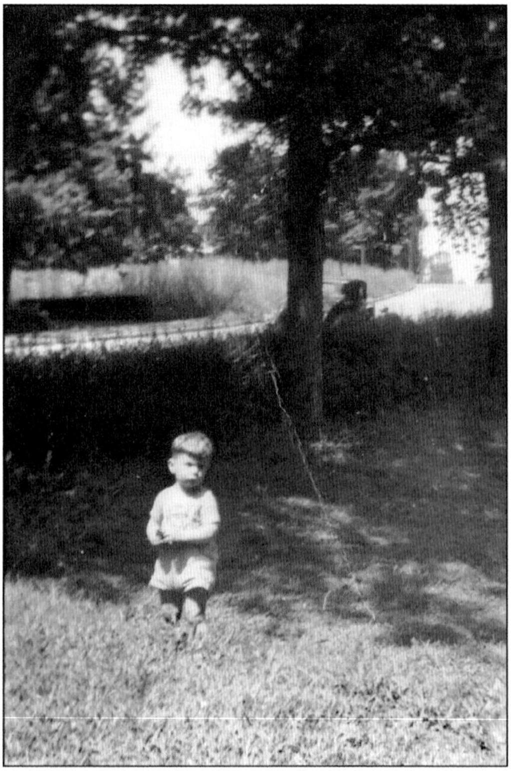

The lot on the corner of Park Boulevard and Vintage Avenue, shown in the upper left corner, wasn't developed until 1950. Until then, it was used as stomping grounds for the children that lived around it. The Swans, who still reside in the family home at 7 Park Boulevard, own the lot next to their house and remember playing many hours of baseball in it. (Swan family.)

Antoinette Barrow Swan grew up in the house that her parents built in 1928 at 7 Park Boulevard. On the back of this photograph she wrote to her future husband while he was overseas in the military, "Your school marm that you left behind! Wish this could be in color. Maybe it would detract from my miserable face. Yellow sweater—red scarf—brown and blue skirt—shall I go on? No." The photograph was taken at a relative's house. (Swan family.)

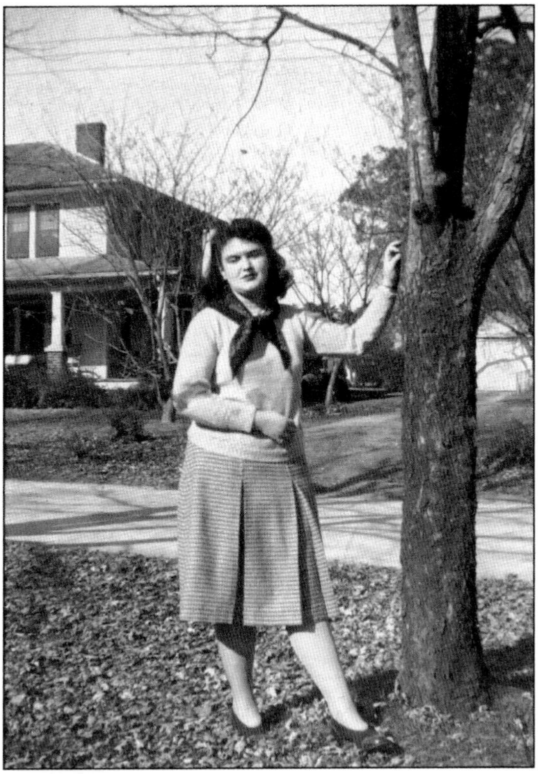

As automobiles grew in popularity, most households in the neighborhood could afford one. The Model T Ford, General Motors's LaSalle, and the upscale Packard were common. LaSalles, created to be the companion car for Cadillac and priced about $1,000 less, were a favorite, although many households on Cascade and Banner Avenues preferred the Packard. Chester Swan sits on his family's car in their driveway at 7 Park Boulevard. (Swan family.)

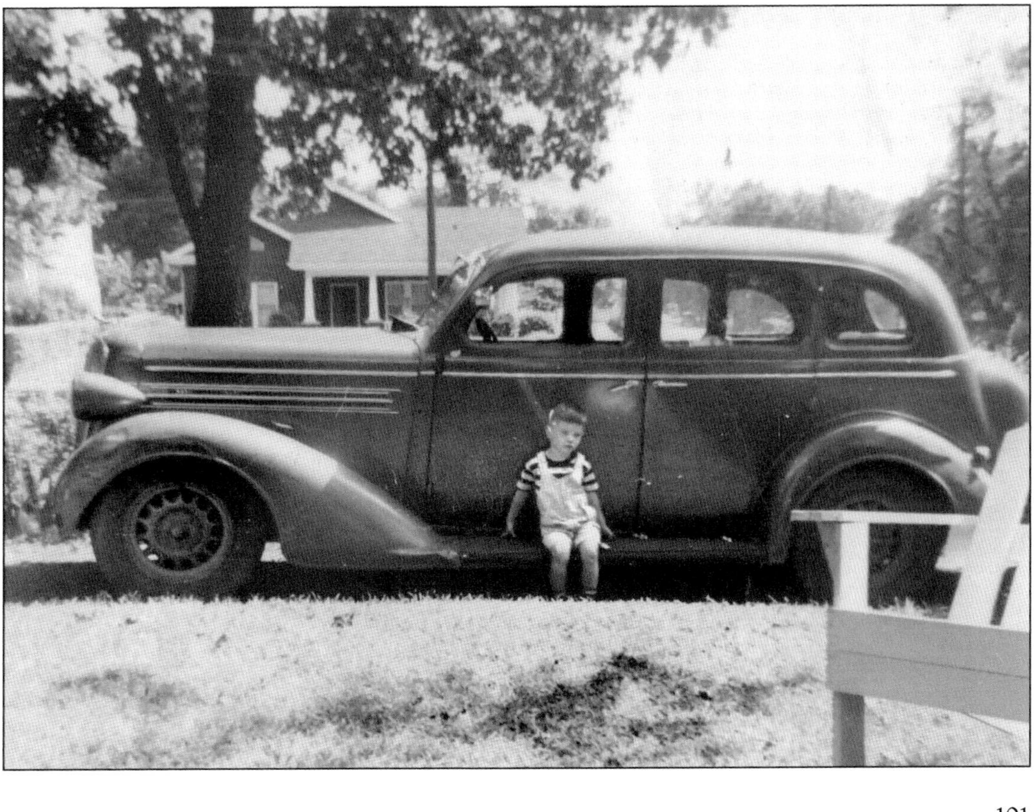

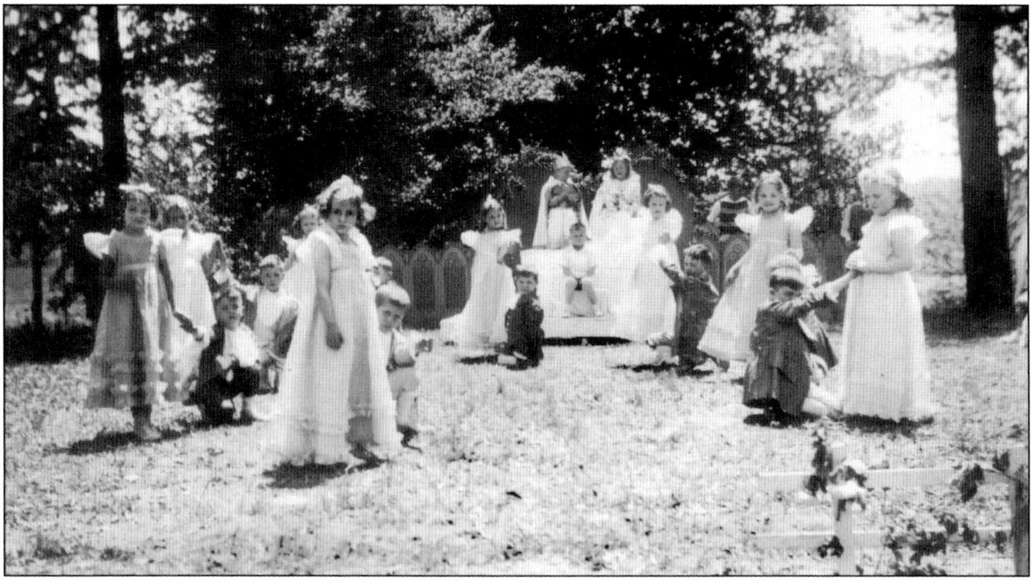

Jean Hayes was elected May Queen in first grade for Central Graded School. Following the British tradition, the May Queen or Princess of May kicks off the May Day celebrations on May 1, which usually includes dancing around the Maypole. The May Queen and her court wear white to symbolize purity. This tradition was popular with Salem College and Academy as well. Jean is shown, along with her king, on the platform in the center of this picture. (Jean Hayes Mahaffey.)

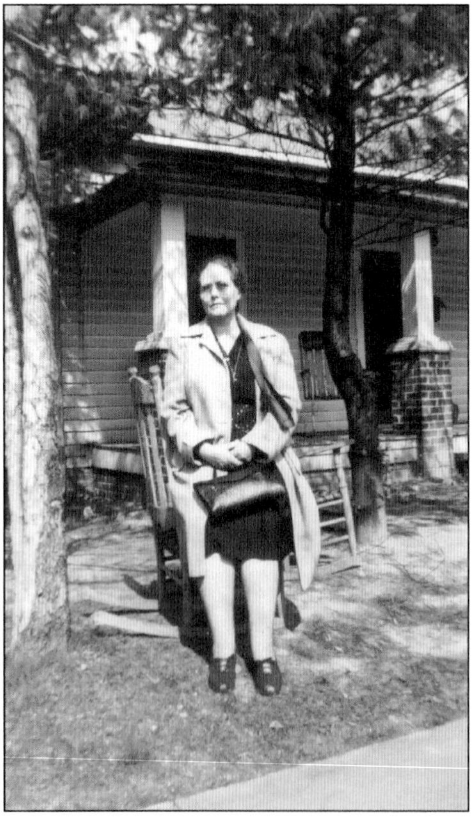

Ruby Borders Hall, Jean Hayes's aunt, who lived at 203 Shawnee Street, lost her young daughter when she stood too close to a fire and her blanket went up in flames. Years later, Ruby died of a similar fate when she fell asleep with a cigarette in her mouth. Their house on Shawnee Street is still standing. (Jean Hayes Mahaffey.)

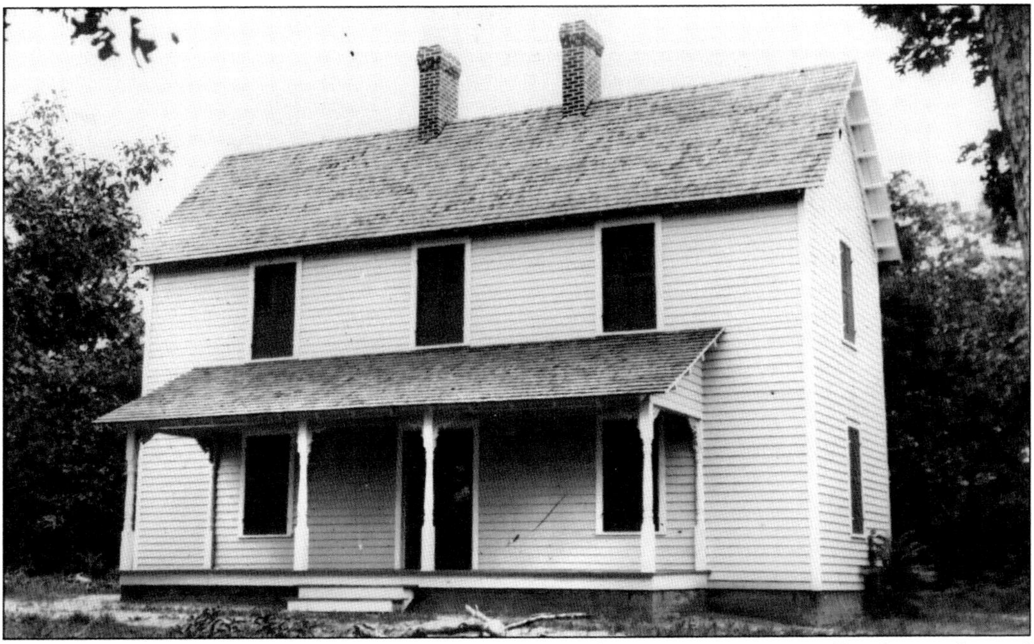

John A. Hartle, a grocery man who owned Hartle's Cash Store on Lexington Road, was charged with fatally wounding Walter Lee Smith, a Winston-Salem barber, at Hartle's home. Hartle reportedly returned to his house from his store nearby to find Smith in the living room with Geneva Hartle and promptly shot him. The interesting thing is that, based on photographs found in the newspaper, the men could have passed for twins. (Collection of the Wachovia Historical Society; photograph courtesy of Old Salem Museums and Gardens.)

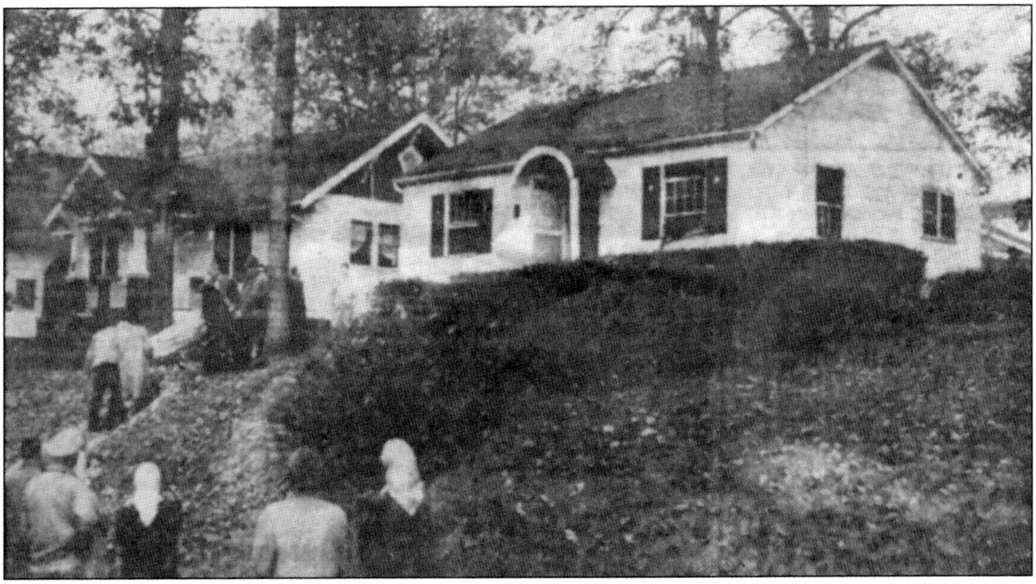

Clarence Eugene Love was 26-years-old when his wife, Marlin, asked for a divorce. Unable to cope, he doused his house, located at 319 Gloria Avenue, with gasoline, lit it on fire, and "shot himself with a pistol through the mouth," as the *Twin-City Sentinel* stated. A similar fate happened to this house when a woman set it on fire many years later. Unable to salvage the house, the lot was sold, and a two-story brick house now stands in its place. (Reich family.)

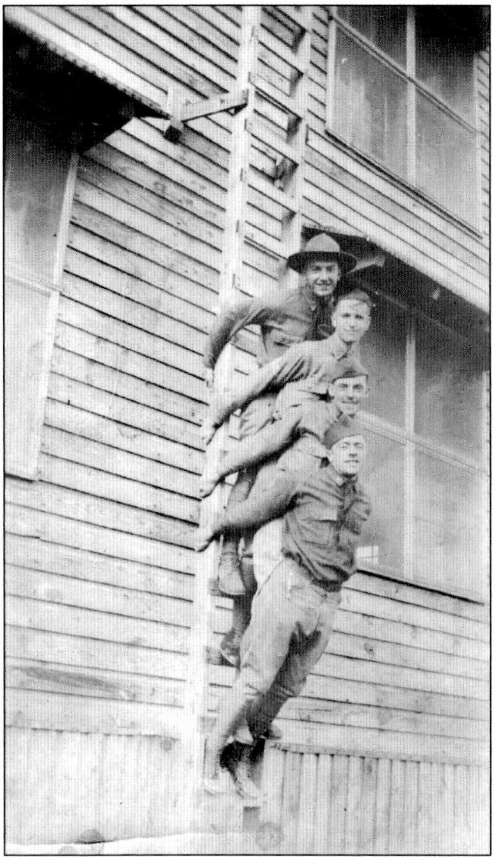

A World War I unit known as the 81st National Army division was organized in August 1917 and drafted soldiers from North Carolina, South Carolina, and Florida. It was named the Wildcat division in recognition of the short-tempered wildcats that live in the southern states and after Wildcat Creek, which ran near Camp Jackson, South Carolina, where they were stationed. A short time later, the men adopted a wildcat silhouette as a shoulder patch, becoming the first insignia worn by troops in the American Expeditionary Force. During the brief months they were in combat, they suffered 248 deaths and 856 wounded soldiers. With the November 11, 1918, signing of the armistice, the soldiers returned home. Merle Whitney Sr. is shown at left at the bottom of the ladder and in the photograph below, first row, first on the left. (Jack Graham Jr.)

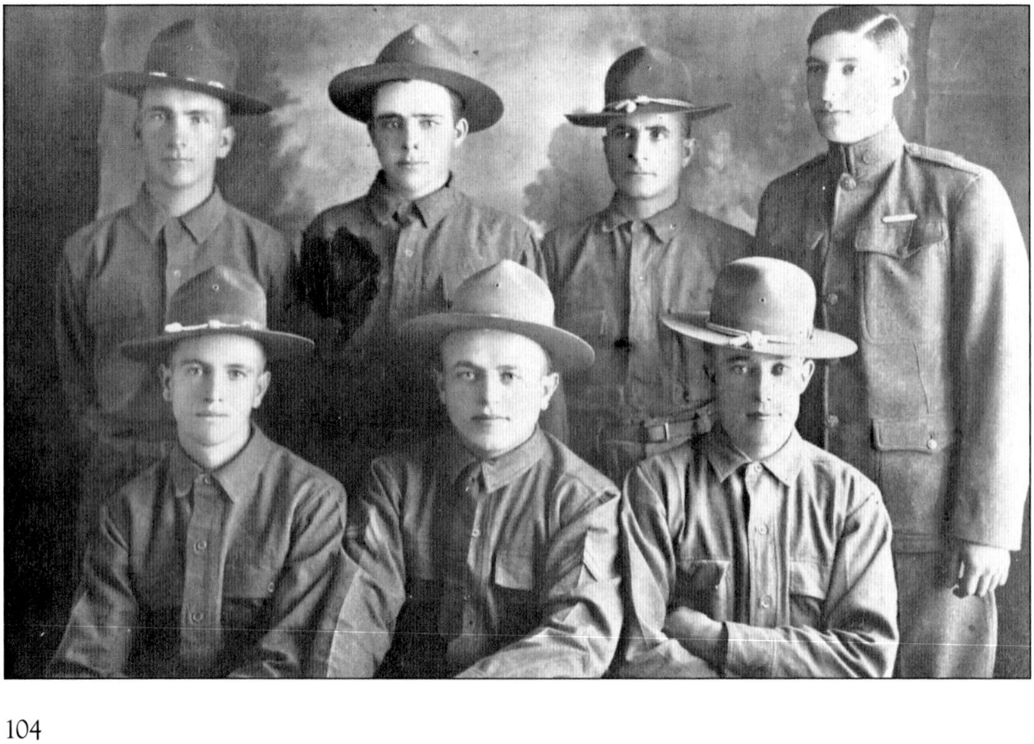

Walter Leonard served in the navy during World War II after graduating from the University of North Carolina at Chapel Hill. He was born January 22, 1918, and served from January 1942 through December 1945 in Norfolk, Virginia, on the USS *Twining* DD-540, in Saipan Tinian Luzon Leyte, Iwo Jima, and Tokyo. He received the Navy Good Conduct Medal, American Campaign Medal, Asiatic-Pacific Campaign Medal with eight stars, and others. (Walter Leonard.)

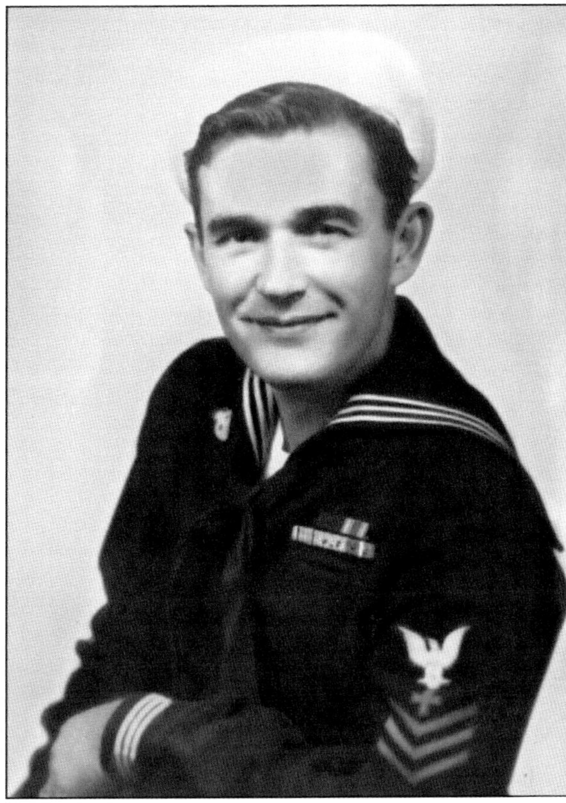

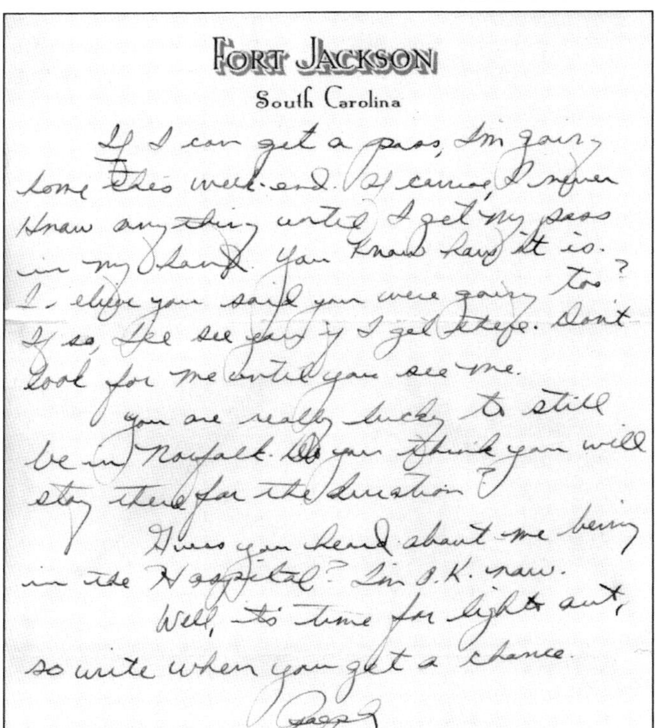

FORT JACKSON

South Carolina

If I can get a pass, I'm going home this week-end. Of course I never know anything until I get my pass in my hand. You know how it is. I believe you said you were going too? If so, I'll see you if I get there. Don't look for me until you see me.

You are really lucky to still be in Norfolk. Do you think you will stay there for the duration?

Guess you heard about me being in the Hospital? I'm O.K. now.

Well, it's time for lights out, so write when you get a chance.

Ralph

When Walter Leonard was stationed in Norfolk during World War II, he received a letter from his younger brother, Ralph, who was stationed in Fort Jackson, South Carolina. In this letter, Ralph writes about hoping to get a pass for the weekend but said "don't look for me until you see me," as passes weren't guaranteed until they were in the soldiers' hands. (Walter Leonard.)

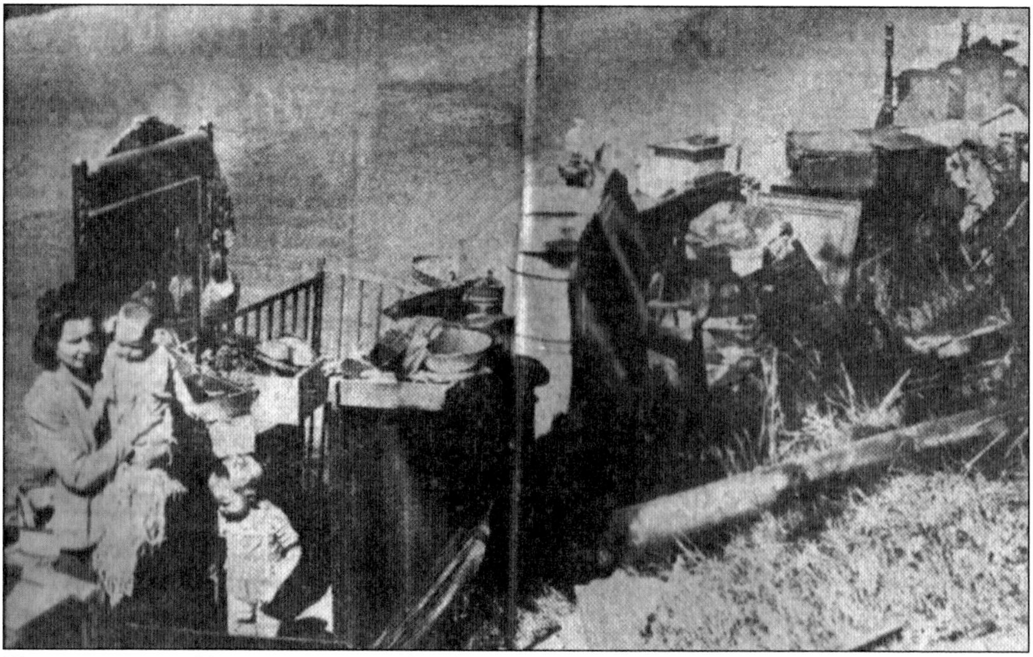

Housing was a problem in Winston-Salem because of a shortage of affordable rentals. J. E. Barber and family had resided at their house on the South Broad Street for eight years when they were evicted on October 4, 1946. A couple of the homes in the Washington Park area were subdivided into apartments during this time to help alleviate the situation, including the Henry E. Fries home. (Reich family.)

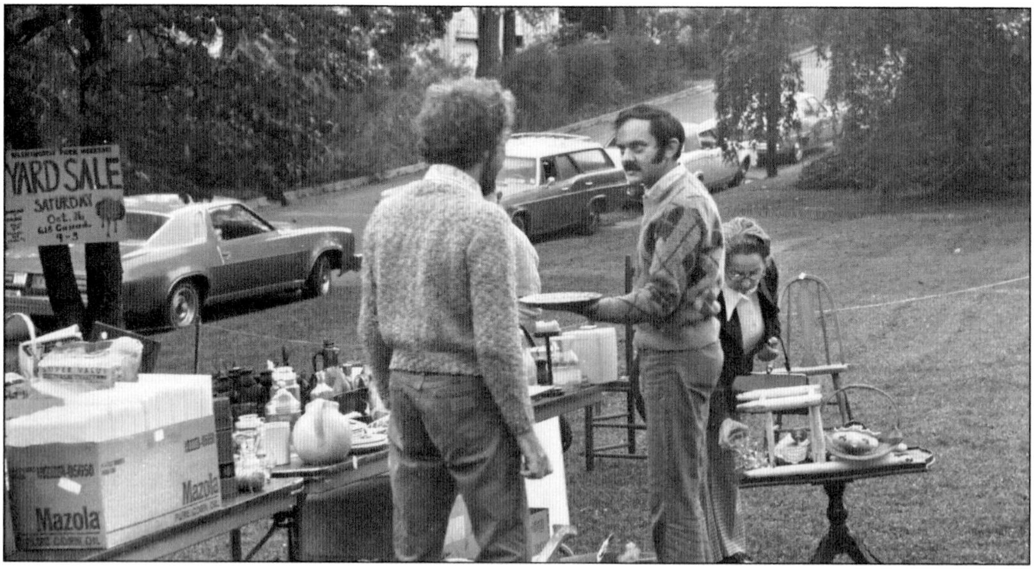

Dr. Clark Thompson (left) and Frederick Medas bought the house on corner of Sunnyside Avenue and South Main Street and restored it to its original condition. It had been condemned for five years, and they were some of the first people in the neighborhood to buy an older home to restore. Thompson was one of the founding members of the neighborhood association and helped with a fund-raising yard sale (shown here) that took place on Cascade Avenue. He was head of the department of religion and philosophy at Salem College. (Washington Park Neighborhood Association.)

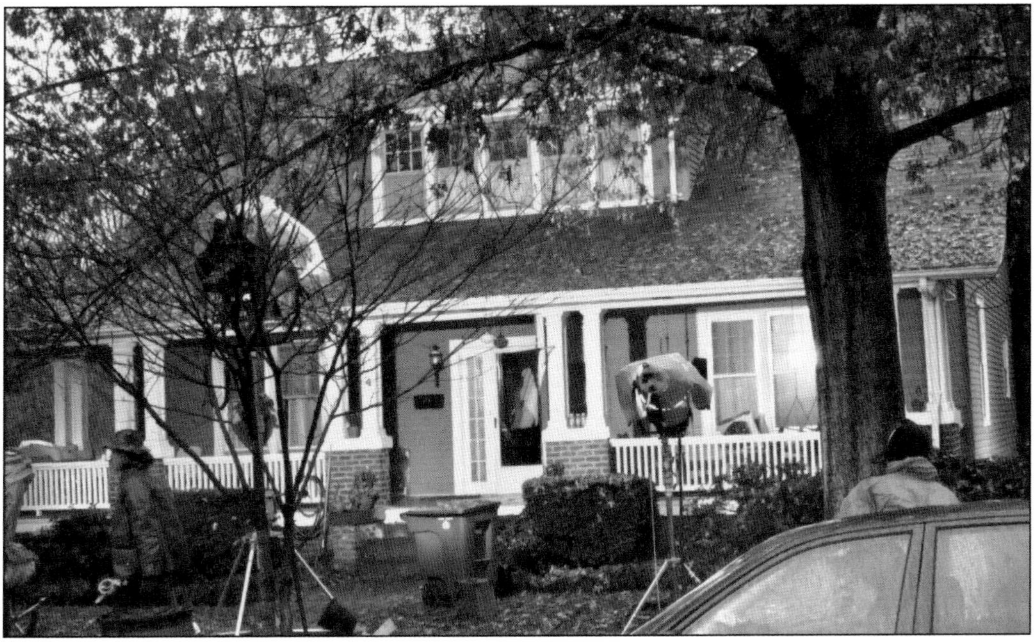

For seven days in November 1997, production crews from Patriot Pictures used several neighborhood locations to film the made-for-television science fiction movie *Target Earth*. It was broadcast on ABC in February 1998. This house, located at 4 Park Boulevard, is currently owned by Gregg Errett and Carmen Caruth, and other houses in the neighborhood were transformed into virtual Hollywood sets. (Gregg Errett and Carmen Caruth.)

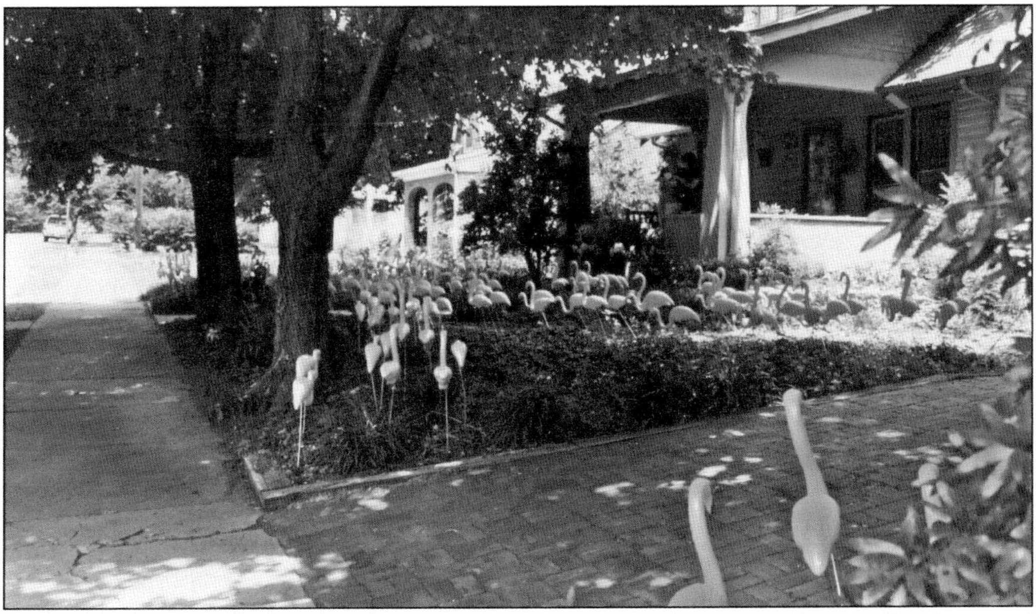

During the first neighborhood garden tour, Myra Gotzinger and Susan and Steve Albee borrowed an entire shipment of pink flamingos from Steve's brother's garden shop in Greensboro. The three neighbors carefully unwrapped each flamingo and placed them throughout both of their yards at 129 and 137 Gloria Avenue. It caused a traffic jam on Broad Street and created much laughter among the tour attendants and neighbors. (Washington Park Neighborhood Association.)

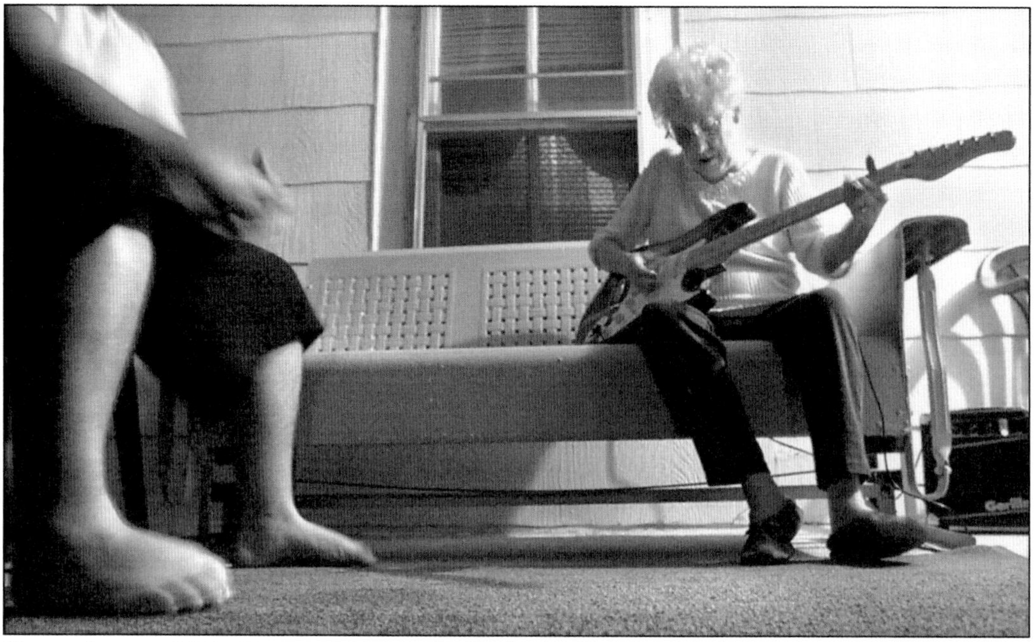

Shown here in 2001, 68-year-old Bessie Hill of 203 Shawnee Street plays an electric guitar on her front porch for neighbor Randy Lawson, who was 17 at the time. Hill, who began playing at age 7, learned by listening to bluegrass on the radio, but she didn't pick up rock 'n' roll until age 30. (© 2001 *Winston-Salem Journal* photograph/Ted Richardson.)

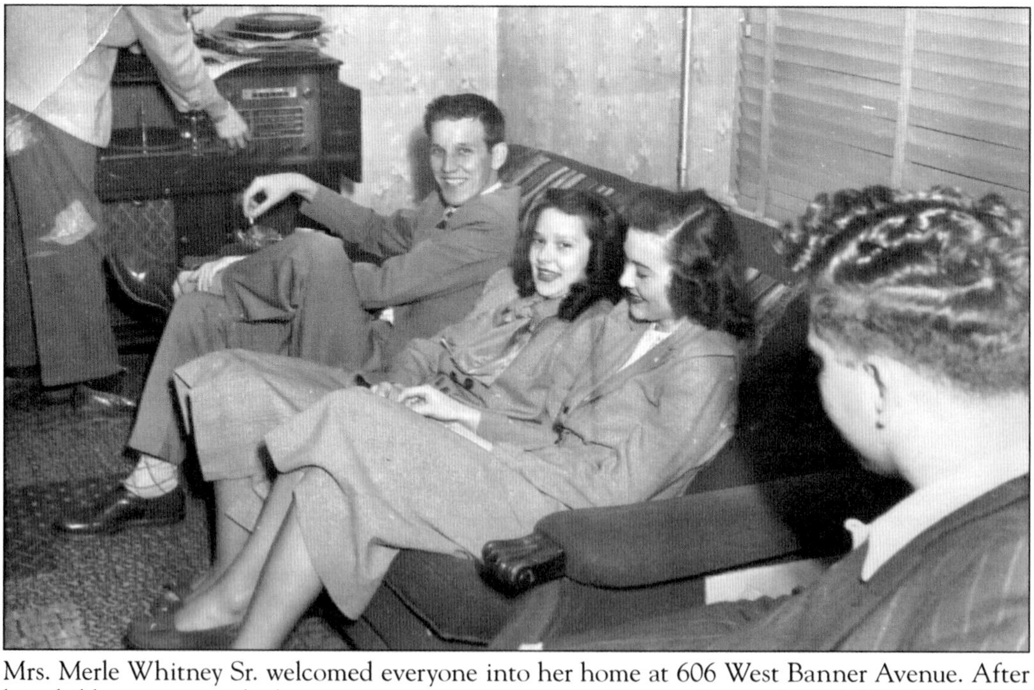

Mrs. Merle Whitney Sr. welcomed everyone into her home at 606 West Banner Avenue. After her children grew up, she became a surrogate mom to teenagers all over the neighborhood. Here some of her "kids" play music in her living room—a favorite pastime shared by many over the generations. (Jack Graham Jr.)

Seven

REVITALIZING AND PRESERVING THE NEIGHBORHOOD

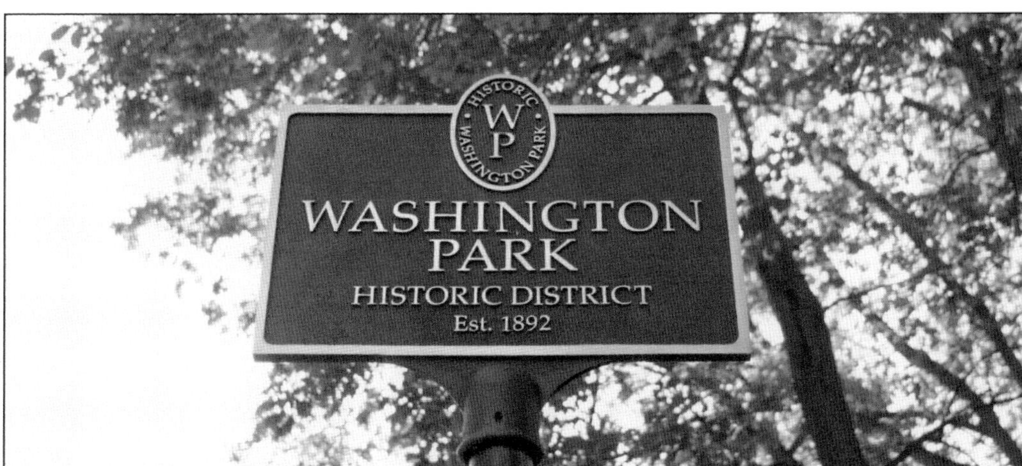

The neighborhood's successful designation in 1992 as a historic district on the National Register of Historic Places ranks as another of the neighborhood association's most significant achievements. Langdon P. Opperman, a preservation consultant hired by the association, said that the volunteer efforts of the neighborhood in obtaining the designation are unique in North Carolina—unmatched by any other group who has sought nomination to the register. Before this, the Washington Park Development Guide was created by Bill McNeil, city planner at the time, and was the first neighborhood development plan in Winston-Salem. Residents of Washington Park helped McNeil with the process as well. Throughout the years, the neighborhood has battled Yarbrough Transfer Company over an encroaching parking lot, turned Doune Street into a cul-de-sac because of heavy traffic, and fought and won the location of I-40, which planned to cut through the neighborhood and park. The value of improved and renovated housing has quadrupled over the last 30 years. (Washington Park Neighborhood Association.)

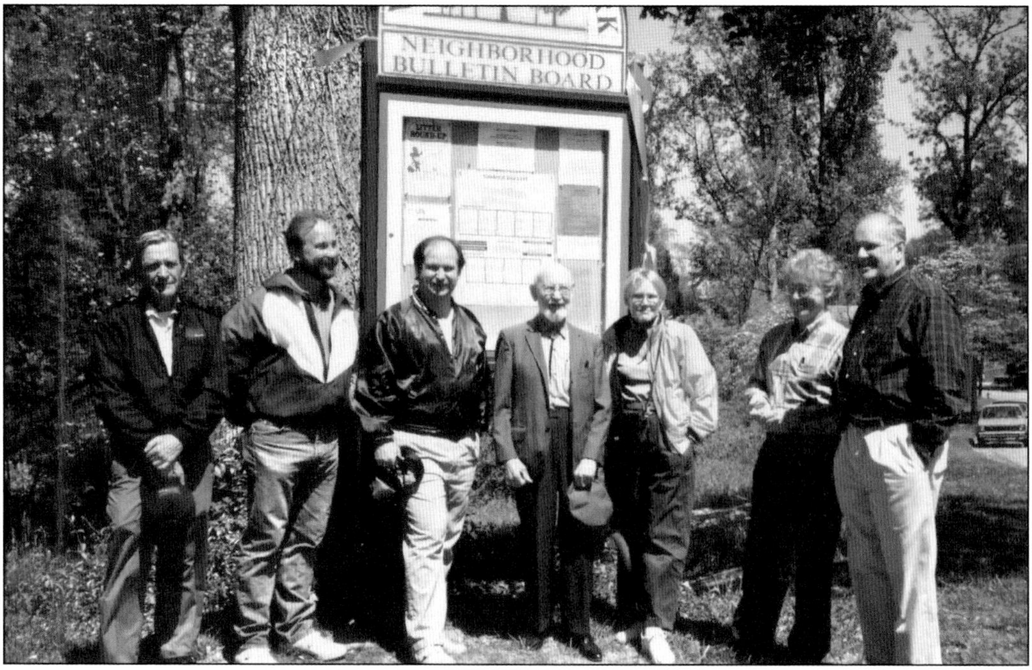

A neighborhood bulletin board was dedicated to three of the association founders: Dr. Frank and Lena Albright and Dr. Clark Thompson. Pictured from left to right are Walter Leonard, James Taylor, Dennis Walker, Dr. Frank Albright, Elen Knott, Frank Frye, and Jack Geis. The bulletin board, located on the edge of the park on Cascade Avenue and Park Boulevard, posts neighborhood events and the newsletter. (Washington Park Neighborhood Association.)

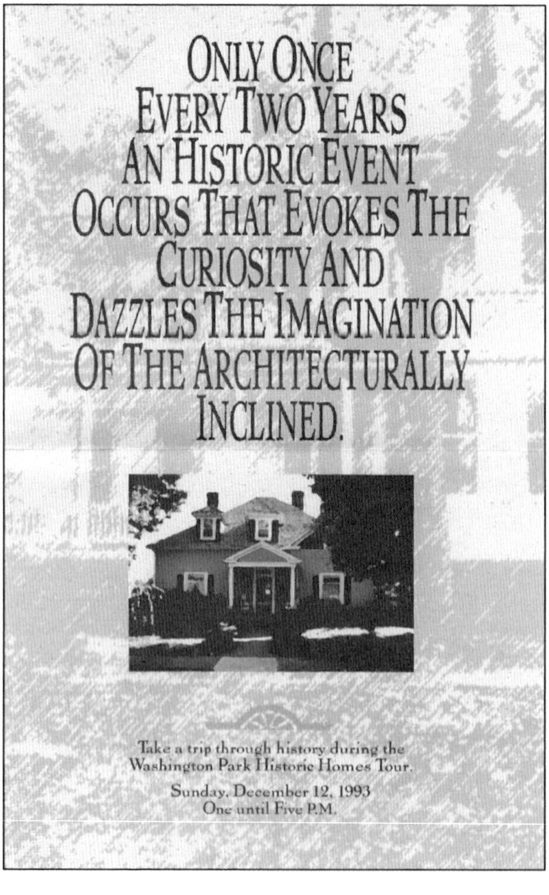

One of the main fund-raisers for the Washington Park Neighborhood Association is opening up homes and gardens in the area for tours. These events, held every couple of years, draw a large crowd and are popular with people all over Winston-Salem. (Washington Park Neighborhood Association.)

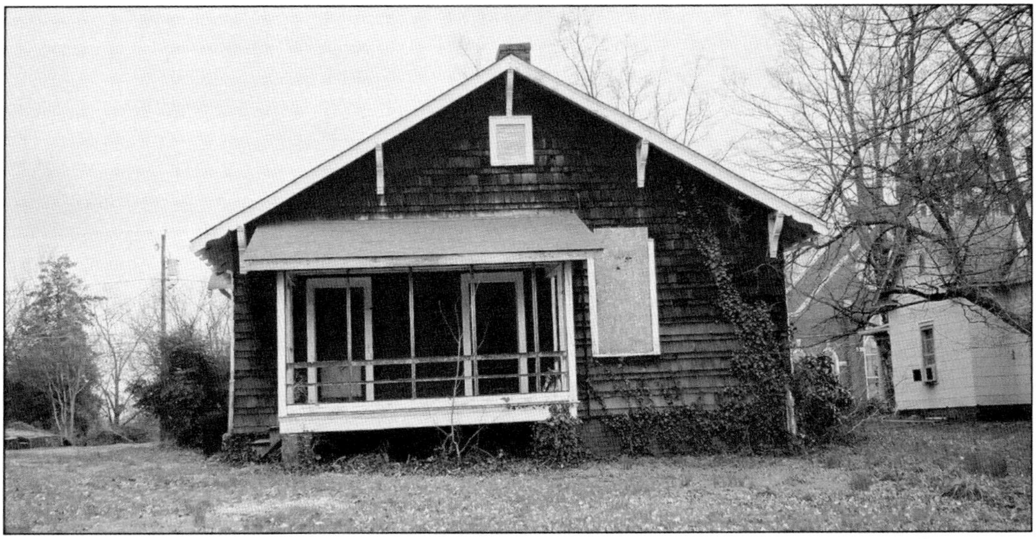

This house, located at 225 West Banner Avenue, was once a notorious drug house. For three years, Kim Mitchell (formerly Hackel) pursued buying it, and when the neighborhood association asked the cops to canvass the area because of drug activity, the owner decided to sell. The dilapidated interior had plaster falling from the walls, rotting floorboards, and white mold covering most of the woodwork. The floor had to be patched, so planks were taken from the back porch to repair the damaged ones. After nine months of extensive renovations, Kim was able to move into it. Out back, she planted smoke bush, Virginia sweet pine, hydrangeas, daphne, and butterfly bushes mixed with assorted perennials within the protected confines of a fenced yard. A stone patio was created in a rustic Arts and Crafts style to complement the house. (Kim Mitchell.)

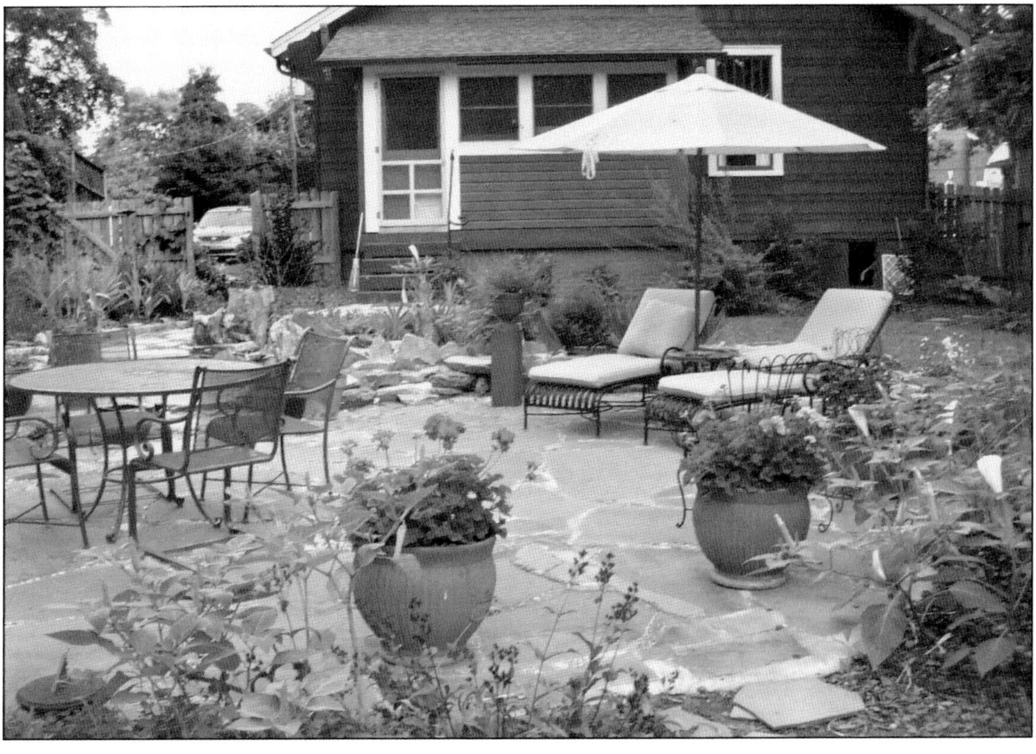

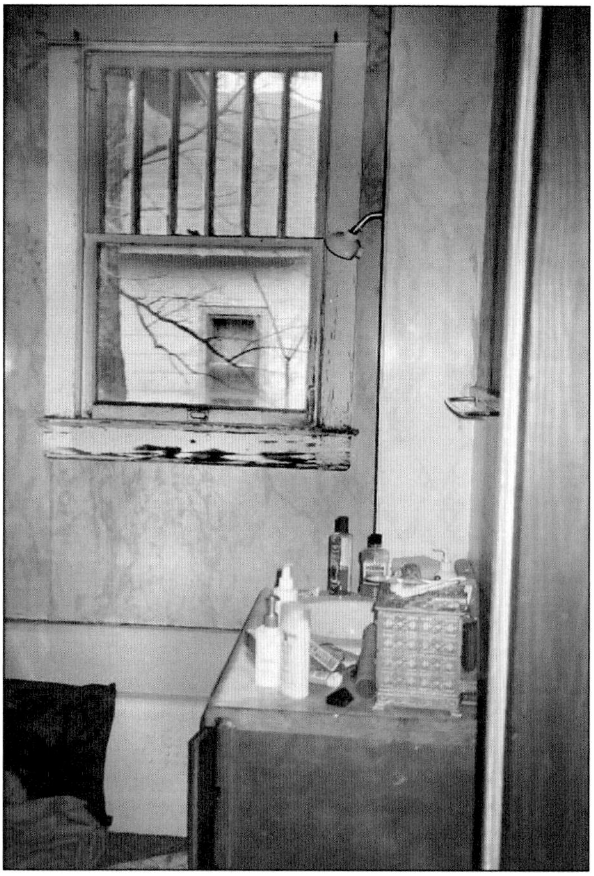

The bathroom was not usable when Kim Mitchell purchased this property at 225 West Banner Avenue. The bathroom was completely gutted and taken right down to the floor joists. Everything went except the window frame. The fixtures were chosen to look like they may have been original to the house; the medicine cabinet was an antique salvaged from a house in Virginia. She hired color expert and historian Robbie King to paint the design effect on the walls and help with many design decisions made throughout the restoration of the house. (Kim Mitchell.)

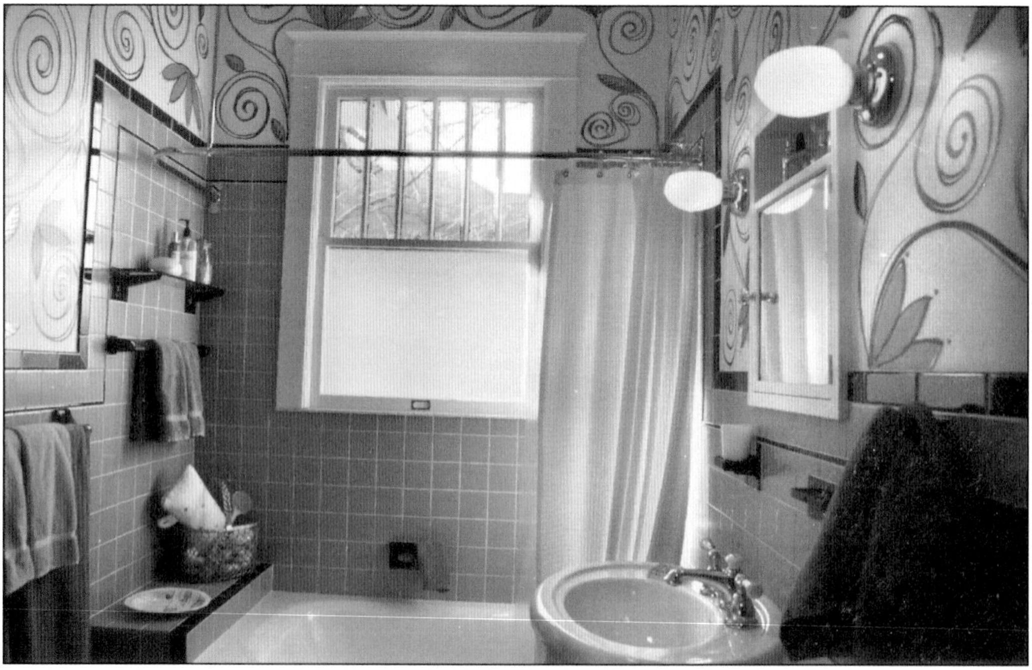

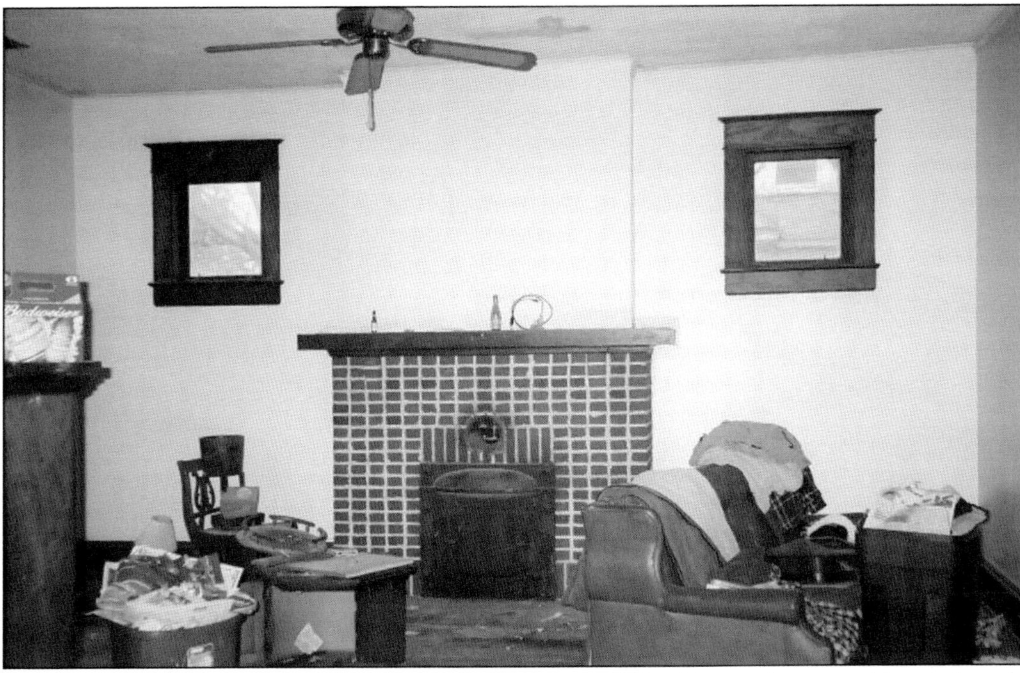

Kim Mitchell bought her 1922 Craftsman bungalow at 225 West Banner Avenue with one thought it mind: Save this house before it's beyond repair. The most she had seen of the house was just inside the front door when she decided to buy it, no matter what it needed. Years before, the roof had collapsed, leaving the home exposed long enough for water to destroy the plaster. The interior doors had been stacked up in the breakfast nook. Trash was waist high, and several dumpsters were needed to remove all the debris before restoration work could begin. Each door had to be taken apart and rebuilt by local carpenter Randy Schuett. The crown molding was custom milled to duplicate what had been removed. The dining room had an old pool table in the middle, and on the walls, spray painted in blue was "Jason's Pool Room." (Kim Mitchell.)

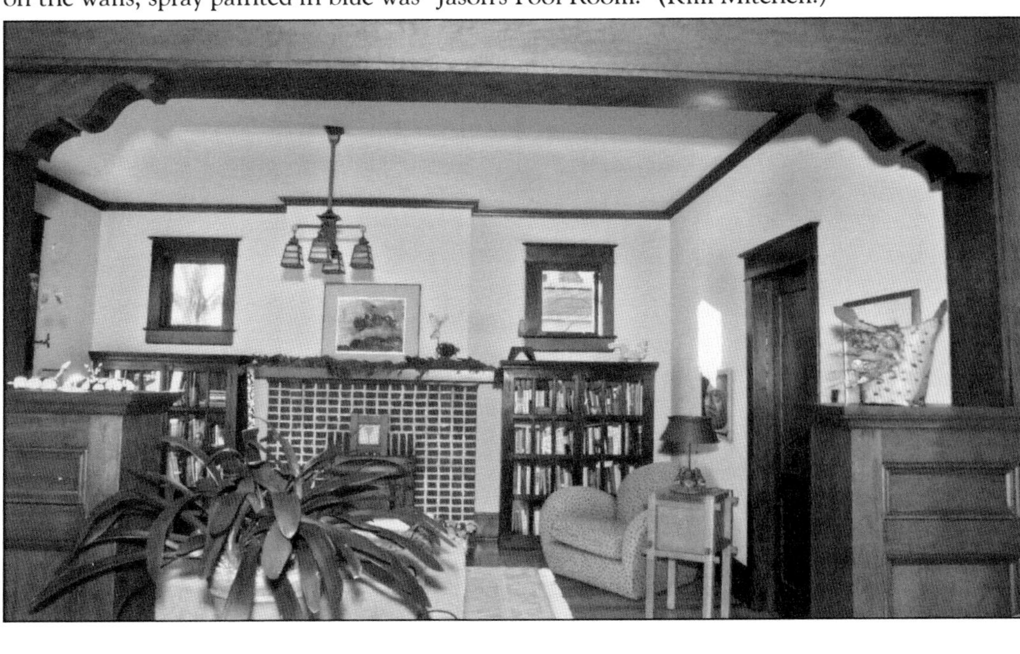

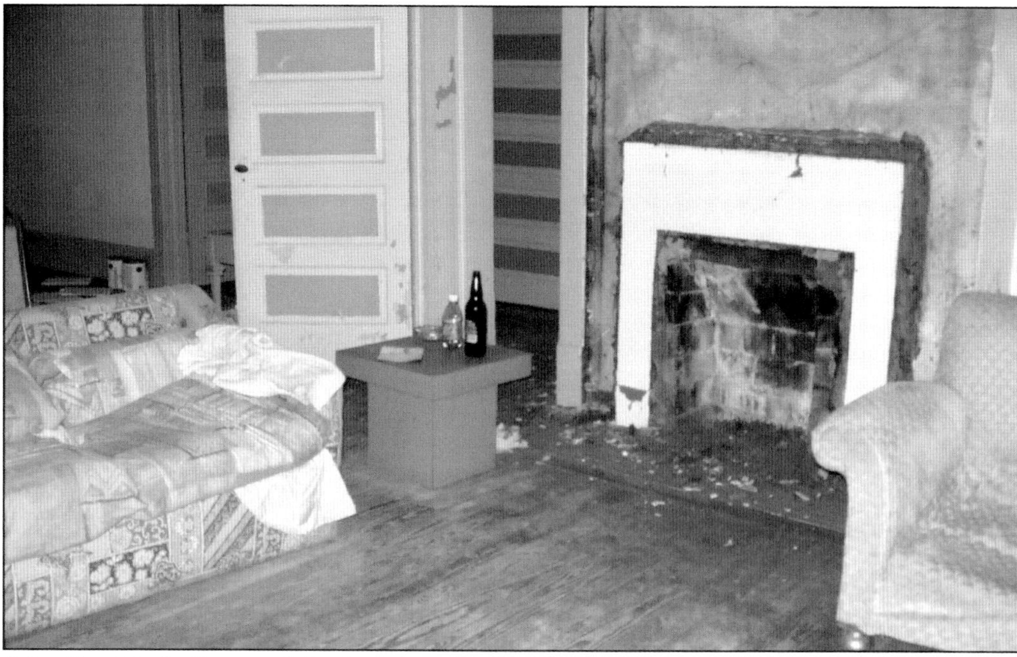

After Kim Mitchell restored the first bungalow, the depilated house next door, located at 229 West Banner Avenue, went into foreclosure. Unwilling to allow it to fall into anyone else's hands, Kim bought it with the intentions of restoring and reselling it. She discovered homeless people had been using the house as a shelter. All the architectural details had been removed, and the rooms had been painted with graffiti in a plethora of neon colors. She was able to buy back all the fireplace mantels and porch brackets from the previous occupant who had removed them. She was finally able to begin the restoration process several dumpsters later. The ceilings were falling down, and dead squirrel carcasses were found in the insulation of the dining room. (Kim Mitchell.)

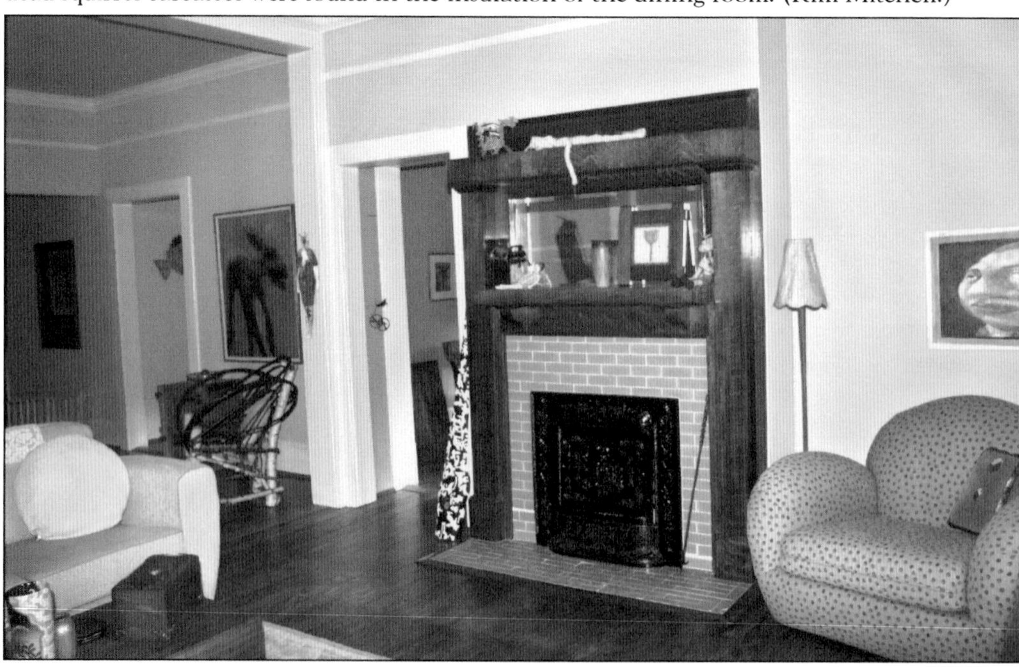

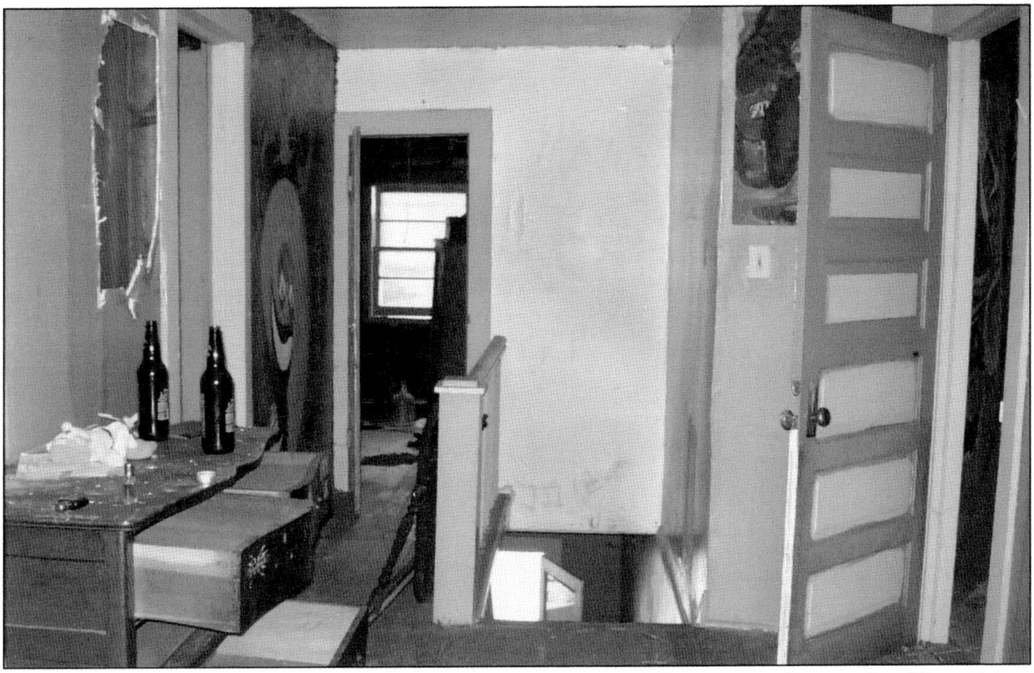

The upstairs of 229 West Banner Avenue was attic space. There were sheets of wallboard just loosely nailed around, and the ceiling was dripping with 90 years of cobwebs. There was a sleeping bag in one of the closets and an art room where the previous tenants drew all over the walls. After cleaning everything out, the roof was replaced, and all-new drywall was installed to make the upstairs a master suite. The woodwork was matched to the downstairs' wood in size and mass, and made the upstairs' detailing look as though it had always been there. The bathroom was added using salvaged antique fixtures, bead board wainscoting, and historic-reproduction tile floors. (Kim Mitchell.)

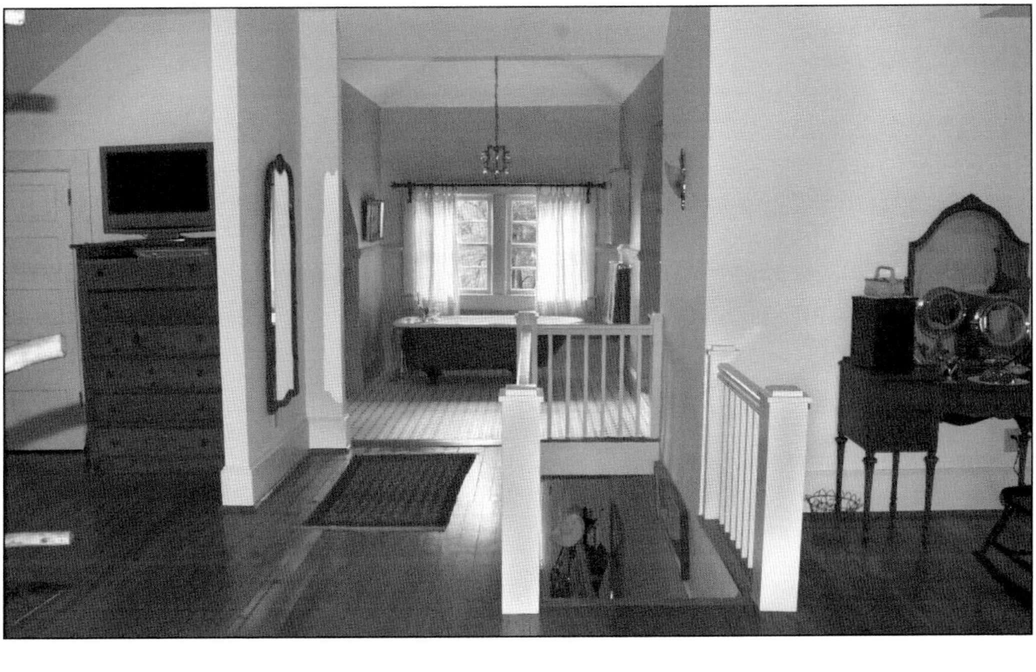

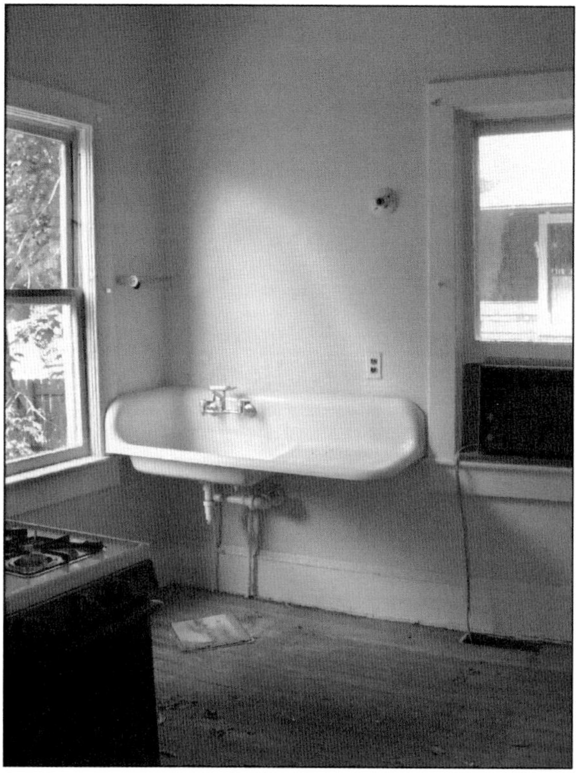

Kim Mitchell's bungalow at 229 West Banner Avenue was built before 1913, and the kitchen had never been updated. No cabinets had ever been installed. The original, rusted-out corner sink remained almost 90 years later. Custom-made cabinetry with inset doors and soapstone countertops were installed to keep the old-style look but bring the kitchen up to modern standards. All new electrical and plumbing work was done throughout the house. (Kim Mitchell.)

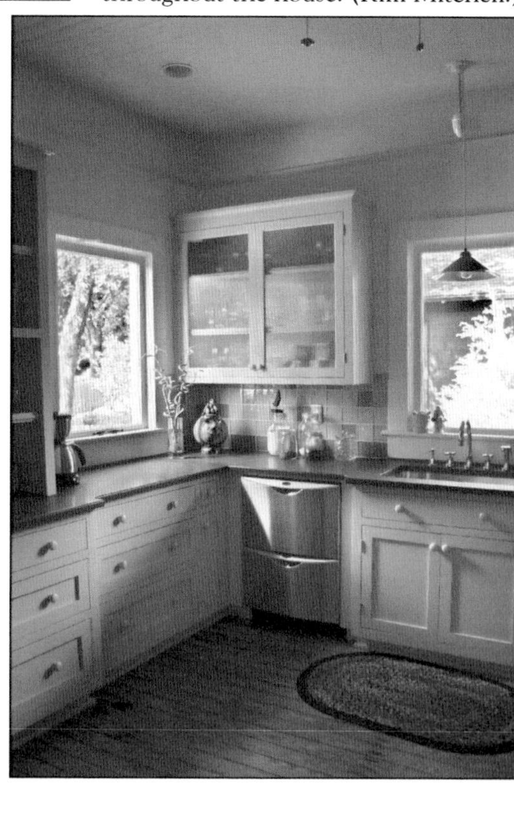

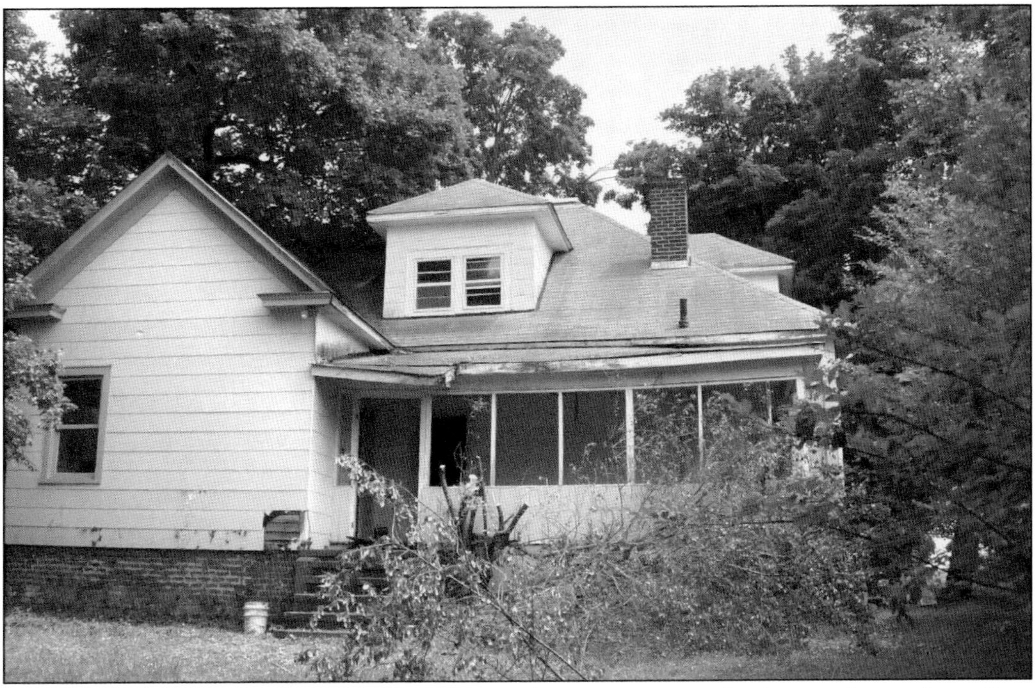

Kim Mitchell's back porch at 229 West Banner Avenue was completely rotted away from floor to roof and was being held together by a large privet bush that had grown into a tree. The entire back porch was rebuilt and made to match the surviving detail of the side porch. The overgrown lot was regraded and years of neglect cleared away. Ivy and wisteria vines were growing under the asbestos siding that was carefully removed to expose the original wood lap siding and cedar shingles on the upstairs gables. Thousands of nails were removed from the siding before restoration could begin on the outside of the house. (Kim Mitchell.)

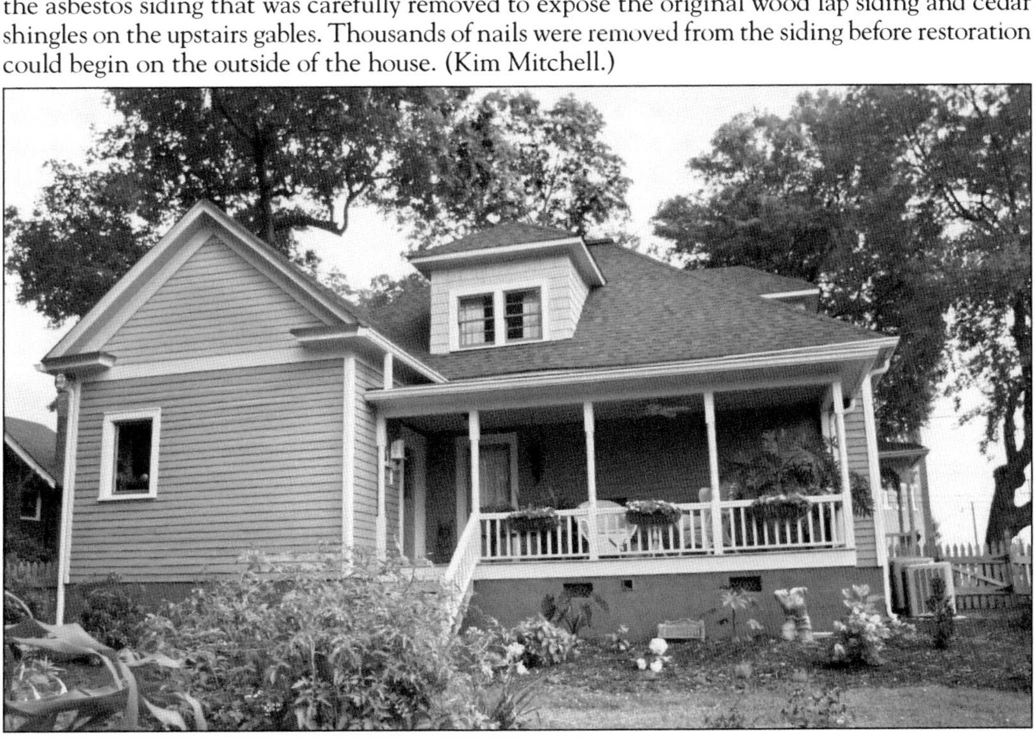

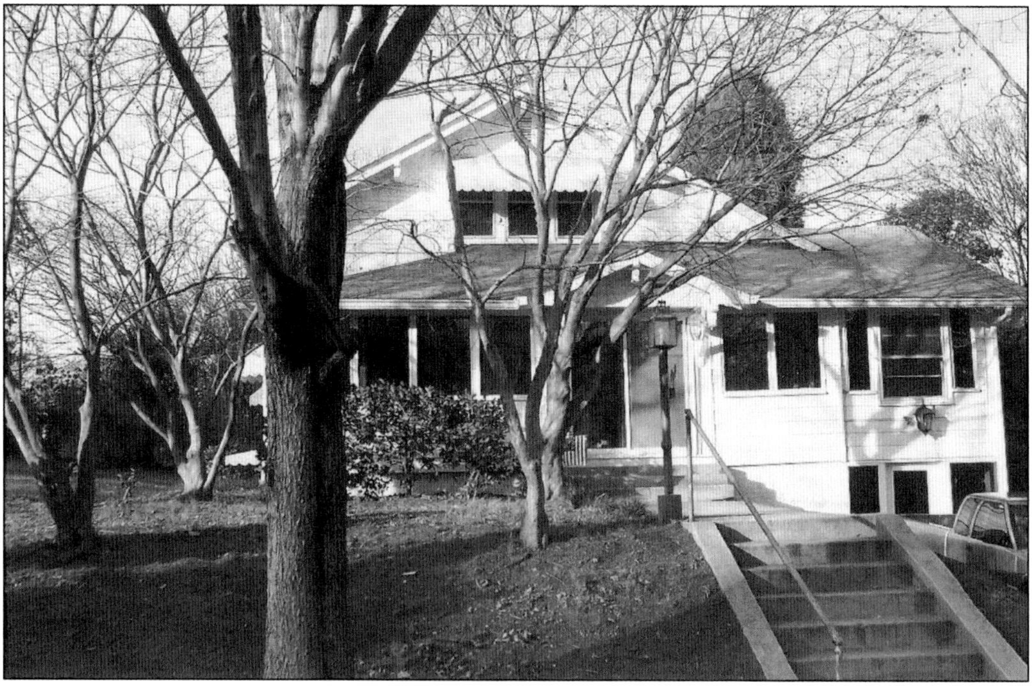

After Gene Hayes bought this house at 209 Vintage Avenue, he enclosed the front porches so he could enjoy them all year long. The area was separated into two rooms: the front of the house was where he spent the majority of his time, and the side room had a spiral staircase leading to the greenhouse below it. When Denis and Nancy Kissane bought the house, they tore out the carpet and the walls and eventually tore down all the walls that separated them from the outside. They plan on building a sleeping porch on the side to enjoy the cross breezes the house receives. (Above, Jean Hayes Mahaffey; below, Denis and Nancy Kissane.)

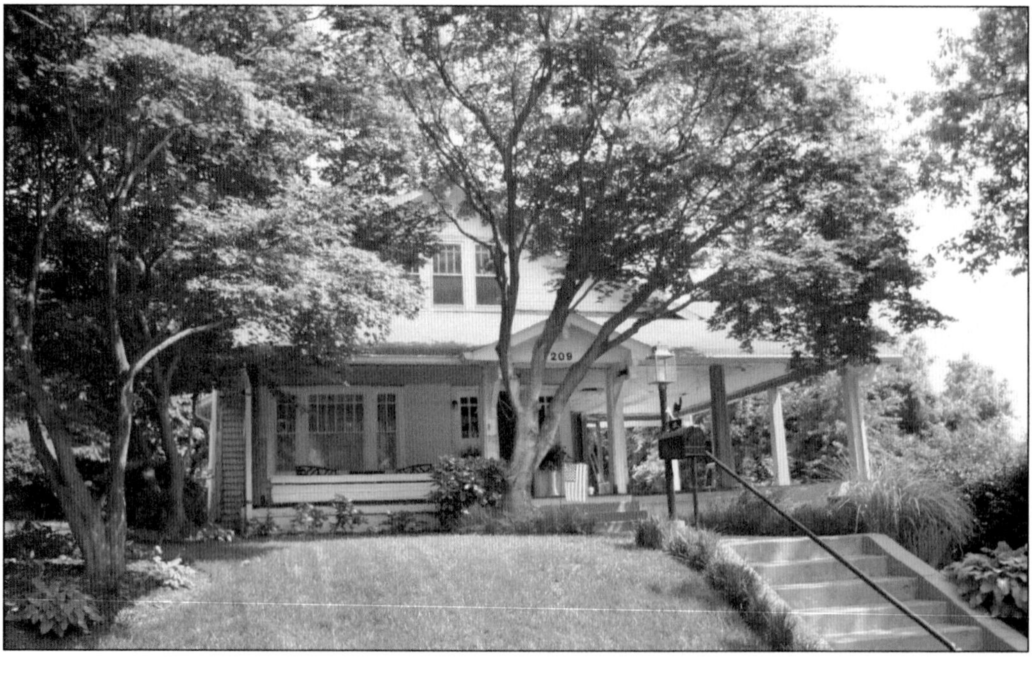

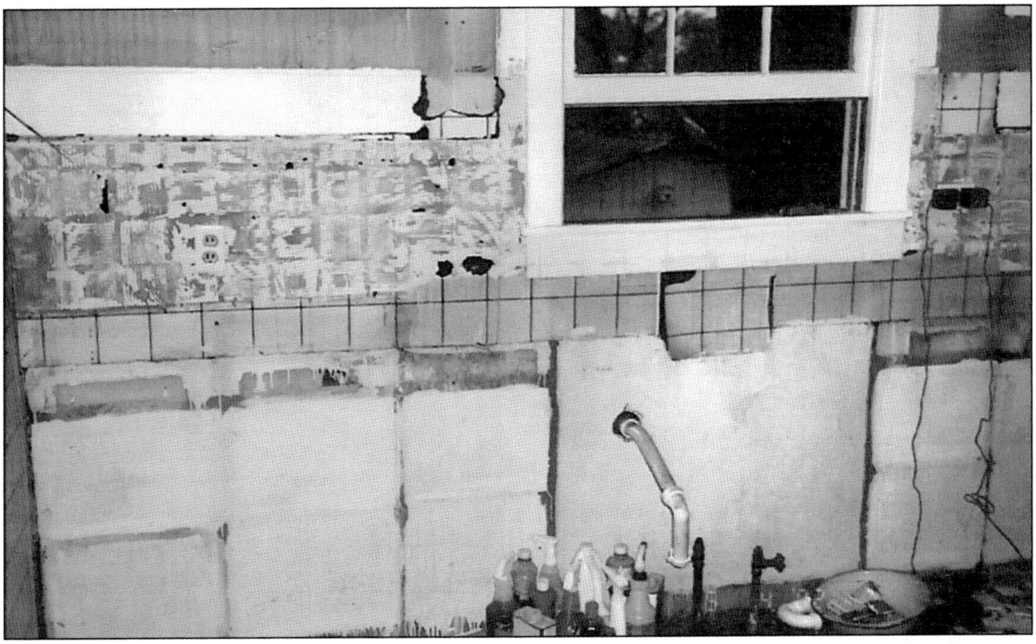

When Debbie and Anthony Transou bought their house at 116 Banner Avenue, they knew it needed some work. The house, built before 1903, had been owned by the George E. Hartman family for many decades. It is believed that the lot was purchased from the Moravian Church, originally extended south to Acadia Avenue, and had been a small farm. It still features the original smokehouse and corncrib. The kitchen, which they remodeled, is said to have been added in 1913. They discovered the original cooking chimney nestled in the kitchen surrounded by sheetrock. Unfortunately, it crumbled when they removed the surrounding materials. The previous owners had already removed the drop ceilings and discovered bead board in all the rooms of the house. (Debbie and Anthony Transou.)

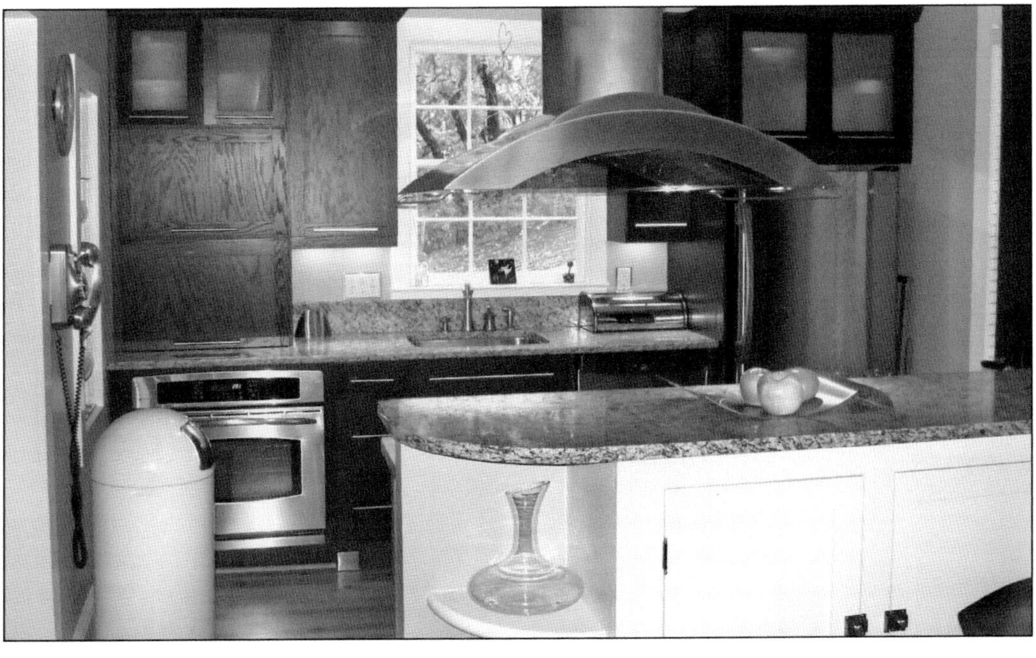

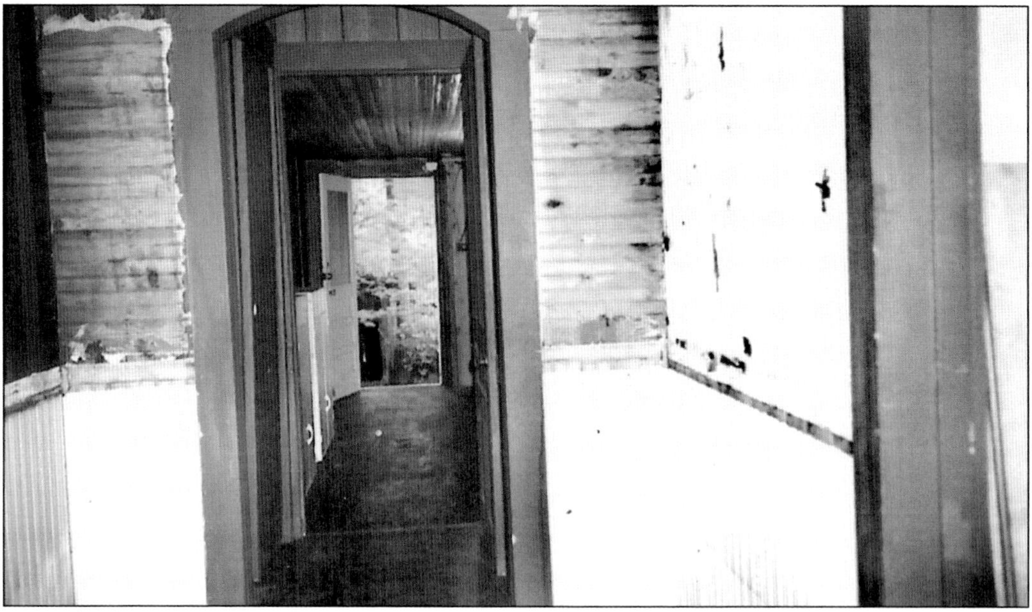

From the front entrance, the backyard of this home is visible through the former porch. The house, located at 116 West Banner Avenue, was built among I-frames, Colonial Revivals, and bungalows and is a rarity because it may be the only dogtrot home in Washington Park. Dogtrots were popular throughout the South because the open bay between two long, flat walls acted as a funnel for cooling breezes. The open bay has since been enclosed, but the configuration of the rooms has been maintained. During the remodeling, owners Debbie and Anthony Transou restored the original bead board walls in the entryway. The ceiling in what used to be the open bay had decayed beyond repair, as had some of the structural boards and sheetrock. Today the house has a warm, open feeling and is structurally sound throughout. (Debbie and Anthony Transou.)

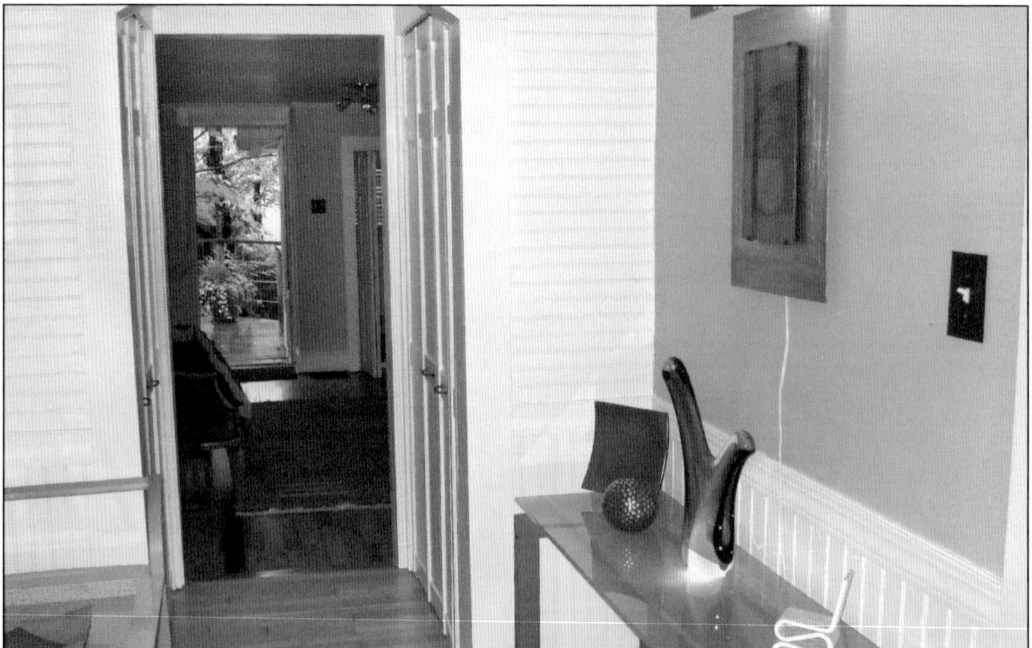

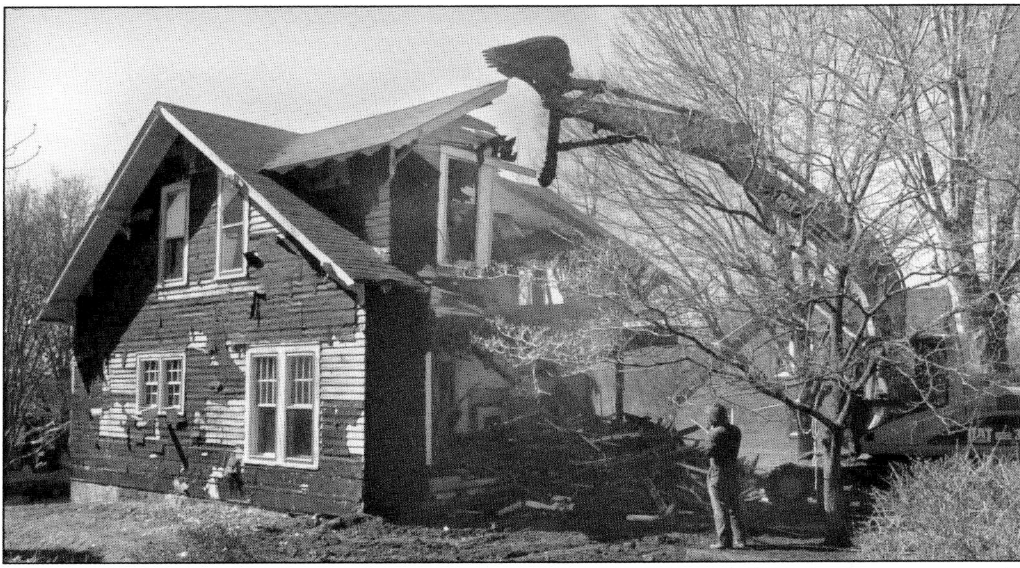

The razing of the 1923 Clarence Morton home at 66 Park Avenue led residents to examine the establishment of a local historic district overlay. Although this would not prevent older homes from being torn down, it could delay the process for up to a year while a review is conducted. The house since has been replaced with a beautiful, cedar-shingled bungalow. Washington Park still retains over 90 percent of its original homes. (©2005 *Winston-Salem Journal* photograph/David Rolfe.)

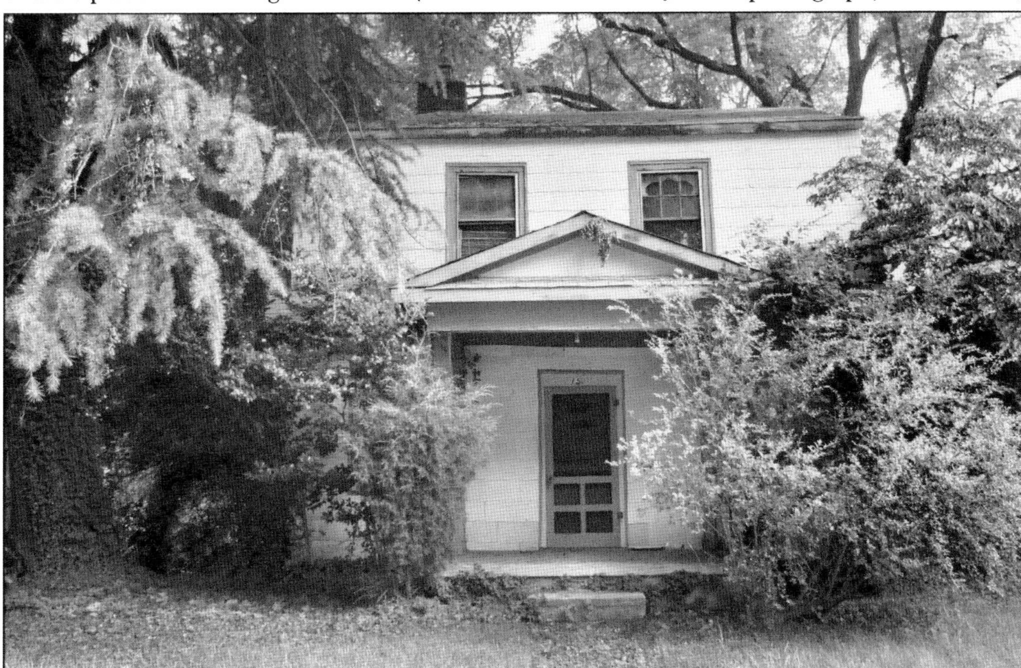

In 2007, this house, located on Gloria Avenue, was demolished because it would have cost more to restore than it is historically worth. It is speculated that this house replaced an earlier house on the site or that it is the earlier house remodeled. The previous owner died, and the new owners are planning to build a bungalow that fits in with the surrounding homes. (Washington Park Neighborhood Association.)

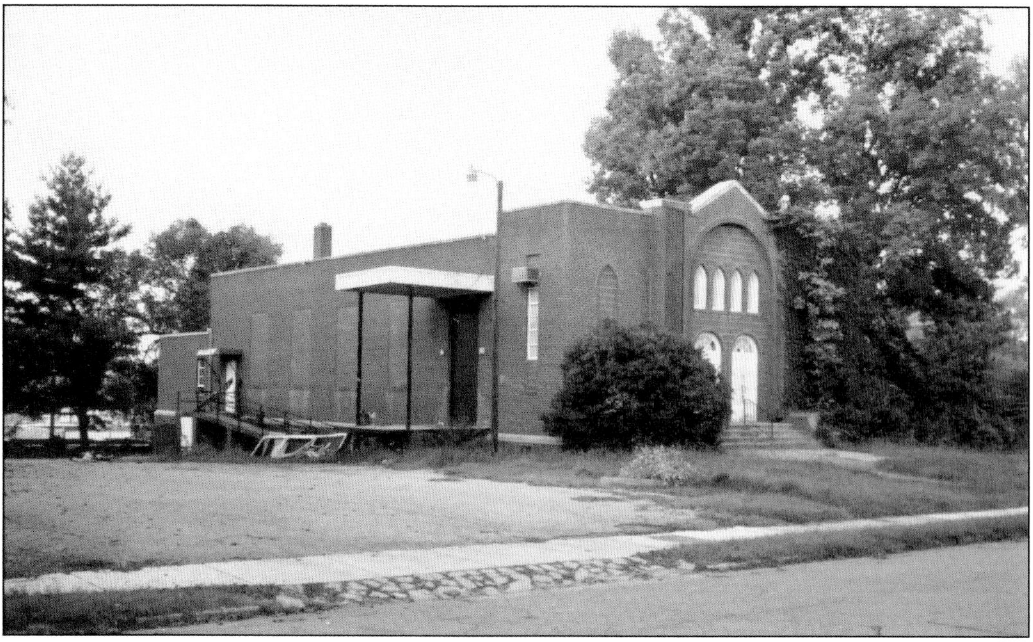

The vintage theater located on the corner of South Main Street and Vintage Avenue was constructed as a Church of Christ in 1947 and sold in 1972 to the North Carolina School of the Arts, which used it first as a recording studio and then as a black-box theater. Through all of this activity, it remained a musty, barn-like building. It was bought by Dr. Stephen Tucker in 1991, and with help from architect William Watkins—both of whom live in Washington Park—nine months of renovations took place to make the building look as it does today. It has a 2,400-square-foot maple floor and a small, permanent stage 40 inches above the floor. The building is used for arts events, contra dances, and square dances, plus it is open to the community for rental. (Stephen Turner.)

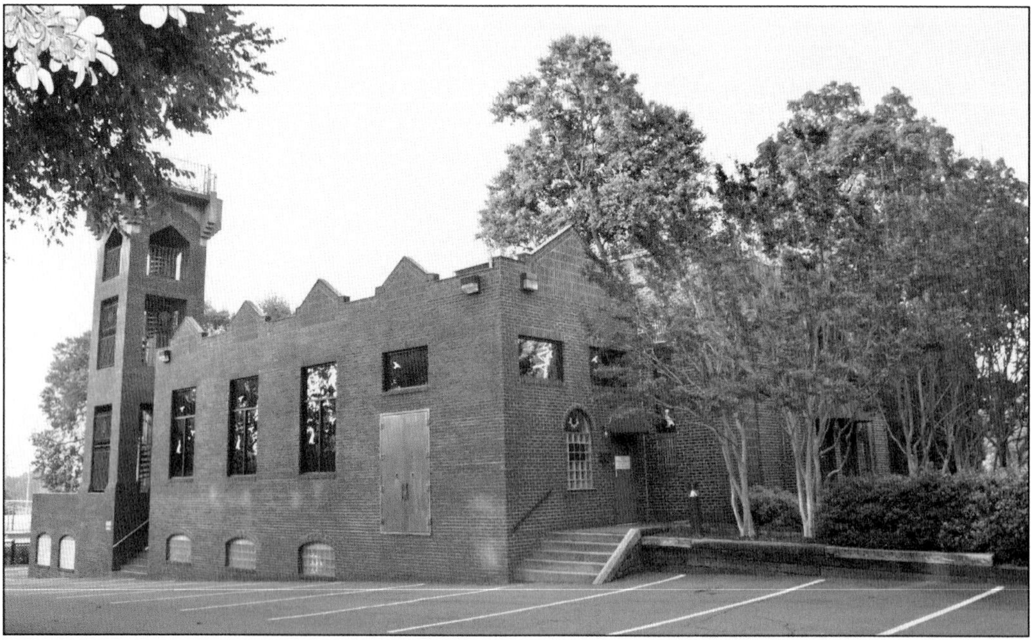

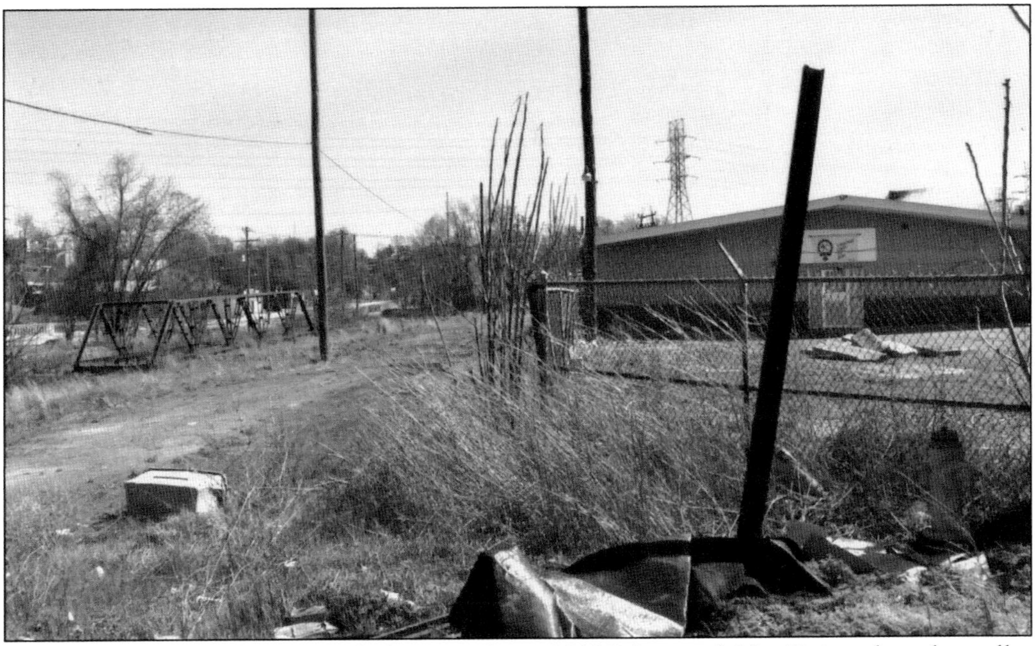

Early in June 1991, Hobie Cawood, then president of Old Salem, and Alex Ewing, then chancellor of the North Carolina School of the Arts, conducted a meeting with top city officials and planners to discuss the forlorn commercial area lying between Old Salem and the arts school. The group saw this area as "tortuous, unaesthetic and bewildering—a depressing introduction to our city" for those entering Winston-Salem from I-40. Peter Batchelor, the chairman of the Southeast Gateway Urban Design Assistance Team, questioned "how such a magnificent site could have become so fragmented by the hand of man. I was looking at a classic example of the process of 'unbuilding' through which a naturally sited community had been ripped apart by roads and inappropriate land development patterns." It was agreed that a comprehensive planning process was needed to rejuvenate the area, and the Urban Design Assistance Team was founded in November 1992. (Debra Collins and Chad Davis of East Coast Capital.)

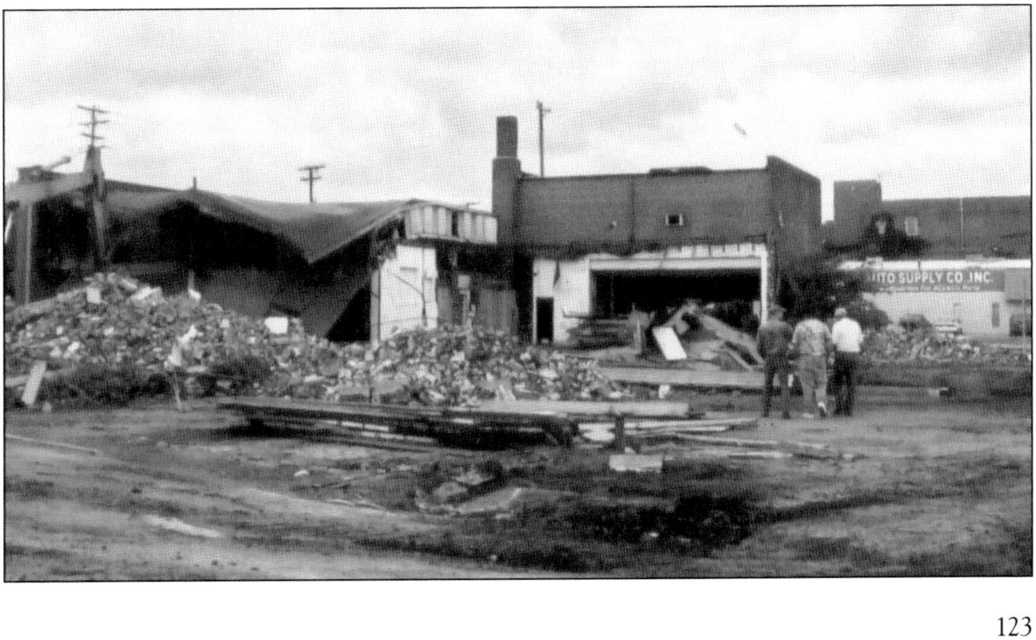

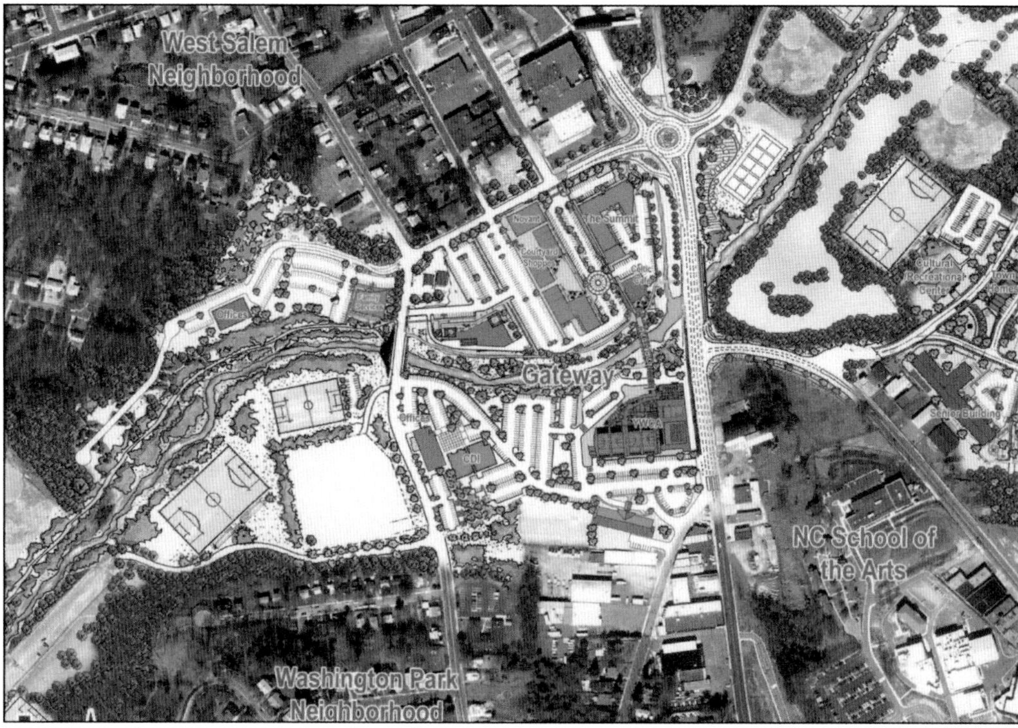

It has been almost 15 years since the Urban Design Assistance Team built their plan of action. The Greenway has been built along Salem Creek from Washington Park to Salem Lake, a pedestrian bridge has been built from Sunnyside Avenue to the North Carolina School of the Arts to allow for foot traffic, the Waughtown Bridge had been closed, a new YWCA had been built, the old buildings have been torn down and construction has started on the Summit—a 24-unit, two-phase condominium residence. Traffic patterns were rerouted, and a roundabout was created between Old Salem and the North Carolina School of the Arts. The strollway provides easy walking or bicycling access to downtown for college students and residents in the area. The goal of building a beautiful, accessible, central location for students, residents, and tourists is reaching completion. (Debra Collins and Chad Davis of East Coast Capital.)

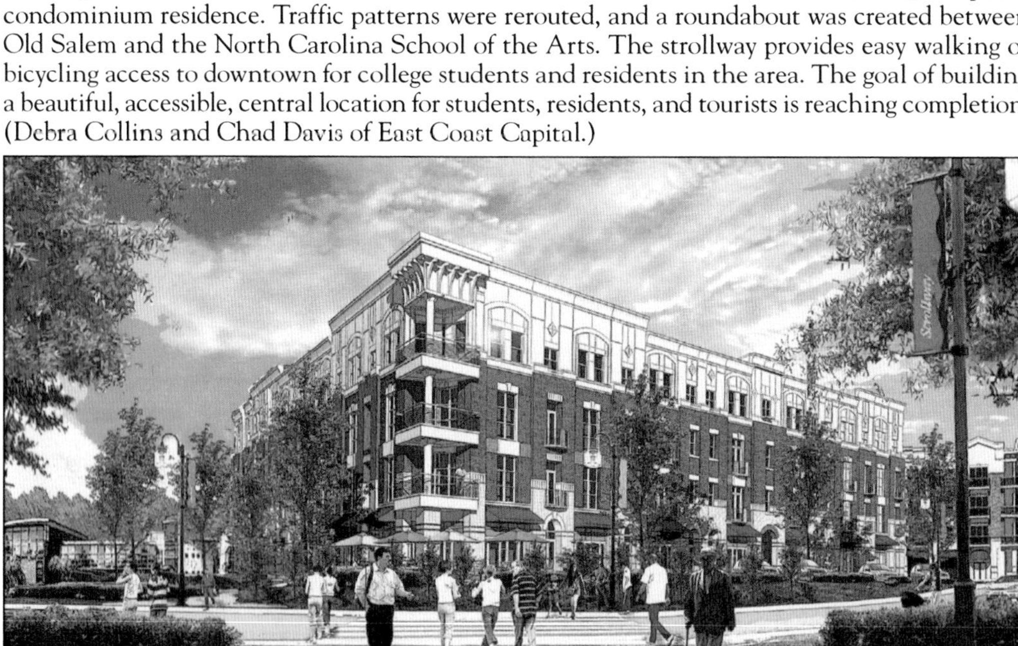

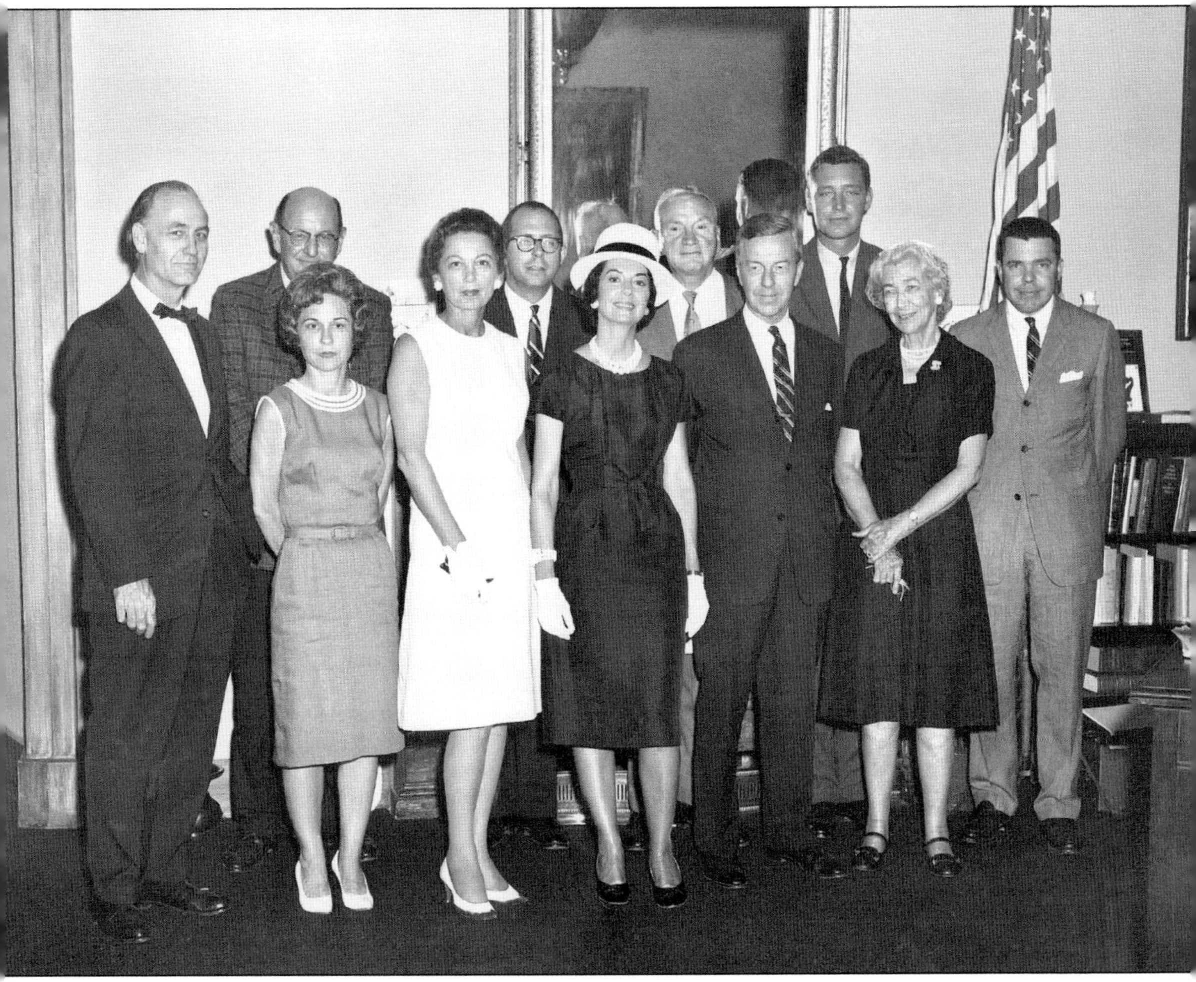

The brainchild of former North Carolina governor Terry Sanford and author John Ehle, the North Carolina School of the Arts was established by the North Carolina General Assembly in 1963. State funds were appropriated and an advisory board of artists was established to recommend a site for the school. Not surprisingly, there was considerable rivalry among the major cities of the state to be the location. The citizens of Winston-Salem, home of the first municipal arts council in the nation, raised nearly $1 million in a two-day telephone campaign to renovate the old Gray High School building and won the location of the school. Composer Vittorio Giannini of the Juilliard School served as the school's first president. During its formative years, the school was also guided by people of vision on its board of trustees: (first row, left to right) Olive Muller, Martha Muilenberg, Sybil Jolly, Dr. James Semans, and Kathryn Boyd; (second row, left to right) Sam Ragan, Ed Richards, Hugh Cannon, Ben Swalin, Smith Bagley, and R. Philip Hanes Jr. (Wallace Carroll and James M. Clark are not pictured). (North Carolina School of the Arts.)

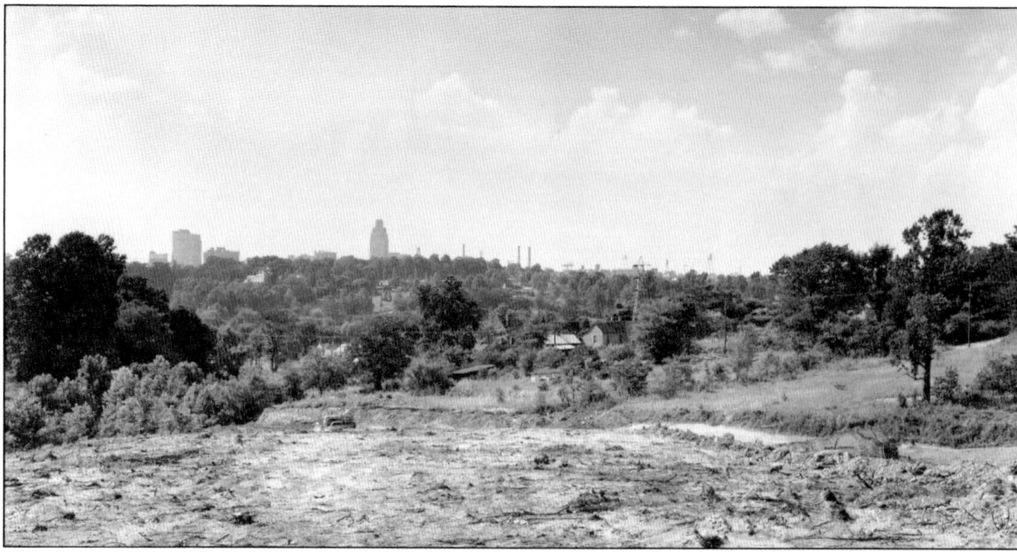

Once the site decision for the North Carolina School of the Arts was won, renovations on the old Gray High School building started, and land was cleared for the residential buildings. The school is now situated on a 67-acre campus overlooking downtown Winston-Salem with over 30 buildings, including residence halls, classrooms, studios, and performing arts venues. (Old Salem Museums and Gardens.)

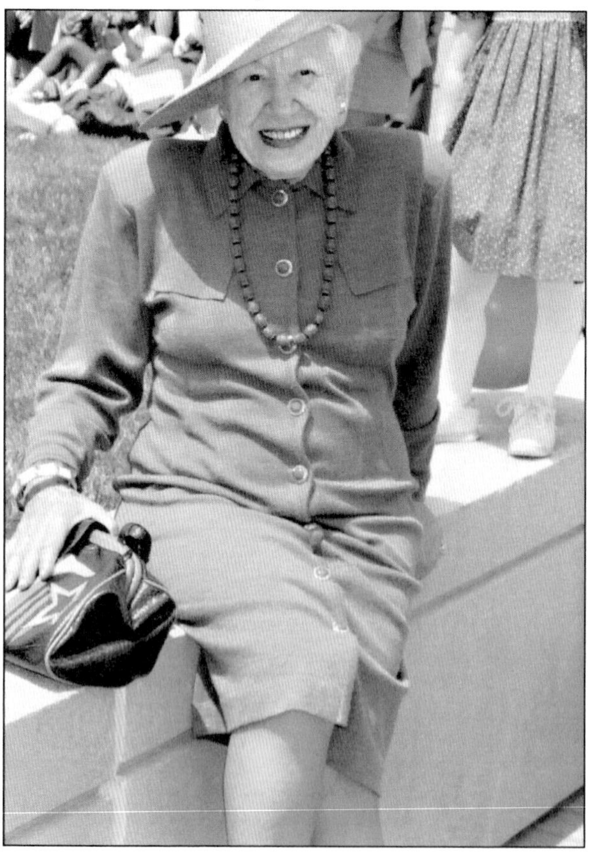

Ruth Julian was a beloved member of the arts community and was a key player in the drive to bring the North Carolina School of the Arts to Winston-Salem and subsequently to her neighborhood's backyard. Those who knew her said that she was a vivacious, lively, social person and loved entertaining. Many people remember her dinner parties and the over 2,000 paintings, drawings, ceramics, and other pieces of art surrounding their home's interior and exterior. (Laura Turner.)

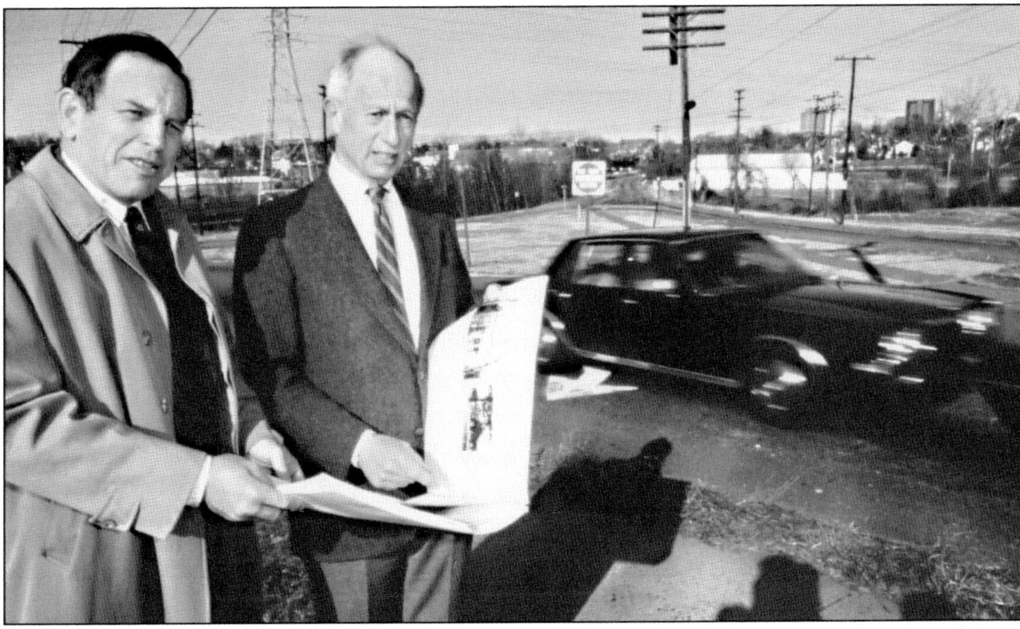

Alex Ewing, former chancellor of the North Carolina School of the Arts (NCSA), and Doug Lewis, former headmaster of the Summit School, stand at the bottom corner of NCSA. The intersection of Waughtown and Main Streets had become "a neglected area that was about as bleak as any strip of mostly vacant commercial space can be." Their vision kicked off the Southeast Gateway Project that is revitalizing the area in 2007. (©1992 *Winston-Salem Journal* photograph/Allen Aycock.)

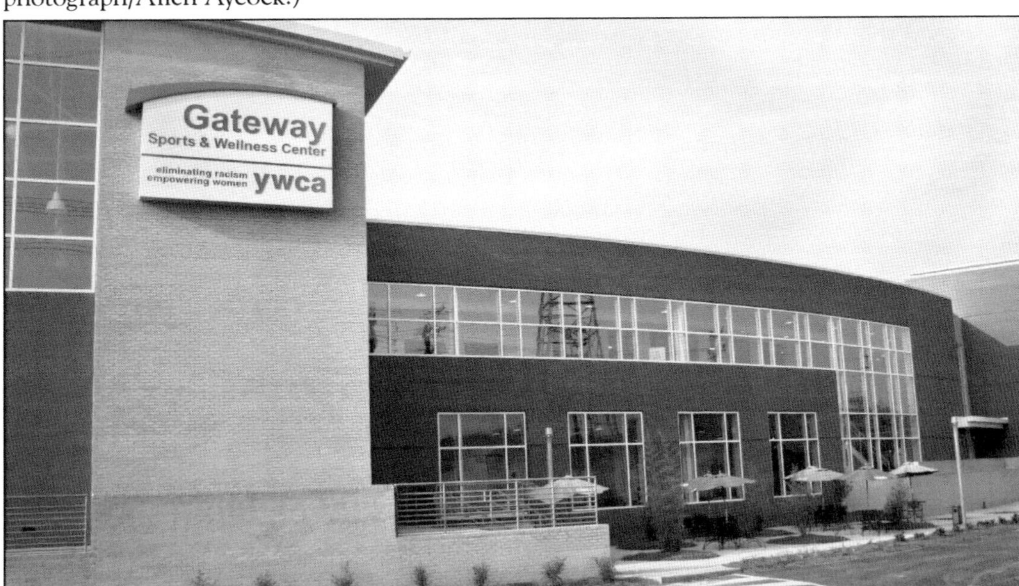

The second completed building in the Southeast Gateway is YWCA's new 90,000-square-foot facility. It opened June 16, 2007, and contains state-of-the-art cardiovascular and strengthening equipment, a competition-sized swimming pool and family water park, tournament basketball facilities, a cyber cafe, and a computerized library. The YWCA's goal is to make this a gathering place for the culturally diverse neighborhoods surrounding it. (Washington Park Neighborhood Association.)

ACROSS AMERICA, PEOPLE ARE DISCOVERING SOMETHING WONDERFUL. *THEIR HERITAGE.*

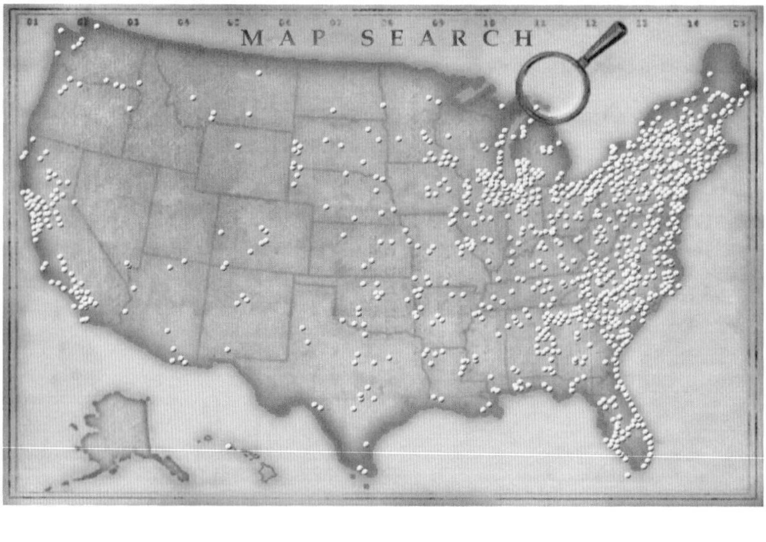